KU-206-003

FRANCISCAN POVERTY

THE DOCTRINE OF
THE ABSOLUTE POVERTY OF CHRIST
AND THE APOSTLES
IN THE FRANCISCAN ORDER
1210–1323

M. D. LAMBERT

Published for the Church Historical Society

LONDON
S·P·C·K
1961

First published in 1961
by S.P.C.K.
Holy Trinity Church
Marylebone Road
London N.W.1

Made and printed in Great Britain by
William Clowes and Sons, Limited, London and Beccles

© M. D. Lambert 1961

B 7565

TO

MY MOTHER AND FATHER

AND TO

THE MEMORY OF WILLIAM EWART GLADSTONE

FOUNDER OF ST DEINIOL'S LIBRARY

HAWARDEN

CONTENTS

ACKNOWLEDGEMENTS

I AM GRATEFUL for advice to Professor E. F. Jacob; for references to Mr W. A. Pantin and the Reverend Dr D. A. Callus, o.p.; for advice and a generous loan of books to Dr D. Douie and Dr M. Reeves; for a scholarship to the President and Fellows of Trinity College, Oxford; and, for much help and encouragement at various times, to Mr M. Maclagan and Mr J. P. Cooper.

I am grateful to the following for assistance on points of translation: Mr S. E. Ievers, Mr A. Menhennet of the Department of German, Mr M. Holland of the Department of French, Mr R. D. Williams and Mr A. E. Wardman of the Department of Classics, in the University of Reading; also Dr J. K. Hyde of the University of Manchester, and Mr J. Heath of Dulwich College. I alone am responsible for any mistakes. I wish also to mention the care of my typist, Mrs Bettles of Oxford.

For unstinted help with proofs and index, I wish to thank Mr W. K. Ford of Worthing, and Mr. M. Twyman of the School of Fine Art, the University of Reading.

I owe more than I can say, in the original writing, to the kindness and learning of the Reverend Dr T. M. Parker. Without him nothing could have been written.

To my parents I owe the opportunity to study and to write, and so much else besides: it is a pleasure to thank them here.

In this, as in all things, my especial thanks go to my wife: she has been the inspiration of the whole work.

University of Reading   M. D. L.

ABBREVIATIONS

AF	*Analecta Franciscana*
AFH	*Archivum Franciscanum Historicum*
ALKG	*Archiv für Litteratur und Kirchengeschichte*
BF	*Bullarium Franciscanum*
BSFS	*British Society for Franciscan Studies*
DTC	*Dictionnaire de Théologie Catholique*
FS	*Franziskanische Studien*
MGH	*Monumenta Germaniae Historica*
PL	Migne, *Patrologia Latina*
RHE	*Revue d'Histoire Ecclésiastique*
RTAM	*Recherches de Théologie Ancienne et Médiévale*
ZKG	*Zeitschrift für Kirchengeschichte*
ZKT	*Zeitschrift für Katholische Theologie*

NOTE ON NOMENCLATURE

DOMINION — Used as a synonym for property rights. Throughout, *dominium, proprietas*, dominion, and property have been used as interchangeable terms.

SPIRITUALS — Used of the rigorist section of the order in the thirteenth and fourteenth centuries. First applied to them by contemporaries in the South of France in the early fourteenth century.

CONVENTUALS — Used of their opponents, and of the majority of the order who observed the Rule according to the Papal interpretations.

FRATICELLI — Used of the Spirituals in Italy who broke away from the main body in order to follow the literal observance in groups of their own. First appears in a contemporary source in the Bull *Sancta Romana* of John XXII, in 1317.

MICHAELISTS — Used of the former Conventuals who, in 1328, under the leadership of Michael of Cesena, broke away from the main body in order to protest against the decision of John XXII on the poverty of Christ.

For details, see F. Ehrle, "Spiritualen und Fraticellen", *ALKG* IV (1888), 138–80; L. Oliger, "Spirituels", *DTC* XIV ii, 1941, coll. 2523–4.

No attempt has been made at consistency in the treatment of personal names: as a rule, the most usual form has been used, without regard to the language of its origin.

INTRODUCTION

IT IS well known that the first century of the history of the Franciscan order was filled with controversies, nearly all related to, or centring on, the practice and theory of poverty. There was the Spiritual–Conventual controversy, which had its beginnings in the lifetime of St Francis, developed in the last decades of the thirteenth century, and was brought sharply to an end by Pope John XXII in 1317–18. There was the controversy over the legitimacy of the mendicant life and the apostolate of the friars, between the secular masters and the mendicant friars in the University of Paris in the mid-thirteenth century. Finally there was the controversy over the poverty of Christ in the fourteenth century, between John XXII, the Dominicans, the Franciscans, and the neutral theologians in the curia.

Each of these controversies has, at various times, attracted the attention of historians. There are numbers of monographs, articles in learned periodicals dealing with different aspects of these disputes, and, behind them all, that great mass of original, printed sources which has been assembled by the devoted zeal of generations of learned Franciscans and—to mention one name above all—Cardinal Ehrle of the Society of Jesus. From time to time, attempts have been made by various hands to assemble and coordinate some sections of this material, and to provide summary accounts, whether of Franciscan history in broad outline, or of certain specialized aspects of that history. Two such accounts which at once come to mind as particularly valuable and successful are those by Père Gratien in 1928 on the history of the development of the order from St Francis to 1318, and by Dr Douie four years later, in 1932, on the more specialized topic of the history of the Spirituals within the order and of their lay supporters outside, from the time of the death of Francis on into the fifteenth century. Of these two, however, Gratien falls away considerably for the later part of his period, from about 1274 onwards, and Douie, though still retaining much value, is being slowly outdated by the output of new material, both primary and secondary, which appears year by year in the pages of the *Archivum Franciscanum Historicum*, in other Franciscan learned periodicals, and in articles and monographs elsewhere.

As far as I am aware no attempt has yet been made to co-ordinate all three of the major controversies and to provide a comprehensive history of Franciscan poverty. One doctrine—that of the absolute poverty of Christ and the apostles—provides a central theme to which all the disturbances of the first century of the order's history are in some way related.

The subject of my work, therefore, is the rise and fall of the doctrine of the absolute poverty of Christ and the apostles within the Franciscan order. The limits I have chosen are 1210 and 1323. The first represents the year in which St Francis and his companions received from Pope Innocent III permission to live according to the form of the holy gospel. The starting point for the doctrine, as far as his order is concerned, lies in the mind of St Francis, and the object of the first part of the work is to describe the nature of the doctrine which he held. It is therefore appropriate to make the year in which his way of life was approved by the Church the starting-point of the whole. The year 1323 selects itself as a concluding point, for this was the year in which John XXII condemned one particular form of the doctrine of absolute poverty, and so checked a tradition of thought about poverty which ran back deep into the thirteenth century.

The definition of John XXII brought to an end the last of the three controversies about poverty: that on the poverty of Christ. Of all medieval controversies, this must rank as one of the oddest, at least to the modern mind. For some time the energies of the greatest scholastics in Christendom were devoted to discussing the issue: Did Christ and the apostles have property in common, or not? The first question which I wished to ask, when I began to study this period, was: Why did the issue of the common property of Christ and the apostles seem to contemporaries a significant item of doctrine, worthy of prolonged discussion in the curia, and a Papal definition? If the purpose of writing history is to gain understanding of the unfamiliar past, then such a question is worth asking; yet no work which I consulted appeared to me to provide an answer.

The answer in fact, I have come to believe, lies primarily in Franciscan history. It was the Franciscan doctrine which was under attack in the curia, Franciscan theologians who defended the propertylessness of Christ, and Franciscans again who, after the Papal definition, carried their resistance to the point of no return, and went into schism. I have, in the first six chapters, described the origin and development of the Franciscan doctrine of absolute poverty, in order to explain the order's vehement attachment to it in the dispute under John XXII. This has carried me through the period of Francis, the time of consolidation after his death, and the secular–mendicant controversy of the mid-thirteenth century. The remaining four chapters describe the process of the decline and discrediting of absolute poverty, and its eventual condemnation. This takes me through the Spiritual–Conventual controversy, and, finally, the poverty of Christ controversy under John XXII. To this sequence strictly concerned with the rise and fall of absolute poverty, I have appended two chapters which, though still concerned with the practical issue of poverty, bear less directly on the main theme. One is the first chapter, which attempts to provide a reassessment of the problem of Francis in the light of continental research; the other is the fourth, concerned with John of Parma and Bonaventura, which has been included in order to give continuity to the history of poverty in the order.

Finally a word of apology. The historian who writes, in comparative comfort and security, about the Franciscan observance of poverty cannot but feel himself at a disadvantage. He has no first-hand experience of this grinding poverty; yet he writes, in part at least, for those who have taken it as their regular way of life. To all such I would address these lines: I have described what I saw, in honesty, and I have tried to understand, where I have no experience.

1

THE PROBLEM OF ST FRANCIS

THERE IS a general feeling in England that Francis, as a subject for serious history, is dead—that he can safely be left to the Quaracchi fathers, and the five-volume biography recently published by the Italian scholar, Arnaldo Fortini.[1] It is now twenty years since any serious work on Francis was published in England. Since the death of A. G. Little, there has been a general lessening of interest. Researchers have transferred their attention to other fields. The boom in Franciscan studies, generally, is over, Little and most of his followers and contemporaries are dead, and the brown volumes of the British Society for Franciscan Studies remain as a memorial to a phase in the investigation of the history of the religious orders which is now over.

It is one contention of this book that such an impression is mistaken.

When work in England on Francis ceased twenty years ago, with J. R. H. Moorman's valuable publication on the sources for his life, it was not because any final conclusion had been reached about the problems of Francis. There were still serious difficulties and they were still unresolved. Every one of the English historians who have dealt with Franciscan history has been a supporter, to a greater or less degree, of the Spiritual tradition about Francis. A. G. Little was; so were Cuthbert and G. G. Coulton; so, in our own time, is Moorman. All of these were in essentials believers in the tradition of Francis as the pure spirit, struggling against suffocating forces of legalism, crying out in the Testament for the true observance of his ideal.

It is not true that there is a settlement of Franciscan problems—that researchers are now much more agreed than they once were. The problem of St Francis stands still, wide open.

---

[1] A. Fortini, *Nova Vita di San Francesco*, Assisi, I-IV, 1959 (1st volume in two separate parts).

Interest has died away, with all kinds of loose ends left hanging
in the air. Vital continental work has never even been noticed
in England. Because all writers in England have followed the
tradition of A. G. Little, it has never been clearly enough realized
how deep the division of opinion among serious scholars really is.
There is no one view about St Francis: it is only chance that one,
the broadly Spiritual one, has been presented in England. In
fact, there are, and remain, two views about Francis—the
Spiritual and the Conventual, and within those broad traditions
there are many individual shades of interpretation.

Because the preliminary work on Francis has all been done, it
does not follow that there is nothing more to be said about him.
All the basic texts about Francis have been published. The writings
of Francis have been edited, with equal skill and thoroughness,
by the Leipzig Professor, Boehmer, and the Franciscan, Lemmens.
All the original biographies are in print, now in a really remarkable
edition by Bihl and the Quaracchi fathers. The Leo-sources, in all
their varied forms, have been edited, and then discussed over
and over again. It is in the last degree improbable that any important MS. on Francis remains to be discovered. But all this, vital
as it is, does not exhaust the subject or even offer conclusions about
the most fundamental problems of Francis.

In this first chapter, then, it is my purpose to make a complete
survey of the progress of studies on Francis since the time of Paul
Sabatier, with specific reference to the issue of poverty, so that
we may know upon what safe ground we can establish our
subsequent study in the doctrine of the absolute poverty of Christ
and the apostles.

Despite more than half a century's work since the appearance
of Sabatier's famous biography,[1] there is still, I would say, no
generally acceptable solution of the problem of St Francis's
intentions. The most pressing question was, and is: what did St
Francis intend his order to be? The sources themselves give
different answers, and more recent historians have been unable to
supply the kind of synthesis that would bridge the gap and provide
an agreed starting-point for Franciscan history.

It is a striking point that non-Franciscan writers have had no

[1] P. Sabatier, *Vie de S. François d'Assise*, Paris, 1894, Eng. tr., L. S. Houghton,
London, 1904.

more success than the Franciscans in emancipating themselves from the division of opinion in the order, which existed in the thirteenth century and continues in a modified form to trouble it to this day. The excess of polemic in this field is partly, but not entirely, explained by the ardent nature of Sabatier himself, whose errors were on the same generous scale as his discoveries, and who aroused a series of equally combative researchers, determined to rectify his exaggerations. Sabatier's intuitive method, his way of vivid generalized expression, having created a classic, tended to become the mode in Franciscan writing, often to its detriment.

An example is his radical approach to the problem of the various forms of rule written by St Francis for the first order in 1210, 1221, and 1223. He would accept only the earliest, the *Regula primitiva* of 1210, as a genuine expression of St Francis's will, the later ones being, in his opinion, more or less the work of the Church. In a characteristic *mot* he says: "In reality, that of 1210 and the one which the pope solemnly approved on November 29, 1223, had little in common except the name."[1] Although the moderate Cuthbert is right to redress the balance in favour of the later forms, it is unfortunate that he chooses to do so with a similar over-dramatic formula: "The revised Rule (that of 1221) was not a treaty of peace: it was a challenge thrown down to those who would change the vocation of the fraternity."[2] Moorman is in the same dangerous tradition when, adopting yet another view-point, he describes this 1221 Rule as "one of those compromises that fail, being acceptable neither to St Francis nor to the dissentient ministers".[3]

What is one to make of these divergent comments? If they are allowed to stand as purely personal reactions, well and good. Their confident tone then corresponds to the "doubtless" of common speech, prefacing some uncertain opinion. What they should not be taken for is primary proof in the argument about St Francis. Sabatier's judgement here is not based on the extant texts of the Rule, except indirectly: it is a deduction from his own conception of the true wishes of St Francis. Just how intuitive a method he

[1] Sabatier-Houghton, p. 253.
[2] Cuthbert, *Life of St Francis of Assisi*, 2nd edn., London, 1914, p. 314.
[3] J. R. H. Moorman, *The Sources for the Life of S. Francis of Assisi*, Manchester, 1940, p. 32.

sometimes used to discover these intentions, his own phrases reveal. On the works of St Francis he says: ". . . when in the writings of the Franciscans we find any utterance of their master, it unconsciously betrays itself . . .,"[1] and, on the 1221 redaction of the Rule, it "marks an intermediate stage. It is the clash of two principles . . . we can separate the divers elements without difficulty."[2] Naturally his critics were not slow to point out that this treatment inverted customary academic method. Their purpose was to sift the sources in order to discover the intentions of St Francis; whereas Sabatier, they claimed, took the object of research at a jump, and then used it to evaluate the sources.

Not only that. Once the sources had been resolved on an ideological basis into genuine Franciscan and extraneous elements, Sabatier cast about for the origin of the latter, and found it in the impositions of Ugolino, the cardinal protector. "If it is asked, who could have made these curtailments, one name springs at once to our lips—Ugolini."[3] The hypothesis proved an embarrassment to modern Franciscans, since not only did it invalidate their form of the Rule as an expression of the founder's will but even attributed the work of distortion to the Church itself. Because of the Ugolino theory the Franciscan controversy took on the overtones of a Catholic–Protestant wrangle, with Sabatier's biography on the Index, and more orthodox interpretations being turned out to replace it.

Sabatier's book served a double purpose. It was a literary work, an immense popular success, which passed into translations all over the world. It was also an academic work and regarded as such by the author. Otherwise he would not have gone on correcting it in a series of new editions lasting from 1894 until his death.[4] As a literary creation, it presents with great force a contest between Francis as prophet and Ugolino as priest. At this level the Ugolino theory performs an invaluable service in assembling the disparate events of St Francis's life into one coherent pattern: first, the growth of conflict between the journey to Rome in 1210 and the return from the East in 1220; secondly, the clash between Francis and Ugolino leading to the betrayal of the ideal in the 1223

---

[1] Sabatier-Houghton, p. 352.
[2] Ibid., p. 254.
[3] Ibid., p. 258.   [4] The final edition, in 1931, was posthumous.

redaction of the Rule; finally the sorrowful *dénouement*, withdrawal, suffering, a last appeal in the Testament, and death.

In effect, Sabatier poses two questions: What was the nature of St Francis's ideal? and, What was the relation between the ideal of St Francis and the will of the Church? The first question is incomparably the more important of the two, yet the format of a comprehensive biography, which requires the author to sustain a unified theme, draws the attention of the reader more to the second. For the same reason, perhaps, the biographers who sought to replace Sabatier, of whom the best examples are Jörgensen[1] and Cuthbert, devote much more time to correcting Sabatier's answer to the second question than to the first.

The whole discussion of the Ugolino theory belongs properly to the realm of literature rather than history. Sabatier's exposition on this point is marked by the prejudices of the Liberal Protestantism of his day: an excessive suspicion of authority, and an exaggerated dichotomy between love and law.[2] The corrections of his critics proceed along predominantly literary lines. Where direct evidence of Ugolino's action and motives is lacking, interpretation becomes a matter of inference. In Sabatier, Ugolino exists as a type-figure of the ecclesiastical politician. In Jörgensen, he has become the honest broker, anxious to mediate between Francis and the group of his followers, led by Brother Elias, who wish to dilute the ideal.[3] In Cuthbert, even Brother Elias has been transformed from Jörgensen's simple villain into a complex personality, at one time attracted and at another time antipathetic to the original ideal.[4] At the end we are left with a more subtle conflict, conducted inside the order, in a half-light of mingled idealism and weakness, in place of the sweeping contrasts conveyed by the 1894 biography.

But the fact remains that the biographers of the twentieth century have allowed themselves to be diverted by Sabatier's hyperbolic phrases from the fundamental question of St Francis's

---

[1] J. Jörgensen, *Den hellige Frans af Assisi*, Koebenhavn og Kristiana, 1907. Eng. tr., T. O'Conor Sloane, 2nd edn., New York, 1913.

[2] It is significant that Sabatier's first work should have been a thesis on the *Didache*: see A. G. Little, *Franciscan Papers, Lists and Documents*, Manchester, 1943, p. 180. I owe this observation to the Reverend Dr T. M. Parker.

[3] Op. cit., p. 226.

[4] Cuthbert, pp. 305–11.

intentions on to an issue which, however profitable and interesting, is essentially secondary. Viewed in the light of the development of the order, it does not much matter who is cast for the role of Judas, provided that it is clearly established that there was a betrayal. The decisive test of a biographer of Francis is the way in which he handles the years between 1220 and 1223, when Francis returned from his missionary journey exhausted, gave the government of the order to Brother Elias, and set about writing the Rule again. Sabatier, Jörgensen, and Cuthbert, however much they differ in other sections of the Life, describe this in similar terms. On the 1223 redaction of the Rule, for example, their contribution consists in toning down Sabatier's criticism. Jörgensen, after enumerating points in which this form falls short of St Francis's ideal, concludes: "The above is not to be understood as if the Rule approved by Rome was quite lacking in the Franciscan imprint",[1] while Cuthbert offers the somewhat halting defence that: "We may say that it gives us more purely the essential Francis of all time if less of the historical Francis of a particular period."[2] Comments such as these concede the justice of Sabatier's case—that the binding Rule of the order (and, therefore, its subsequent observance) did not correspond to the true wishes of St Francis.

While the Ugolino theory underpins the literary structure of the 1894 biography, this conviction of Sabatier's lies behind all his Franciscan work, both literary and academic. He dissociated himself from those who would treat Francis as some sort of forerunner of Protestantism,[3] and in later editions of the biography considerably modified his judgements on Ugolino; but he was not prepared to surrender his opinion that the ideal of St Francis was formed once and for all in the Rule of 1210 and the heroic days at Rivo Torto.

Sabatier's first edition of the biography was based solely on sources which were in print at the time; its most immediate effect,

---

[1] Jörgensen-Sloane, p. 254.

[2] Cuthbert, p. 386.

[3] "And yet those who would rely exclusively on these passages, and plenty of other similar ones in the works of the saint to make a kind of precursor of Protestantism out of him, would be completely wrong. I know it is a reproach which has been made to me. If I have deserved it, I am sorry, and I will try to make amends for my fault." P. Sabatier, "L'Originalité de Saint François d'Assise", *Franciscan Essays* I, *BSFS* Extra Ser. I, Aberdeen, 1912, p. 9.

however, was to instigate a search for new MS. sources, which should either prove or disprove his theories. Sabatier himself had the first success. In 1898 he published a MS. known as the *Speculum perfectionis*, a collection of sayings of Francis and stories about him grouped under the virtues which they illustrated. A MS. *incipit* gave to the original work the startling date of 1227; the text itself seemed to have been written by Brother Leo, Francis's secretary and his closest companion. Sabatier believed that he had discovered the earliest and most authentic piece of evidence about Francis and published the first edition of the *Speculum* at Paris under the title *Speculum Perfectionis seu S. Francisci Assisiensis Legenda Antiquissima auctore Fratre Leone.*

The new source appeared to support to the hilt Sabatier's belief that Francis in his last days, after his return from the East, had repudiated the current observance of the order. This was the key passage. The author of the *Speculum*, having described a reply of Francis in which he apparently demanded a poverty more strict than that of the Rule, went on to give the following explanation:

If any brother should wish to ask why St Francis did not have so strict a poverty observed by the brothers in his lifetime . . . we who were with him reply as we heard from his mouth, since he said this and many other things to the brothers, and also had many things written in the Rule, which he asked from the Lord with earnest prayer and meditation for the good of the order, saying that they were according to the will of the Lord; but after he showed them to the brothers, they seemed to them heavy and intolerable, not knowing then what things were to come in the order after his death. And because he greatly feared scandal in himself and in the brothers, he did not wish to contend with them but yielded unwillingly to their will and excused himself with the Lord.

But, that his word might not return empty to the Lord that he put in his mouth for the good of the brothers, he wished to fulfil it in himself, so that he might thereby obtain reward from the Lord. And at the last he rested in this and his spirit was consoled.[1]

---

[1] Ed. cit., chap. ii, pp. 6–7. On all other occasions reference to Sabatier's version of the *Speculum* will be made according to the first volume of the second edition, revised after his death by A. G. Little. P. Sabatier, *Le Speculum Perfectionis ou Mémoires de Frère Léon sur la Seconde Partie de la Vie de Saint François d'Assise*, tome I, Texte Latin, *BSFS* XIII, Manchester, 1928; tome II, Étude Critique, *BSFS* XVII, Manchester, 1931. The differences between the various forms of the Leo-sources are not our prime concern: Sabatier's *Speculum* has been taken as representative of this literature.

The purpose of most of the rest of the work was to display in detail the true wishes of St Francis about poverty. Understandably enough, Sabatier believed that he had discovered a decisive proof for his theory of St Francis.

But other discoveries followed Sabatier's. In 1901 the Franciscan, Lemmens, published another version of the *Speculum perfectionis*, and with it two other short works, the *Intentio regulae* and the *Verba sancti Francisci*, both supposedly written by Brother Leo.[1] Later, A. G. Little and the Franciscan, Delorme, discovered yet other versions of the *Speculum* stories, the latter, in the form in which it was discovered, being attributable to the years 1311–12.[2] The MS. *incipit* of Sabatier's version of the *Speculum* was found to be a scribe's error for 1318.[3]

It became clear that the document which Sabatier had discovered, so far from being the one original biography by Leo, was a single piece of a whole new literature, dating in its extant versions, not from the period immediately after Francis's death, but from the late thirteenth or early fourteenth centuries. It became clear, also, that none of this fresh literature had the indisputable authenticity for which Sabatier had hoped. Although the new literature broadly supported his account of Francis's views rather than that of his opponents, it all contained doubtful elements. Closer examination of the *Speculum* revealed in the body of the text an awareness of later events in the history of the order which could hardly be accounted for by the gift of prophecy alone. The anecdotes appeared perhaps a little too relevant to later controversies about the observance of poverty to be accepted *in toto* and in the exact form in which they are given. Even Sabatier was compelled to excise from his version the first chapter, describing the miraculous appearance of Christ at Fonte Colombo to confound the dissentient ministers and authenticate the Rule.[4]

---

[1] *Documenta Antiqua Franciscana*, ed. L. Lemmens, Ad Claras Aquas, 1901. Pars I: *Scripta Fratris Leonis socii S.P. Francisci*. Pars II: *Speculum Perfectionis* (*Redactio I*).

[2] For details, see Moorman, *Sources*, pp. 11, 128–30, 134–5. It should be added that the two documents edited by Little and Delorme do not bear the title of *Speculum perfectionis*; but they have close affinities with the *Speculum* and can justly be regarded as part of the same literature.

[3] Op. cit., pp. 130–3.

[4] *Speculum*, ed. Sabatier (1928), pp. 1–3. Sabatier here puts the chapter in brackets.

The dates of two of the new documents, Sabatier's and Delorme's, appeared significant. The date of 1318 for Sabatier's would put it into relation with the Bull of John XXII, *Quorumdam exigit*, which set obedience above poverty and allowed Franciscan ministers to coerce zealots for poverty.[1] Delorme's date of 1311–12, drawn from internal evidence, would make his version contemporaneous with the peak of the poverty conflict carried on by rival groups of Franciscans at the curia in Avignon and at the Council of Vienne.[2]

It soon became apparent that the prejudiced elements in the newly-discovered Leo-sources, instead of forming one excisable portion, were scattered throughout the whole. The Fonte Colombo episode, which puts into the mouth of Christ the slogan of the zealots for poverty—"ad litteram . . . sine glossa"—appears also, for example, in the *Verba* edited by Lemmens, as an integral part of the argument.[3] Few accepted Sabatier's belief that the *Speculum* only required the elimination of the Fonte Colombo chapter to be restored virtually to the state in which it left the hand of Brother Leo. Yet, despite these weaknesses, it remained true to say that in the new sources historians appeared to get nearer than ever before to witnesses who were in a position to give a final verdict on the intentions of St Francis. The first companions were alone with Francis for all the primitive period up to the great expansion of the order from about 1215 onwards, and then again for the rest of his life after he gave the government of the order to Elias in 1221. Their testimony accounts for a great part of the information in the official thirteenth-century Lives. Thomas of Celano, it would seem, wrote his second Life from the rolls of reminiscences of the companions.[4] Bonaventura, in the prologue to his Life, describes how he checked the facts with those of the companions who had survived to his own time.[5] The decree of the chapter-

---

[1] See chap. 10, below. *Quorumdam exigit* was issued in 1317. Four zealots who refused to accept its provisions were burnt in 1318.

[2] See chap. 8.

[3] *Documenta Antiqua Franciscana*, ed. Lemmens, Pars. I, *Verba*, para. 4, pp. 101–3.

[4] See Moorman, *Sources*, pp. 112–13.

[5] Bonaventura, *Legenda Maior*, prologus, 4, lines 1–6, in *Legendae S. Francisci Assisiensis saeculis XIII et XIV conscriptae*, Analecta Franciscana X, Ad Claras Aquas, 1926–41, p. 559. All references to the official biographies, *I* and *II Celano*, and Bonaventura, will be made according to this edition. The *Legenda Maior* will be cited normally by chapter, paragraph, and page of this edition.

general of Paris in 1266, which accepted Bonaventura's Life as
the official biography and ordered the destruction of all others,
partly justified their decision on the same ground, that this version
had been based on the oral witness of the companions.[1]

References in early authorities suggested that the rolls of reminiscences, originally set down in answer to an appeal of the
chapter-general in 1244, on which Thomas of Celano based his
second Life, were not destroyed but survived, first in the convent
of the Clares, and later in the Sacro Convento. These authorities
quote sections of the rolls, and their quotations turn out to be
identical with passages in the *Speculum perfectionis*, the *Intentio
regulae*, and the *Verba*.[2] These authorities are all Franciscans
deeply involved in the conflict about poverty in the later thirteenth
century. They have an interest in saying that these writings show
the true wishes of St Francis. At the same time there is too much
supporting evidence for their witness to be wholly discounted.
There are thus both primitive material and later interpolations,
or distortions, contained in the Leo-sources. But how would it
be possible to separate the wheat from the chaff? No one could
provide an easy answer. The Leo-sources, therefore, fail to provide
a knock-down answer to the problem of St Francis. The difficulties
inherent in their use, we see, are as great, or greater than, those
met with in the official biographies.

What of these official biographies? Like the Leo-sources, they
bear the imprint of the stormy history of the Franciscan order.
When, for example, the second Life of Celano appeared, the order
had already passed through a number of disturbing scenes. Even
the most tranquil of the biographies, Bonaventura's *Legenda maior*,
mentions that after Francis wrote a first draft of the Rule the

---

[1] "Item precepit generale capitulum per obedientiam, quod omnes legende
de beato Francisco olim facte deleantur, et ubi extra ordinem inveniri poterunt,
ipsas fratres studeant amovere, cum illa legenda, que facta est per generalem
ministrum, fuerit compilata prout ipse habuit ab ore eorum, qui cum b.
Francisco quasi semper fuerunt et cuncta certitudinaliter sciverint et probata
ibi sint posita diligenter" (*sic*). "Definitiones Capitulorum Generalium Ordinis
Fratrum Minorum 1260–1282", ed. A. G. Little, *AFH* vii (1914), 678; Paris,
no. viii.

[2] For details, see Jörgensen's Appendix to his Life, "Authorities for the life
of St Francis of Assisi": Jörgensen-Sloane, pp. 356–78, and esp. pp. 382–90,
with refs. given. On these established points, Jörgensen's account has not been
outdated by Moorman.

minister-general Elias lost it "by carelessness"[1]—surely a very odd thing to do. Later there was a mysterious dispute over the translation of the body of Francis in 1230; there was disorder over the re-election of Elias; then came his deposition in 1239 and final excommunication. There had been two major Bulls issued by Gregory IX and Innocent IV to dissipate doubts about the Rule, and revolutionary changes in the order's legislation after the fall of Elias.[2]

All this was bound to have some repercussions on the presentation of the life of Francis by Celano. The most obvious instance of the effect of these events is the suppression of information about the execrated Elias. Undoubtedly Elias played a considerable part in the life of Francis, whether for good or ill—he joined early, was chosen by Francis as provincial for Syria, and then, after the rule of Peter Catanii, as minister-general. The first Life of Celano mentions Francis's esteem for him, and his special blessing of him.[3] Yet in the second Life his name is not so much as mentioned.

The argument against *II Celano* as a completely reliable source for Francis is this: if Celano was prepared to alter the account of events in this negative way, by suppressing information about Elias, might he not also be led by the pressure of the history of the order after the death of Francis to alter the account of his views on poverty? The positive bias required might be quite slight and largely unconscious. It is a delicate matter. The difference of emphasis is small between Francis, for example, urging his followers, as other saints have done, to go beyond the observance prescribed in the Rule, and Francis denouncing that observance as a distortion of his ideal.

On any view of the interdependence of the sources, the element of bias cannot be discounted. If *II Celano* is preferred to the Leo-sources, there is the possibility of distortion both in the memory

---

[1] Bonav., *Leg. Maj.*, iv, 11, 576.
[2] See below, chap. 3.
[3] *I Cel.*, 108; *AF* X, 83–4. Ref. to the two Lives by Celano has been given according to the paragraphs in the Quaracchi edn. Line refs. have been used only where necessary; these have been enumerated by paragraphs in the Quaracchi edn., and not by pages. The subdivisions of the text of *II Celano* differ markedly from those in L. Amoni's edn: a concordance is given, *AF* X, p. xxxiv.

of the companions and in the subsequent writing-up by Celano. If the miscellaneous Leo-sources are preferred, then one has to contend with the late date of the extant MSS. and the prejudice of the compilers, as well as the possible prejudice of Leo and the companions.

For this purpose it is not of the first importance which way the bias leans. The supporters of the Leo-sources will feel that Celano has played down the opposition of Francis to the Rule of 1223 and the ministers, while the adherents of Celano will think that the Leo-sources have greatly exaggerated this opposition.

There is even room for a third point of view, that Bonaventura, although he had access to no new sources, by omitting all reference to controversy in his Life, presented an account less misleading than either *II Celano* or the Leo-sources, who sharpened and misinterpreted such doubts and hesitations as Francis expressed about the observance of the order between 1221 and 1226.

The dilemma remains. Ever since the Bollandists rediscovered Celano in the eighteenth century, lost sources, which were suppressed or ignored in favour of the official Life by Bonaventura, have been brought once more to the light of day. The researchers who toiled so patiently in the libraries and archives of the last two centuries have given us now a great mass of primary material for the life and thought of Francis. But these sources are either contradictory; or appear in late MS. versions; or are suspect on other grounds. What can be done to use this refractory material? This is a central problem. Can we discover any one authentic source for Francis's mind? Or can we, in any way, break down hitherto unusable material to discover authentic sections embedded in it?

We have seen the problem. Now we may examine the solutions which have been proposed for it.

The great need is for some objective criterion which can be used to resolve the contradictions in the sources—some yardstick which will enable us to decide which source, or part of a source, is authentic, and which not. If such a yardstick cannot be found, then the sources cannot be used with that confidence and certainty which is desirable. It is important, therefore, that one should be found. In practice, however, I do not believe that any of the solutions hitherto put forward have been fully effective. This view does not seem to have been generally accepted in England.

Nevertheless, I think that if we examine these proposed solutions, and apply to them the criticisms of continental writers, we shall find that it is true.

I would distinguish three principal solutions. One is concerned with the Leo-sources; another with the *Verba* and the *Intentio*; a third with the Testament of Francis. I propose now to examine each of these three solutions in turn, and to test their validity.

First, the solution concerned with the Leo-sources. A. G. Little [1] summarized it most briefly and effectively in a lecture given to the British Academy in 1926, on the occasion of the seventh centenary of the death of Francis. It was a masterly lecture by a great scholar. It has carried great weight in England, and the methods expounded in it form the foundation for the later work of J. R. H. Moorman.

Little spoke as a moderate supporter of Sabatier, who recognized his faults and rejected, for example, his views on Ugolino and his first, extravagant claims for the *Speculum perfectionis*. [2] In arguing for the superiority of the Leo-sources over *II Celano*, he had selected from the mass of stories and sayings about Francis those where his judgement could be most clearly illustrated. His plea was, probably deliberately, a minimal one.

One suggested line of attack related to the content of the stories. If the same story was presented in two versions in two different sources, of which one displayed the saint in a more human, and the other in a more respectable light, the presumption was that the first represented the original version, and the second the copy. One such anecdote appears both in *II Celano* and in three redactions of the Leo-sources, the MSS. discovered by Sabatier, Lemmens, and Little. It illustrates St Francis's gift of foreknowledge. On a dark and stormy night, as he lay dying in the bishop's palace at Assisi, he took a fancy to some parsley, and asked for one of the brothers to go and pick some for him there and then. The cook at first demurred, but, on St Francis insisting, did as he was told and put his hand on the first herb that he came to—and discovered the parsley. The essential variation in wording

---

[1] A. G. Little, "Some recently discovered Franciscan documents and their relations to the Second Life by Celano and the Speculum Perfectionis", *Proceedings of the British Academy*, xii (1926), 147–78.

[2] See A. G. Little, "Paul Sabatier, Historian of St. Francis", *Franciscan Papers, Lists and Documents*, Manchester, 1943, pp. 179–88.

occurs in the version of Francis's reply to the excuses of the reluctant cook. The version in *II Celano* is edifying; the one in the Lemmens and the Little redactions of the Leo-sources is not. Little prefers the Little MS. even though it is only a fifteenth-century one. He goes on to say:

> The external evidence is weak. The internal evidence is conclusive. It is impossible to doubt that we have here a copy of the original narrative on which Celano worked. And one obvious inference to be drawn from a comparison of the two versions is that Celano had no scruples about altering the words of St Francis as they were reported to him, when he saw an opportunity of making them more edifying.
> So the complaint of a sick man, "You should not make me say a thing so often", becomes a little homily on obedience.[1]

A similar glossing of his originals by Celano was deduced by Little from a story of Ugolino's visit to the Franciscans, which appears in two versions, one in Delorme's or Sabatier's MSS., the other in *II Celano*. Little concludes: "The real difference between the two points of view is this: Celano lays stress on the asceticism of the early friars: the Delorme–*Speculum perfectionis* version lays stress on the poverty and their equality with the poorest of the poor which resulted from it."[2]

One may observe the subtlety and minuteness of this analysis. The criterion for deciding which is the primitive, and which the worked-up version, consists in a few words only. Even when the test has been applied, it only enables the historian to decide on the superiority of a source over the others in respect of one anecdote.

The general tenor of Little's argument is that the Leo-sources represent in essentials a better tradition than *II Celano*. On some points, he admits, the Leo-sources have merely copied *II Celano*. Sabatier's *Speculum perfectionis*, for the parsley episode, copies the glossed version of *II Celano*.

In general, Little's use of internal evidence is open to much the same objections as the higher criticism of gospel sources. The parallel has long been noted between the study of the sources for the life of Christ and those for the life of Francis. Coulton used the analogy of Franciscan sources to show the possibility of similar

---

[1] Art. cit., p. 155.
[2] Ibid., p. 159.

suppressions of fact in the sources for the life of Christ.[1] Both Sabatier and F. C. Burkitt were scholars with some knowledge or experience of higher criticism in both fields of study. Conversely, some of the strongest opposition to the application of the methods of the higher criticism to the Franciscan problem through the Leo-sources has come from scholars like Faloci-Pulignani, Van Ortroy, or Bihl, who were reared in a theological tradition that refused to admit such methods to the study of gospel sources.[2]

The difficulty of the higher criticism is finding an adequate control. Probably not much more can be done in Franciscan research by investigation of MSS.; progress will be made only on the lines of Little's lecture, by internal criticism of individual "pericopes". But the nature of the method is such that every variation in the form of the individual pericope can be accounted for in more than one way, without doing violence to the known facts.

It is not generally realized that even Little's instances have been powerfully controverted. In the course of a seemingly unknown article which appeared in the *Archivum Franciscanum Historicum* for 1927 and 1928, Bihl took step by step every example adduced by Little to show that Celano had altered the original versions of the pericopes contained in the Leo-sources; and provided for each one some reasonable alternative explanation.[3] On the parsley episode, for instance, he attributed the discrepancy between *II Celano* and the Little MS. to a condensing of Francis's words in Celano by the later compiler of the Little MS.[4] On the account of Ugolino's visit, he explained the discrepancy between *II Celano* and the Delorme MS. as a scribal error in the Delorme MS. which has misplaced a line from the pericope immediately preceding.[5]

Generally, he turned Little's hypothesis upside down and argued

---

[1] G. G. Coulton, "The Story of St Francis of Assisi", F. J. Foakes Jackson and Kirsopp Lake, *The Beginnings of Christianity*, Part I, *The Acts of the Apostles*, vol. II, 1922, pp. 438–61.

[2] I am indebted to the Reverend Dr T. M. Parker for information on this point.

[3] M. Bihl, "Disquisitiones Celanenses", *AFH* xx (1927), 456–61, xxi (1928), 4–19.

[4] Art. cit., *AFH* xxi, 5–8.

[5] Ibid., pp. 10–13.

that *II Celano* is the original, and the Leo-sources are the copy.

Over much of the ground the reader may still prefer Little's explanation to Bihl's. Certainly, to accept Bihl's theory in full means jettisoning all the Leo-sources that have been discovered since 1898, with the exception only of the *Verba Sancti Francisci* and the *Intentio Regulae*, which have been generally accepted as genuine works of Brother Leo. The point, however, remains that after reading Bihl's attack no one can feel that internal criticism of the Leo-sources will supply the need for a generally recognized means of resolving the contradiction in Franciscan sources. The attack came from a reputable source: Bihl, for many years the editor of the *Archivum*, could not be described as a crude conservative.

Moreover, it was made at Little's strongest feature, since his examples had naturally been selected as the most cogent for his theory of the relation between *II Celano* and the Leo-sources. Bihl was able to counter with rival examples, where *II Celano* seemed to put Francis in a less conventional light than the Leo-sources. If this view could be sustained, it would make nonsense of Little's theory, for the one fact which, by this time, was accepted by supporters of Celano and of Leo alike, was that *II Celano* was older than the extant redactions of the Leo-sources.

Little in the same lecture touched on another line of approach which, at first sight, appeared to have the element of objectivity required to silence opposition. This was the study of style. He said:

> If one document uses the rhythms which were generally regarded as marks of good style in the middle ages, and another version of the same story does not use those rhythms, the probability is that the rhythmical version is derived from the unrhythmical rather than *vice versa*. No medieval writer would deliberately change what he regarded as good style into bad style, though if he were not a "bonus dictator" the need of compressing a narrative might compel him to do so.[1]

He then gave a demonstration of the efficacy of this test applied to *II Celano* and the Leo-sources.

But here again Bihl was prepared with a number of objections. Although Little believed that the rhythms of the *cursus* appeared many more times in *II Celano* than in the Leo-sources, he was too

[1] Little, art. cit., p. 157.

honest not to admit that: "Leo was a competent 'dictator' and could use the rhythms of the *cursus* when he chose."[1] Bihl made play with this admission. He noted how the *cursus* might make its appearance by sheer chance, and argued that not enough was known about its nature and use in the Middle Ages to enable historians to erect any general theory upon it.[2]

There the matter rested. No fundamental advance has been made since Bihl's article was published. The conservatives and the Leo-supporters have continued their work on existing lines without, apparently, much contact between each other. Bihl and the Quaracchi editors produced a definitive edition of the formal biographies of Francis in which scant reference is made to the Leo-sources.[3] Moorman, in his work on the sources, applied the methods of Little's lecture in order to develop a new hypothesis about the *Legend of the Three Companions*, the most intractable source of all; but he neither developed nor criticized Little's methods. No one, in effect, has met Bihl's attack on Little's methods or, perhaps, even noticed it; it was unfortunate that it should have been embedded in an article dealing with a whole range of other matters. Moorman in his turn was attacked by Bihl[4] on much the same grounds as Little had been although with rather less discrimination.[5]

There are two sides to the question. Little, and Moorman following him, are tackling an unusually complex problem, and it may be that to ask for definitive proofs, as Bihl does, is to cry for the moon. On the other hand, until the methods outlined in the British Academy lecture have been developed in greater detail, and until the "*cursus* method" in particular has been subjected to a closer analysis, it seems prudent to conclude that internal criticism of the biographical sources does not provide us with a solution.

Unfortunately there can be no shirking the result of this

[1] Ibid., p. 163.

[2] Art. cit., *AFH* xx, 456–61, *AFH* xxi, 10.

[3] See above, p. 9, n. 5.

[4] M. Bihl, "Contra duas novas hypotheses prolatas a Ioh. R. H. Moorman adversus 'Vitam S. Francisci' auctore Thoma Celanansi, cui substituere vellet sic dictam 'Legendam 3 Sociorum'", *AFH* xxxix (1948), 3–37, and review, ibid., pp. 279–87.

[5] We may note Doucet's later comment, that Moorman's book was "reviewed here a bit severely perhaps", *AFH* xlvi (1953), 105.

melancholy decision. The first proposed solution has to be dismissed.
The mass of the Leo-sources have to be put on one side as unreliable, because no means have been found of discovering what sections of them, if any, record the actual words of Brother Leo.

We may now turn to examine the second solution—that concerned with the *Verba* and the *Intentio Regulae*. Both have been
recognized as genuine works of Leo. Both have a clear purpose in
recording the intentions of Francis about the observance of
poverty. The *Intentio* includes the solemn declaration of Francis's
dissatisfaction with the observance of his day.[1]

The case of these works raises for the first time the issue of the
credibility of the testimony of Leo and the companions. Directly
associated with the exposition of Francis's views on poverty in the
Verba is the doubtful story of Fonte Colombo. The specious clarity
of the story, the reiteration of "ad litteram . . . sine glossa", the
existence of an echo at the spot, above all the value of the episode
as giving the assurance of Divine approval to the rigorist party,
suggest a confusion of fact, allegory, and the subsequent wishes of
the teller.[2] As Sabatier said, "Indignation and despair carried
these poor mystics away. . . ."[3] If the Fonte Colombo account in
its present form is factually incorrect, will the exposition of
Francis's intentions which is linked to it be any more accurate?

Even if, excepting the *Verba*, we turn our attention to the
Intentio, difficulties still remain.

Leo and the surviving companions lived through the same disturbing events which may perhaps have led Celano in his second
Life to sharpen the words of Francis on poverty. They had even
more reason than he to regret the changes which carried the order
on so far from the simplicity of their early days with Francis. Once
he was dead, they had no clear-cut place in the order—except to
go on recounting their memories to fresh generations of Franciscans. They played no part in the development of the missions, the

---

[1] *Documenta Antiqua Franciscana*, ed. Lemmens, *Intentio*, para 4, p. 86. However,
R. B. Brooke, in her *Early Franciscan Government*, Cambridge, 1959, p. 87, n. 1,
describes the *Verba* as a "pseudo-Leonine collection", and promises a study on
it. My text here was written before the appearance of this book.

[2] F. C. Burkitt, "Fonte Colombo and its traditions", *Franciscan Essays* II,
BSFS Extra Ser. III, Manchester, 1932, pp. 41–55. But see Brooke, *Early
Franciscan Government*, p. 94, where the writer was unable to arouse an echo at
Fonte Colombo—an alarming discovery.

[3] *Speculum*, ed. Sabatier (1928), p. xvi.

entry to the universities, the growth of learning. They were not suited to hold office, and therefore were the less likely to understand the difficulties of those who were in office. Oliger well describes the influences at work in the minds of the companions when they came to set down their recollections of Francis:

> It should be no surprise to us to find among such accounts some statements whose authorship one would scarcely, at first sight, attribute to Brother Leo, that gentle companion of St Francis and "pecorella Dei". They can be understood better if we recall the frame of mind in which Leo in his old age reinterpreted what St Francis had said in a general way about the future state of the order, giving these sayings a more forceful interpretation than the Holy Father, and a concrete and particular application. Here is an example. On seeing some followers of the sect of the *Spiritus libertatis*, Leo was shaken and alarmed, and said: "Those are the apostles of Satan, who our father St Francis prophesied would come, who, misguided themselves, will lead many others astray", etc. This was no falsification on Brother Leo's part, but the effects of a psychological law, which is observable in other men, and cannot be neglected if we are to understand the literature of the Spirituals about St Francis.[1]

A similar process of misunderstanding, it may be suggested, can be seen at work in the chronicle of the English Franciscan, known as Thomas of Eccleston. Recalling how his hero, the provincial, William of Nottingham, used to say that he believed that Christ would raise a new order to stir up the Franciscans, Eccleston fails to grasp his meaning and begins to run through the list of lesser-known orders to see which one it could be.[2] Here in this narrative the words of the leader and the reflections of his simple follower are given distinct from each other; we are at the first stage of the process of transformation. The case of Francis and Leo is in many respects akin to that of Eccleston and William of Nottingham, with the difference that Leo had kept the words of his master in his mind and meditated on them until they passed into his own thought. The ideas of Francis and the reflections of Leo had become inseparable by the time he committed them to writing.

[1] Angelo da Clareno, *Expositio Regulae Fratrum Minorum*, ed. L. Oliger, Ad Claras Aquas, 1912, p. lxiv.

[2] *Fratris Thomae vulgo dicti de Eccleston tractatus, De Adventu Fratrum Minorum in Angliam*, ed. A. G. Little, Manchester, 1951, p. 102.

Therefore, we may say, the *Verba* and the *Intentio* cannot be secure guides: the possibility of unconscious distortion in the mind of their author prevents us from recognizing them as decisive evidence for the mind of Francis.

The biographical sources must therefore be put on one side. There remains a third solution. If adequate, it would by-pass the difficulties aroused by all the Lives.

Before the discovery of the new MS. Leo-sources, in the 1894 biography, Sabatier described the study of the writings of Francis as the key to the problem. He said, in the opening sentence of his Appendix on the sources: "The writings of St Francis are assuredly the best source of acquaintance with him; we can only be surprised to find them so neglected by most of his biographers."[1] When the new *Speculum* literature began to find its way into print he regarded it as a remarkable confirmation of the judgement he had already formed from his analysis of the writings of Francis. Because his opinion was fixed by this criterion, the doubts subsequently expressed about the new discoveries affected him no more than the criticisms which were made earlier on against the fragments of the Leo-sources which were in print when he composed the first edition. He recognized the force of some of the technical arguments levelled against the Leo-sources; but he felt that in the long run they were bound to be vindicated because on the vital issues their interpretation corresponded to the testimony of Francis himself.

On the fundamentals, Sabatier was supported by an objective critic, W. Goetz, who in a series of articles in 1901 and 1903 set out to provide a fresh investigation of all the documents for the life of Francis.[2] However often Goetz turned aside to attack incidental errors of Sabatier, he agreed with him in thinking that the writings of Francis were the proper standard by which to assess the rest of the sources. Speaking of the later biographical tradition, he decided: "What he wrote himself is the only reliable standard of measurement for the truth of this tradition."[3]

[1] Sabatier-Houghton, p. 351.
[2] "Die Quellen zur Geschichte des hl. Franz von Assisi", *ZKG* xxii (1901), 362–77, 525–65; xxiv (1903), 165–97, 475–519; xxv (1904), 33–47; also, "Die ursprünglichen Ideale des hl. Franz von Assisi", *Historische Vierteljahrschrift* vi (1903), 19–50.
[3] *ZKG* xxii, 368.

Like Sabatier, Goetz believed that the clue to Francis's thought was contained in three of his writings, the two extant Rules of 1221 and 1223, and the Testament which was dictated after these, in the months before his death. The way in which he expounded his interpretation of the nexus between the three documents carried more weight because he avoided both Sabatier's over-statements and his penchant for regarding Francis as a victim of the hierarchical self-seeking of Ugolino. The minimal established facts seemed to him to be as follows: Ugolino had a share in writing the Rule of 1223, as we know from his own statement in the Bull *Quo elongati*, issued four years after the death of Francis, in 1230.[1] This Rule, which was confirmed by the Pope, differs materially from the earlier form of 1221, which was not. The Testament shows Francis at the end of his life anxious for the purity of his ideal.[2]

Goetz's general conclusion was that a source in which Francis spoke directly was to be preferred to one in which he spoke under influence from outside. The Testament, where he spoke without any apparent impediment, was therefore a better source than the Rule of 1223, in which his voice mingled with that of Ugolino. In so far as the Testament was in conflict with the Rule of 1223, the Testament was to be preferred as a statement of his ideal. An examination of the wording of the two documents confirmed the external evidence. The stylistic roughness of the Testament, the loose sequence of thought, demonstrated that it came direct from the mouth of the saint, while the more clear-cut arrangement of the Rule of 1223 suggested the intervention of a learned adviser. The Rule of 1221 and the Testament had more in common with each other than with the Rule of 1223.

This is not far distant from the view of Sabatier, when he said: "If we would find the Franciscan spirit, it is here, in the Rule of 1221, and in the Will that we must seek for it."[3] Above all, it was the Testament which guaranteed the Sabatier interpretation. "In this record . . .", he said, "the Poverello reveals himself absolutely. . . ."[4] Goetz was equally convinced

[1] *Bullarii Franciscani Epitome*, ed. C. Eubel, no. iv, p. 229a.
[2] *Historische Vierteljahrschrift* vi, 42–3.
[3] Sabatier-Houghton, p. 327.
[4] Ibid., p. 334.

of its value. He used it not only as a textual standard to try the
rest of the *Opuscula*, but also as a definitive statement of the Franciscan ideal. "For although this Testament is very far from exhaustive, it nevertheless summarizes in a compressed form Francis's
desires for the future of his order and the ideals to which his soul
clung so very firmly."[1]

On the interpretation of the Testament and its relation to the
Rule of 1223, Goetz was more cautious than Sabatier. The latter
said simply that: "The Will is not an appendix to the Rule of
1223, it is almost its revocation."[2] If we look at the actual text
of the Testament, we shall see much to support Sabatier's view.
Even though Francis declared that he did not intend to issue
another Rule but only to urge the brothers to a better observance
of the Rule they had—which was the Rule of 1223[3]—still he
delivered the Testament to posterity with all the solemnity
associated with a legally binding document. He expects it to be
kept with the Rule, and read with it at chapter meetings.[4] He
orders the ministers "per obedientiam" not to change its wording.
When in the body of the text he comes to speak of the observance
of the order, his thoughts turn not towards the Rule of 1223 but
to the earliest form of all, that of 1210, and to the simple, heroic
days before the great expansion of the fraternity. There is an
unmistakable note of nostalgia as he recalls this time. "And those
who came to receive this life gave all that they might have to the
poor. And they were content with a tunic, patched inside and out,
with cord and breeches. And we did not want to have more."[5]
Sabatier saw in these words something deeper than the natural
predilection of a dying man for the early years of his conversion,
because of the implied contrast with the clauses of the two later
forms of the Rule, which allowed the professed to have two tunics

---

[1] *ZKG* xxii, 376.

[2] Sabatier-Houghton, p. 275.

[3] *Testamentum*, 11. The definitive text, used throughout, is that given by
K. Esser in his *Das Testament des heiligen Franziskus von Assisi. Eine Untersuchung
über seine Echtheit und seine Bedeutung*, Münster-i-W., 1949, pp. 100–3. The
divisions of the text he takes from *Analekten zur Geschichte des Franciscus von Assisi*,
ed. H. Boehmer, Tübingen, Leipzig, 1904, pp. 36–40.

[4] *Testamentum*, 12.

[5] *Testamentum*, 4. Esser in his comparison of the Testament and the Rule of
1223, *Testament*, p. 132, perhaps underestimates this nostalgia for the primitive
Rule.

if they wished, and did not insist on novices actually giving all their goods to the poor.[1]

Elsewhere one may detect a reaction against the current practice of the brothers. With great sternness Francis forbade the brothers to accept privileges from Rome "per se neque per interpositam personam":[2] the years following Francis's return from the East were the beginning of the flood of Papal Bulls and letters of protection that fill so many volumes of the *Bullarium Franciscanum*. He warned them to observe the poverty they had promised in the Rule in their churches and dwelling-places:[3] in these years the process was gathering momentum which converted the Franciscans from a band of wandering preachers into a settled order with permanent stone friaries and churches. Finally he expressed his determination to block the way to development away from the primitive ideal by prohibiting all glossing of the Rule.[4]

Thus, if attention is concentrated on certain of its clauses, the Testament may be taken to reveal Francis as a full-blown Spiritual Franciscan. His last words, taken in one way, did include most of the elements of the programme of the reforming groups which appeared in the order in the last quarter of the thirteenth century: the stress on poverty, on the literal observance of the Rule, and the rejection of Papal glosses and privileges. When Sabatier concluded that it was possible to resolve the contradiction in the sources and to decide in favour of a Spiritual interpretation of the Franciscan ideal, he did, therefore, have some weighty evidence on his side.

Of the three solutions which we have discussed, this last is thus the most effective. It takes as the standard of authenticity for Francis a writing of his own. It does, to all appearance, cut out the possible prejudice of later writers by relying on a source in which the saint speaks directly to us, free of interventions from outside.

---

[1] ". . . dicant illis verbum sancti Evangelii, quod vadant et vendant omnia sua et ea studeant pauperibus erogare. Quod si facere non potuerint sufficit eis bona voluntas." *Regula Bullata*, 2; *Analekten*, ed. Boehmer, p. 30, lines 14–17. "Et illi, qui iam promiserunt obedientiam, habeant unam tunicam cum caputio et aliam sine caputio, qui voluerint habere." Ibid., lines 30–2. See also *Regula prima*, 2; *Analekten*, ed. Boehmer, p. 2, lines 16–19, p. 3, lines 5–7, 10–12.

[2] *Testamentum*, 8.

[3] *Testamentum*, 7.

[4] *Testamentum*, 12.

But even this last solution has in recent years been shown to be defective. The credit for achieving this goes to Kajetan Esser, a Franciscan from the Rhineland, who in 1949 published a study of the Testament of St Francis.[1] The work itself was not greatly noticed when it came out. It has not even received a review in a single English historical periodical. Here, however, it will be suggested that the work has been quite unduly neglected. It reveals its author as a worthy successor to Ehrle and Oliger as historians of the Spiritual Franciscans. It creates a new situation in Franciscan studies. It is the first successful answer to Sabatier.[2]

A necessary preliminary to a study of the Testament is to establish the authentic text. Such doubts as survived the investigation of Goetz early in the century have been dispelled by Esser, who assembles the MSS. for the fourteenth and fifteenth centuries, and covers the MS. gap in the thirteenth by a sequence of citations in early Franciscan authors. Esser's new text emerges little different from that in the accepted editions of Boehmer and Lemmens. With this done, the way is clear for a reassessment of the meaning of the document as a whole.

Esser's theme is that the Testament, so far from being a summary of the Franciscan ideal, is a work of occasion, a "spontane Gelegenheitschrift".[3] A comparison with the two Rules of 1221 and 1223 shows that it omits vital features of the life of the friars, such as the prohibition of money, included in all forms of the Rule. If the evidence of the Leo-sources, in the redactions of the *Speculum* and of the *Legenda antiqua* of Delorme, can be trusted, this was in fact not the only "last will" put out by Francis. At Siena, in the last year of his life, probably about April or May 1226 after a haemorrhage had caused the brothers to fear for his life, he had a few sentences dictated as an expression of his last wishes for the order. Despite their brevity, Esser claims, these do summarize the essentials of Franciscan life, in love, poverty, and subjection to the Church. The contrast between this, the Pre-Testament of Siena, and the Testament proper demonstrates that in the latter Francis was not providing a complete survey of his ideal, because his

[1] See above, p. 22, n. 3.
[2] What follows is a personal assessment of Esser's work; I do not know what the author himself would say, and I have, of course, no authority to speak for him. I should like to make an acknowledgement here of my indebtedness to his work.
[3] Esser, *Testament*, p. 129.

gaze was taken up by transient questions of the hour. The Testament, being thus dated, cannot be accepted as a full manifestation of the will of the founder.[1] It must lose its pre-eminence among the sources and be put back on an equal footing with the rest of the works of Francis, the Letters, the Admonitions, and the Rules.

Sabatier and his school had always made much of the fact that in the Testament Francis spoke free of any interference from outside. Moorman, for instance, after describing the inadequacy of the Rule of 1223, goes on to reconstruct the contrasting mood of recollection following solitary prayer, "calm and unimpassioned", in which he put together the Testament.[2] Esser relies on the Leo-sources to disprove such assertions. He points out that Spiritual sources like these are unlikely to make up the story of the Pre-Testament of Siena, when it diminishes the unique position of their favourite writing, the Testament proper. The account of the Siena episode, with the companions begging Francis to give them "some memorial to which we may have recourse after your death,"[3] suggests strongly that the writing of the Testament also was influenced by the companions around his death-bed. At this time, removed from the active government of the order, he was almost exclusively in the company of friars "Spiritual" in outlook, and opposed to development of the primitive life. The accounts which we have of his life at this time give a picture of a sick man near his end, anxious for the future of his order. At such a time the effect of the words of constant companions is greater than in times of full health. If Esser is right in his dating, the actual dictation of the Testament took place literally in the last days at the Portiuncula,[4] at a time therefore when these factors would have full play. What could be more natural than that the companions should ask Francis for a decisive document that would defend them for the future against the hostility of their opponents in the order, and that Francis should yield to the companions of his last hours?

Indeed the external influences on the writing of the Testament came from both sides, from the two embryonic groups of the

---

[1] Ibid., pp. 10–11, 108–9, 130. Comparison with the Rule of 1221, pp. 135–7, and with the Rule of 1223, pp. 130–5.

[2] Moorman, Sources, pp. 34–5.

[3] Esser, Testament, p. 117.

[4] Esser, Testament, pp. 107–15.

companions and the ministers, who were the forerunners of the
Spirituals and the Conventuals. According to the *Intentio*[1] Francis
intended to command his followers to build their churches and
houses of mud and wattle. He altered his draft version into a
general injunction to poverty in deference to the plea of the
ministers that in many provinces wood was more expensive than
stone. One can still say that the Testament has come more directly
from the mouth of Francis than the Rule of 1223, but the margin
of difference has narrowed, and is more than offset by consid-
eration of Francis's physical and mental state at the time of
writing.

Comparison with the rest of Francis's writings, given by Esser
in closer detail than ever before, bears out the impression that the
Testament, instead of giving a calm statement of principle, has
selected and over-emphasized existing features of his thought.
The final exhortation to keep the writing carefully and understand it simply can be readily paralleled elsewhere, only here there
is an unusually preceptual tone and the addition of the prohibition of glosses. The refusal of Papal privileges, although it is new,
can be paralleled in the actions of Francis; but his practice was
not as uncompromising as his command in the Testament. The
abnormal circumstances of its production had heightened the
existing strain of radicalism in the nature of the saint, which on
other occasions led him to reject even the most legitimate compromises with the world.

Finally more detailed analysis of the text reveals the presence
of ideas hardly accounted for in Sabatier's version. Beside the
memories of Rivo Torto, which put heart into the Spirituals, are
injunctions to obedience, which are hard to reconcile with the
practice of these later followers of Francis. Circumstances led
them to put the observance of poverty before obedience to
superiors. The stress in, for example, Ubertino da Casale, is on an
internal obedience, somewhat to the detriment of the external.[2]
Francis in the Testament explicitly recalls his followers to a direct,
external obedience to their superiors. He says:

---

[1] *Documenta Antiqua Franciscana*, ed. Lemmens, Pars I, *Intentio*, para. 15, p. 98.
[2] "Moreover, his conception of internal obedience, which is not sufficiently
controlled by external obedience . . . can favour illuminism." Godefroy, "Ubertin de Casale", *DTC* XV, ii, 1950, col. 2029.

And I firmly wish to obey the minister general of this fraternity and the guardian that it shall please him to give me. And I so wish to be captive in his hands, that I could not move or act outside obedience and his will, because he is my lord. . . . And all the brothers should be held thus firmly to obey their guardians and to do the office according to the rule.[1]

"Captive in his hands" is a formula almost Ignatian in its severity, and, if one is to continue with Sabatier's comparison, a good deal more stringent than the relevant clauses of the Rule of 1223.[2]

Sabatier always saw the Testament as a protest. Picking his way through the writings of the later Spirituals, he was able to discover phrases which seemed to put the Rule and the Testament above all ordinances of the Church. Such words corresponded too closely to his own religious ideas for him to be able to avoid over-valuing and distorting them, and even, by an inversion, to read them back into Francis's own mind. Of the Spirituals and the Testament he said:

Very confusedly, no doubt, but guided by a very sure instinct, they saw in these pages the banner of liberty. They were not mistaken. Even today, thinkers, moralists, mystics . . . may not refuse to acknowledge in him the precursor of religious subjectivism.[3]

For the understanding of Francis he quoted one sentence of the Testament, which opens his account of the early life of the friars.

And after the Lord gave me some brothers, no one showed me what I ought to do, but the Most High himself revealed to me that I ought to live according to the form of the holy gospel,[4]

and commented: "The individual conscience here proclaims its sovereign authority."[5]

Esser admits the existence of an element of protest here, but not a protest against the Church. Francis is thinking of the section among the ministers who wished him to affiliate the order more closely to some existing Rule. He is asserting the sufficiency of the Franciscan Rule against those who wished to borrow from St Benedict and St Bernard, just as he had done in his famous

---

[1] *Testamentum* 9, 10.
[2] *Regula bullata*, 10; *Analekten*, ed. Boehmer, p. 34, lines 7–20.
[3] Sabatier-Houghton, p. 335.
[4] *Testamentum*, 4.
[5] Sabatier-Houghton, p. 335.

outburst before Ugolino and the ministers at the chapter-general described in the *Speculum*.[1]

His concept of revelation was not such as to exclude the intervention of the Church. On the contrary, it was through a series of instruments that God's will was made plain to him. In the same way as the commonplace incidents of the Umbrian scene recalled to his mind the words and actions of Jesus, so equally trivial occasions served to show him his mission. The means might be the words of the Gospel at Mass,[2] the practice of sortilege,[3] the words of the Bishop of Assisi,[4] or the advice of his companions, Silvester and Clare.[5]

When, at the end of the Testament, he came to order his brothers not to put glosses in it or in the Rule, he used similar wording to that employed above in his account of the genesis of the Rule of 1210. "But as the Lord gave it to me simply and purely to speak and to write the rule and these words, so you are to understand them simply and without gloss. . . ."[6] Yet we know from St Francis's own words[7] and from the evidence of *Quo elongati*[8] that, instead of being written down directly from the mind of Francis, the Rule of 1223 was hammered out with the aid of both the chapter-general and of Cardinal Ugolino. Clearly these representatives of the Church and the order were seen by Francis as agents conveying to him the will of God. Actually no clear distinction is made in the Testament between the Rule of 1210 and that of 1223.

The general effect of this discussion is to weaken the force of Sabatier's thesis of the unbridgeable gulf between the primitive ideal and the regulations later foisted on Francis by Ugolino and the Church.

However Francis's "no one showed me what I ought to do"

---

[1] *Speculum*, ed. Sabatier (1928), chap. lxviii, pp. 194–8.

[2] *I Cel.*, 22; *AF* X, 19. For further refs. and illustrations see Esser, *Testament*, p. 163, on which this discussion is based.

[3] *I Cel.*, 92; *AF* X, 70.

[4] ". . . ab initio meae conversionis posuit Dominus in ore episcopi Assisii verbum suum ut mihi consuleret bene et confortaret in servitio Christi." *Speculum*, ed. Sabatier, (1928), cap. x, para. 14, p. 31.

[5] Bonav. *Leg. Maj.*, xii, 2, 611, and see below, p. 58, n. 1.

[6] *Testamentum*, 12.

[7] See *Epistola ad ministrum; Analekten*, ed. Boehmer, p. 29, lines 1–5.

[8] See above, p. 21, n. 1.

be taken, it has to be put beside two other paragraphs, numbers
three and ten in the divisions adopted by Boehmer and Esser,
which strongly inculcate reverence to the Roman priesthood and
care in delivering up Franciscans suspect of heresy to the cardinal
protector. Francis's adherence to the Roman Church is primarily
adherence to a sacramental Church. His reverence is given to
its priests especially because of their office as ministers of the
Eucharist. "And I do so for this reason, that I see nothing cor-
porally in this world of the most high Son of God, except his most
holy body and most holy blood, which they receive, and they alone
administer to others."[1] Reverence for the Eucharist is one of the
most frequent themes of the writings of Francis—a feature to
which Sabatier all unconsciously gave insufficient weight.

One of the most valuable features of Esser's work is his willing-
ness to admit inconsistencies in Francis. Sabatier hardly suggests
the possibility of such changes of view from the inside. In his interpretation the man Francis is only acted upon from outside: from
the completion of his conversion until his death there is only one
"true Francis". Such inconsistencies as appear in his utterances,
like the elements Sabatier considered un-Franciscan in the Rule
of 1223, or the injunction to corpse-like obedience, are explained
in external terms, as the result of pressure from Ugolino, or a
momentarily overwhelming effect of adverse circumstances.[2] The
most fundamental assumption of his biography is that Francis is
consistent. Once the ideal has been formed, in the Rule of 1210,
it does not change. It follows that any development away from it
must have been imposed on Francis from outside. Any view which
accepts the fact that Francis was inconsistent is bound seriously to
weaken Sabatier's thesis.

To sum up, therefore, Esser's book has done away with the
special position of the Testament among the writings of Francis.
This is the last of the individual documents which gave us hope
of finding a decisive standard of measurement for the mind of
Francis. One by one, we have examined them all, and have found
them in some way wanting. Firstly, the weaknesses of *II Celano*
and the conventional biographies were detailed. Then, the Leo-

---

[1] *Testamentum*, 3.
[2] E.g. "This longing for corpse-like obedience witnesses to the ravages with
which his soul had been laid waste." Sabatier-Houghton, p. 261.

sources were found to be unreliable because of the defects inherent in the application of higher criticism. The *Verba* and the *Intentio* were shown to be subject to the prejudice of Leo and the companions. Finally, the writings of Francis were examined. The commanding position amongst them of the Testament for pro-Sabatier scholars was demonstrated; and it was shown how in 1949 Esser's book had thrown it down.

We have now, in our argument, established an important conclusion for Franciscan studies. There is no certain yardstick for St Francis's wishes. There is no one document which we can select as a completely reliable guide. Does this mean that we cannot make any approach to St Francis? Does it mean that there is no possibility of investigating his ideas? No: it is still possible to use the sources, though we must always bear in mind the traps and pitfalls inherent in their use. Despite the contradictions in them, there are still themes which are common to them all.

To pursue our original purpose of discovering St Francis's views on poverty and on the poverty of Christ, we must therefore abandon the use of original documents taken individually. Instead, we must take ideas of Francis, whenever we can, which run through all the documents, or as many as possible. We must try to see what was the total background of his thought. In doing this, we must be prepared to drop some conventional academic methods, and to adopt an approach closer to St Francis's own way of thinking.

2

ST FRANCIS AND THE POVERTY OF CHRIST

THE WORK of textual criticism on the sources for St Francis is now largely over. That essential work done, we are embarking on a more difficult and dangerous territory still, that of the investigation of Francis's mind. More and more, it is becoming clear that the central problems in this field are not derived solely from the accidents of the biographical sources, important as those are, but are embedded deep in the personality of Francis himself.[1] The new and valuable work in this field, therefore, will not be done through textual investigation, but through the means of other, less familiar, methods—the investigation of Francis's use of words and symbols. What is needed is a re-creation of Francis's thought-world.

Curiously enough, nowhere is this more needed than on the central issue of poverty. Nearly all accounts portray well the spiritual significance of poverty for St Francis, and none have done this so well as the Franciscans themselves; but there has been a gap in the investigation of the material conditions of the poverty which St Francis desired.

The first object of this chapter is to discover the views of Francis about the poverty of Christ. This can best be done through a number of other, lesser, investigations. For convenience, the chapter has been divided into sections. The first discusses the nature of St Francis's way of thinking—an indispensable preliminary to any investigation of his ideas. The second deals with his ideas on the poverty of his followers, and especially the question of the total renunciation of property in which has, perhaps, never yet been adequately discussed section, the origins of this poverty in the *apostolic* ished. Finally, the fourth section deals directly with issue:

[1] On this, see particularly the pregnant observations of J. Lortz in the preface to Esser's book on the Testament.

St Francis's belief in the absolute poverty of Christ and the apostles.

1. ST FRANCIS'S WAY OF THINKING

It is a dangerous thing to make unrestricted use of scholastic methods in analysing the nature of Francis's intentions. Many of the historians who have given us outlines of the ideal of Francis have been Franciscans themselves, trained in systematic theology and naturally enough employing the categories of scholasticism. Felder,[1] Holzapfel,[2] Balthasar,[3] and Gratien[4] are examples of writers of this kind, who have prefaced their studies in Franciscan history with an account of the wishes of Francis, couched in the language of the Schools. The best example is Gratien, who says of Francis:

> Then from this ideal he draws a whole programme of life, nothing less than a plan of action whose aim, principles and means are all clear to him.[5]

Gratien does, certainly, recognize that Francis could not have begun to give an exposition of his ideal in such a manner. He continues:

> He never formulated it systematically as we shall see further on, but it can be easily discovered from studying his actions and those of his companions.[6]

Nevertheless the outline which follows is an academic, abstracted survey of the essential principles of Franciscan life. As such it is of the utmost importance, not only in Gratien, but also in Felder, Holzapfel, and Balthasar, for their judgements on later Franciscan history are bound to depend to some extent on the primary judgement passed on the wishes of the founder.

Yet Francis was never able to think or to write in such terms.

---

[1] H. Felder, *Geschichte der wissenschaftlichen Studien im Franziskanerorden bis um die Mitte des 13. Jahrhunderts*, Freiburg-i-B., 1904.

[2] H. Holzapfel, *Handbuch der Geschichte des Franziskanerordens*, Freiburg-i-B., 1909.

[3] K. Balthasar, *Geschichte des Armutsstreites im Franziskanerorden bis zum Konzil von Vienne*, Münster-i.-W., 1911.

[4] Gratien, *Histoire de la Fondation et de l'Évolution de l'ordre des Frères Mineurs au XIIIᵉ siècle*, Paris, Gembloux, 1928.

[5] Op. cit., p. 29.

[6] Op. cit., pp. 29–30.

He could distinguish only with great difficulty, if at all, between the essential and the dispensable elements in Franciscan life; this is one reason why the Rule was such an unsatisfactory juridical document. His thought was always immediate, personal, and concrete. Ideas appeared to him as images. A sequence of thought for him, as Esser demonstrates for the Testament,[1] consists in leaping from one picture to the next. At the start of the Testament he recalls his conversion. This at once suggests a picture: the lepers who represented the first great obstacle, which God helped him to conquer. ". . . because when I was in sins it seemed too bitter to me to see lepers. And the Lord himself led me among them. . . ." Next in time sequence came his leaving the world.[2] This suggests a picture once more: the churches which he repaired after he had left the world, a task which was the sign of his conversion. He leaves this thought unspoken and the image carries him on to speak of the prayer he said in the churches: "And the Lord gave me such faith in churches, that I would simply pray and say. . . ."[3] From the churches spring the next image—of the priests who serve them. They in turn summon up another, of the Eucharist which they administer.[4] The content of the Testament is thus held together in an association based on Francis's visual imagination. Whether Esser is correct at all points in his reconstruction of the thought-process does not matter greatly for this purpose; enough has been done to show the superiority of his approach to a more thematic and academic treatment, such as Cuthbert gives.[5]

What has been said of the Testament can be amply illustrated elsewhere, in Francis's writings and in the Lives. When, for instance, he wishes to explain his way of living to Innocent III, he turns his plea into a parable[6]; on other occasions, when he wishes the brothers to understand his intentions, he chooses to do so by symbols. The luxury of the brothers' table is demonstrated to them by Francis disguised as a poor stranger.[7] The wickedness of touching money is conveyed by an acted parable imposed on an offender by Francis as a penance.[8]

---

[1] Testament, pp. 125–9.
[2] "Et postea parum steti et exivi de seculo." Testamentum, 1.
[3] Testamentum, 2.   [4] Testamentum, 3.
[5] Cuthbert, Life, pp. 449–55.   [6] II Cel., 16–17; AF X, 140–1.
[7] II Cel., 61; AF X, 167–8.   [8] II Cel., 65; AF X, 170.

4

These symbols were, of course, of different kinds: some are shadowy allegories, like the salutation of the three women by the ... a in *II Celano* and Bonaventura,[1] valuable as an illustration of the heightened mental state in which Francis and his closest companions habitually lived. Some stand for real events in the life of Francis, like the preaching to the birds,[2] but are pure *jeux d'esprit*, unrelated to the life of the order. Others again are not intended to convey any meaning to the outside world, but relate solely to Francis's own inner life. The supreme example in this last category, where the symbol has become the reality, is the stigmata—which Francis was so anxious to conceal from the world.[3]

That the use of symbols is not a preacher's device but a spontaneous expression of his thinking is shown particularly by those occasions on which his own decisions were prepared in the inner mind and then brought to consciousness in dreams. At least two important steps were heralded in this way. Before he decided to resign the official leadership in 1220, he dreamt of a little black hen, which, try as she might, was too small to cover all her brood with her wings.[4] A little later, his deficiencies as a legislator were revealed to him in another dream in which he tried vainly to feed his starving brothers with crumbs of bread that slipped through his fingers.[5] In him the line between subconscious and conscious was thin; so much did his preaching depend on the inspiration of the moment that it was not uncommon for him to find himself dumb before a crowd of his hearers.[6] Boehmer laid great stress on the visual and ecstatic quality of Francis's thought, on what he called "die Lebendigkeit, Frische und Kraft der Phantasie",[7] and "die gesteigerte Sensibilität des Dichters".[8] He who leaves this aspect of his personality out of account, he said, will not fully understand him.[9]

---

[1] *II Cel.*, 93; *AF* X, 185–6. Bonav., *Leg. Maj.*, vii, 6, 589.

[2] *I Cel.*, 58; *AF* X, 44–5.

[3] "Studiosissime namque abscondebat haec ab extraneis, celabat cautissime a propinquis. . . ." *I Cel.*, 95; *AF* X, p. 73, lines 16–17.

[4] *II Cel.*, 24; *AF* X, 144–5. Sabatier's interpretation: Sabatier-Houghton, p. 244.

[5] *II Cel.*, 209; *AF* X, 250–1. Sabatier's interpretation: Sabatier-Houghton, pp. 258–9.

[6] *I Cel.*, 72; *AF* X, 54.

[7] *Analekten*, ed. Boehmer, p. xlix.

[8] Ed. cit., p. l.

[9] Ed. cit., p. xlix.

Modern writers on Francis have generally recognized the justice of Boehmer's comment; but it may be that they have not drawn out the full implications of his characterization for the study of Francis's intentions. To do so will involve a shifting of attention away from the Rules and the fine differences between them. The sensitivity of Karl Müller and Sabatier to the points of contrast between the Rules of 1221 and 1223 does not seem to have been shared by contemporaries. Reflection on the nature of Francis's thinking suggests that the life of the friars as a whole was in the forefront of his mind rather than the detail of any Rule. It was because his ideas flowed naturally in picture form that he had such difficulty in writing any Rule at all. As Sabatier said, "Never was man less capable of making a Rule than Francis."[1] If one looks at the wording of the Rules when they did emerge from the founder's lonely struggles, one notices a strong emphasis on "vita fratrum minorum". The Rule of 1221 begins: "This is the life of the gospel of Jesus Christ . . .", and the Rule of 1223, somewhat less dramatically, "The rule and life of the friars minor is this . . .".[2] The second chapter of the accepted Rule, similarly, is headed by the sentence: "Of those who wish to accept that life, and how they ought to be received."[3] When the ministers asked him to adopt some existing Rule for the fraternity, he was vehement in his rejection of them all. "And so I do not want you to mention any rule to me, neither St Benedict's nor St Augustine's nor St Bernard's nor any way and form of living but what the Lord has mercifully shown and given to me."[4] All this can be understood more readily if seen against the background of the personal, concrete images in which the Franciscan ideal was comprised in the mind of the founder.

A further consequence of adopting this approach to Francis is some discrediting of the Spiritual tradition of the observance of the Rule "ad litteram". If, as has been suggested, all versions of the Rule are of secondary importance compared to the personal, living example, then talk of Francis's demand for the literal observance of his Rule must be regarded as a projection of the struggles

---

[1] Sabatier-Houghton, p. 253.

[2] *Regula prima*, prologus; *Analekten*, ed. Boehmer, p. 1. *Regula bullata*, 1; *Analekten*, ed. Boehmer, p. 29.

[3] *Regula bullata*, 2; *Analekten*, ed. Boehmer, p. 30.

[4] *Speculum*, ed. Sabatier (1928), chap. lxviii, p. 196, v. 6.

of the rigorists in the later thirteenth century. In their eyes the living tradition had been poisoned by the actions of the relaxed friars, and their only hope of remaining faithful was to cling to the written remains of the founder. Under the pressures of the conflict documents took on a significance which they had not possessed for Francis. The words "ad litteram" never appear in his writings. Although he often asks his readers to keep his writings carefully[1] and, in the case of the Testament and the Rule of 1221, prohibits any alteration of the text,[2] it is plain that he regards them as only partial indications of his wishes. When, in the Testament, he orders the brothers to understand the Rule "simpliciter et sine glosa"[3] he means that they should receive it directly as it was written, without the interposition of a learned commentary, which by investigation of detail would distort the unity of the whole. He does not require a verbal adherence; in the Rule of 1221 his request to the friars is given "to learn the tenor and sense of those things, which have been written in that life for the salvation of our soul . . .".[4] Spirit should speak to spirit. The meaning should be taken "non via speculationis, sed via unctionis".

Both the Rules, the Rule of 1221 more than the Rule of 1223, are not properly legislative documents: they are truly part of the series of Admonitions. Francis was a supreme spiritual master of small groups: but he was unable to provide the impersonal organization required to maintain a world-wide order. His genius was alien to all abstraction.

True obedience he understood very well. Indeed, questions about obedience occupy a significantly greater space in his writings than those about poverty.[5] The natural *milieu* for its expression, however, was a personal relationship.

---

[1] E.g. *Epistola ad fideles*, epilogus; *Analekten*, ed. Boehmer. pp. 56–7. *Epistola ad capitulum generale*, epilogus; *Analekten*, p. 62, lines 1–6.

[2] *Testamentum*, 12. *Regula prima*, 24; *Analekten*, ed. Boehmer, p. 26, lines 18–22.

[3] *Testamentum*, 12. The meaning of "simplex" in the writings of St Francis will be found well explained by K. Esser, L. Hardick, *Die Schriften des hl. Franziskus von Assisi*, Werl-i.-W, 1951, pp. 172–4. For further details of this work, see below, p. 48.

[4] *Regula prima*, 24; *Analekten*, ed. Boehmer, p. 26, lines 10–12.

[5] "Thus it is not surprising if questions of obedience play a much greater part in the writings of St Francis than questions of poverty." Esser in *FS* xxxix (1957), p. 14, n. 50.

Coulton first noticed an anecdote from Wadding which displays to advantage both the carefree fashion of living of the founder's circle and his individual interpretation of obedience to a superior. A certain Brother Stephen had once acted as cook for some months to Francis in a hermitage. Their habit was to pass the morning in silence and prayer until they were summoned by a gong to their meal. About the third hour Francis would leave his cell, and if he did not see a fire in the kitchen, would gather a bundle of herbs and give them to the cook for their meal. Often Brother Stephen prepared some eggs and a stew for them, and Francis would sit down gladly with the rest, and praise the cook for his care. But on one such occasion he told him that he had done too much, and ordered him not to prepare anything for the following day. The next day Francis, coming to sit cheerfully with his companions, found nothing on the table but a few crusts of bread, and asked Brother Stephen why he had prepared nothing for them. When the cook reminded him of his order of the day before, he only said: "Discretion is good and one should not always do what superiors say."

This is very far from the uniform obedience that is demanded of any large community, and Coulton's conclusion, that no order could exist on such a basis, is no more than is warranted by the facts.[1]

Any discussion of St Francis's views, then, should take account of these fundamental features. St Francis thought naturally in personal, concrete terms. Ideas appeared to him as images. Documents had only a secondary importance for him, and the natural medium for him to employ in conveying his ideas to the friars was the acted parable, the mime, or the symbol.

This being so, some of the difficulties inherent in the use of the sources disappear. We have seen in our first chapter that each one of these sources is in some way defective and cannot be taken as wholly authentic evidence for the mind of Francis. But if we remember that all the documents, even St Francis's own writings, are only a pale reflection of that total "vita fratrum minorum"

[1] G. G. Coulton, "The Story of St Francis of Assisi", Foakes Jackson and Kirsopp Lake, *Acts* II (1922), 441; L. Wadding, *Annales Minorum* ad ann. 1258, no. ix, 2nd edn., IV, Romae, 1732, p. 92. A better text, used here, is in L. Oliger, "Descriptio codicis S. Antonii de Urbe una cum appendice textuum de S. Francisco", *AFH* xii (1919), p. 384, n. 59.

which the founder wished to convey to his friars by personal example, then hope appears. What we wish to do is to establish the fundamental ideas about poverty and the poverty of Christ which lie behind all the writings and reported sayings of Francis. If certain basic themes and ideas run through all our sources, or at least a fair proportion of them, we have reasonable ground for saying that they are the authentic products of St Francis's mind. If, in particular, an idea appears in sources which are in other respects contradictory, we may feel that we have safely negotiated the prejudices of the sources. Therefore, in the following investigation of St Francis's views on poverty, we shall trace a theme through as many sources as possible.

2. ST FRANCIS'S IDEAS ON POVERTY

We may now turn to examine the view of poverty held by Francis. The Francis who in the *Epistola ad fideles* so confidently and directly urges all Christians to a perfect life will speak with the same voice when he comes in the Rules to instruct his brothers in the poverty of the order. We can, indeed, accept it as an axiom that the more radical the version of poverty that is presented to us, the more likely it is to reflect the true wishes of Francis.

This conclusion, based on quite general deductions from his personality, is confirmed by the language which the founder used to convey his ideal to his followers. Their wandering, insecure life "as strangers and pilgrims in this world" he called "that summit of the highest poverty",[1] a phrase which it would be impossible to use of anything but the most rigorous poverty. The prohibitions of the religious life, in the matter of poverty more than all, he gives in universal terms: "nullus", "nihil", "nullo modo", and the like.

The Rule of 1221, taken as a whole, gives the impression that Francis wished his friars to cut adrift entirely from the commercial system of the world. He is insistent, for example, that the need for giving advice to postulants about the disposal of their goods should not involve the brothers in secular business,[2] and in his final

---

[1] "illa celsitudo altissimae paupertatis", *Regula bullata*, 6; *Analekten*, ed. Boehmer, p. 32, lines 17–24.
[2] ". . . multum caveant sibi fratres, ne de suis negociis temporalibus se intromittant . . .", *Regula prima*, 2; *Analekten*, ed. Boehmer, p. 2, lines 12–13.

admonition he openly treats the affairs of the world ("secularia negotia") as one of the snares set by Satan to tempt the brothers.[1] When he does use legal and commercial terms in the Rules or in his expositions to the friars, he delights in standing them on their head, so that words like *hereditas*,[2] *commercium*,[3] or *mutuum*,[4] lose their customary meaning and take on a significance drawn solely from the spiritual world of the Franciscans.

The recurrent theme of his disquisitions on Franciscan poverty, that the members of the order should be able to associate on equal terms with the poorest of men in the outside world, automatically presupposes a standard of living in the order not far removed from destitution. Although the idea originates in the preparatory years before his conversion, when he went and stood in the place of a beggar in the porch of St Peter's,[5] a passage in the Rule of 1221 makes it clear that he does not regard it solely as an item of his own personal observance. In chapter nine he tells the brothers that they should rejoice "when they find themselves among mean and despised persons, amongst the poor and weak and infirm and the lepers and those that beg in the street".[6] These are not the ordinary poor but the lowest of all, the wreckage of society. The biographical sources show him eager to engage in a contest to achieve the most strict poverty,[7] and saddened when he meets a man in the world who is poorer than the Franciscans.[8]

The assumption, that the poverty of the Franciscans should be taken to the limits of necessity, can be seen at work in the more detailed prescriptions of the Rules.

An example is the prohibition of money given in the Rule of 1221. The actual touch of money tokens is forbidden. "And if we should find coins anywhere, let us pay no more attention to them

---

[1] *Regula prima*, 22; *Analekten*, ed. Boehmer, p. 21, lines 2–8.

[2] "Et elemosina est hereditas et iustitia, que debetur pauperibus. . . .", *Regula prima*, 9; *Analekten*, ed. Boehmer, p. 10, lines 15–16.

[3] "Commercium est inter mundum et fratres; debent ipsi mundo bonum exemplum, debet mundus eis provisionem necessitatum." *II Cel.*, 70; *AF* X, 173.

[4] "Oportet, frater, ut reddamus mantellum pauperculo cuius est. Mutuo accepimus ipsum, donec pauperiorem invenire contingeret." *II Cel.*, 87; *AF* X, 182.

[5] *II Cel.*, 8; *AF* X, 135.

[6] *Regula prima*, 9; *Analekten*, ed. Boehmer, p. 10, lines 2–5.

[7] *II Cel.*, 83; *AF* X, 180.

[8] *II Cel.*, 84; *AF* X, 181.

than to the dust we tread under our feet." [1] Here the term used is
denarius: the context makes plain its meaning. But everywhere
else in this chapter of the Rule the forbidden object is not merely
denarius, but *pecunia* and *denarius*, put in double harness. The
brothers are not to take or receive or cause to be received "pecuniam aut denarios", neither for clothing or books nor as a reward
for any kind of work.[2] They should not have or consider themselves
to have more value "in pecunia et denariis" than in stones.[3] If
any brother should collect or keep "pecuniam vel denarios", all
the brothers should treat him as an apostate.[4] Here again the
context makes plain the meaning. If *denarius* is a simple money
token, *pecunia* represents all forms of goods that can be employed
as substitutes for coin.[5] This is a radical measure indeed. It involves
a total withdrawal from the world of buying and selling[6]: the
poverty which in the older orders still retained their com-
munities in the framework of the economic system outside has
here been replaced by one in which the economic contact is of
the thinnest possible kind.

Although the twelfth-century reforms of the order of St Benedict, like the Carthusians or the Cistercians, did renounce certain
forms of wealth, such as feudal rents, their renunciations were,
in comparison with those of the Franciscans, incomplete and
partial. To find a closer parallel to Franciscan poverty one would
have to go to the twelfth-century movement of the wandering
preachers and their offshoots, the heretical sects and the orthodox
groups, the Poor Catholics, and others. Even here, where the
common lines of thought with the ideal of Francis are most
apparent,[7] discrepancies are considerable. None of these groups
was of any great size, and none of them had the world-wide

---

[1] "Et si in aliquo loco inveniremus denarios, de hiis non curemus tanquam
de pulvere, quem pedibus calcamus. . . ." *Regula prima*, 8; *Analekten*, ed.
Boehmer, p. 9, lines 3–5.

[2] Ibid.; *Analekten*, ed. Boehmer, p. 8, lines 18–22.   [3] Loc cit., lines 22–4.

[4] *Regula prima*, 8; *Analekten*, ed. Boehmer, p. 9, lines 6–9.

[5] Compare the definitions of the civil law. *Denarius* is *pecunia numerata* but
"'Pecuniae' verbum non solum numeratam pecuniam complectitur. . . ."
Dig. L, 16, 178; *Corpus Iuris Civilis*, I, *Digesta*, ed. T. Mommsen, P. Krueger,
Berolini, 1928, p. 916.

[6] And, incidentally, acquits Francis of the charge of fetichism. This is an
austere measure; but it is not an illogical one.

[7] On the links between Francis's ideas and earlier movements, see W. Lampen, "De quibusdam sententiis et verbis in opusculis S. P. N. Francisci", *AFH*

extension which Francis intended for his order from early on in his religious life, when he divided up the world into provinces for his followers.

Among the heretics the most rigid adherents of poverty, the *perfecti* of the Cathars, on the very margin of Christianity, were supported in their austerities by *credentes*, a body of second-class believers who suffered no economic restrictions. But it was only out of charity, for the care of the sick and the clothing of the brothers, that Francis could be induced to provide any form of regular support in the world outside for his followers, and the attachment that he provided, in the shape of the *fidelis persona* in 1221 and the *amicus spiritualis* in 1223,[1] was in its beginnings tenuous indeed.

Without money and without regular support outside, the means of accumulating a surplus of material goods were greatly restricted. The normal sources for the maintenance of life were of a deliberately transient and insecure nature: they consisted in rewards in kind for menial labour outside the settlements, eked out with the products of begging expeditions.[2] The Rule of 1221 forbids the friars to take posts of authority and assumes that their work will leave them free to say their hours.[3] Early followers, like Brother Giles, always took on irregular tasks, such as grave-digging, basket-weaving, and water-carrying, none of them providing any security in times of dearth.[4] The prescribed method of begging, passing indiscriminately from door to door, "petendo elemosinam ostiatim", as Francis said in the Testament,[5] precluded mitigation

---

xxiv (1931), 552–7; A. Quaglia, *L'originalità della Regola francescana*, Sassoferrato, 1943, pp. 57–120; *Expositio Quatuor Magistrorum super regulam Fratrum Minorum (1241–1242)*, ed. L. Oliger, Roma, 1950, Appendix, "Regula S. Francisci anni 1223 fontibus locisque parallelis illustrata", pp. 171–93.

[1] See *Regula prima*, 10; *Analekten*, ed. Boehmer, p. 11, lines 15–17. *Regula bullata*, 4; *Analekten*, ed. Boehmer, p. 32, lines 2–5.

[2] "Et pro labore possint accipere omnia necessaria preter pecuniam. Et, cum necesse fuerit, vadant pro elemosina sicut alii pauperes." *Regula prima*, 7; *Analekten*, ed. Boehmer, p. 7, lines 20–3. This whole chapter assumes that the work will take place outside the settlements.

[3] "Omnes fratres, in quibuscumque locis steterint apud alios ad serviendum vel laborandum, non sint camerarii nec cellararii nec presint in domibus, in quibus serviunt . . . Sed sint minores et subditi omnibus, qui in eadem domo sunt." *Regula prima*, 7; *Analekten*, ed. Boehmer, p. 7, lines 7–11. See chap. 3: *Analekten*, pp. 3–4.

[4] See W. W. Seton, *Blessed Giles of Assisi*, BSFS VIII, Manchester, 1918, p. 11.

[5] *Testamentum*, 5.

of the instability of the life through recourse to wealthy, regular
patrons. Francis realized that to employ such a method of seeking
alms would bring insults and refusals on the heads of the brothers;
he regarded their discomfort as a means of training in the religious
life, and comforted them with thoughts of their reward in the
future life.[1] On one occasion *II Celano* records him as using this
method of begging as a phrase covering all Franciscan poverty.
The words are put into an elliptical form characteristic of the
founder, and it may well be that the drama of the occasion, when
Francis appeared disguised as a beggar to upbraid the friars at
Greccio for the luxury of their table, fixed this line in the memory
of the companions. As he revealed himself, Francis said: "I saw
the table decked and ready, and I did not recognize it to be that
of poor men who beg from door to door." In Celano's Latin the
line runs: "Mensam vidi paratam et ornatam, et pauperum ostiatim euntium non esse cognovi."[2]

The prohibitions hitherto discussed, if they did not render the
possession of property futile, would at any rate much diminish
its value. By the terms of both the Rules the friars would be forbidden to receive from their property rents either in money or in
goods which might be sold for money. The order to take up some
kind of menial work assumes that the friars' place of business would
be outside the home of their community; and, therefore, if they
had lands they would have no time to work them themselves, in
the manner of the Cistercians and other reformed Benedictines.
For owners of property of any significance at all to take to begging
would be a doubtful practice: the Grandmontines with their
meagre possessions were allowed to have recourse to mendicancy,
but only as an emergency measure.[3]

It is with these assumptions in mind that we may examine the
meagre sentences which Francis used to instruct his followers in
their attitude to property. If we exclude the renunciation of

---

[1] *Regula prima*, 9; *Analekten*, ed. Boehmer, p. 10, lines 10–15.

[2] *II Cel.*, 61; *AF* X, p. 168, lines 17–18.

[3] "Si vero Deus . . . ad tantam inopiam vos devenire permiserit, ut omnino
victus deficiat, episcopo in cuius diœcesi locus habitationis vestræ fuerit,
prius eam ita manifestare potestis . . . Quod si vos super hoc exaudire noluerit
postquam biduo in cella jejunaveritis, duo de fratribus in religione firmiores
ad quaerendum humiliter exeant, per molendina scilicet et domos, ostiatim
velut cæteri pauperes eleemosynas petentes." *S. Stephani Grandimontensis
Regula*, 13; *PL* CCIV, 1145.

individual property as already catered for in the instructions for the reception of postulants, there is left only one sentence in each of the two Rules in which this matter is discussed. The renunciation of individual property by those who wished to enter a religious order was a commonplace in the West. What we are most interested in at this juncture is St Francis's attitude to the property of a whole community. Later, the renunciation of all common property was taken as a distinctive mark of Franciscan poverty. The question we should ask is: did Francis himself intend this renunciation of all common, as well as individual property? It is surprising to find how little Francis has to say on this point. In the Rule of 1221 the instruction is given in the chapter devoted to the manual labour of the friars, and is concerned with the ownership of their settlements alone. Francis says: "Let the brothers be careful, wherever they may be, in hermitages or in other settlements, not to appropriate a settlement to themselves or maintain it against anyone."[1] In the Rule of 1223 the implications are wider, and the instruction is no longer concerned exclusively with the Franciscan settlements. Here he says: "Let the brothers appropriate nothing to themselves, neither a house nor a settlement nor anything."[2]

Such brief exhortations hardly provide the material for a detailed account of the founder's views on property-owning in his order. On this topic he is silent everywhere else in his own writings. On reverence for the Eucharist, on obedience, on humility, he has much to say, but on property he has nothing to say outside the two extant Rules and the Testament. These are difficult and controversial documents. The circumstances of its writing, as we have seen, make the Testament an insecure guide, and it is impossible to say how far Francis was influenced by external factors in the writing of the Rules. Further, the weaknesses which are apparent in his writings are merely accentuated if one is to go farther afield and attempt to use the biographical sources, written so much later and in the full knowledge of the later controversies. When, for example, *II Celano* puts into the mouth of Francis words

[1] "Caveant sibi fratres, ubicumque fuerint, in heremitoriis vel in aliis locis, quod nullum locum sibi approprient nec alicui defendant." *Regula prima*, 7; *Analekten*, ed. Boehmer, p. 8, lines 5–7.

[2] "Fratres nihil sibi approprient nec domum nec locum nec aliquam rem." *Regula bullata*, 6; *Analekten*, ed. Boehmer, p. 32, lines 17–18.

like *proprietas* or *usus*[1] which he never employs in his own writings, and which played such an important part in the later history of his followers, there is no means of telling whether they have been interpolated in some way or whether Francis did in fact employ these technical terms in conversation with the companions. The only comparatively safe way of turning the biographical sources to profit when treating the subject of poverty is to take stories they give about Francis as a whole and interpret in each case their general bearing.

On the issue of property the number of such stories is not very great. *I Celano* records one incident relevant to this point; *II Celano* has a small group of episodes, which are summarized by Bonaventura in the *Legenda Maior* and also appear with some differences in the Leo-sources.

I Celano's story shows Francis observing to the full his own injunction in the Rule of 1221 about not turning visitors away from the Franciscan settlements. At Rivo Torto, where they occupied a tumble-down shed as a regular dwelling, a peasant one day drove in an ass as a sign that he wished to take up occupation; without demur Francis and the rest got up and left the place to him.[2]

Another story, about their next home at the Portiuncula, provides a more sophisticated picture of Francis's attitude to property-owning. Here, when he was handed the dilapidated church of St Mary by the Benedictines of Monte Subasio, he insisted that the monks should continue to hold all property rights in it while he paid them an annual rent of a basket of fish. The monks would have been willing to make a free grant of the property, which Francis intended to turn into the permanent centre of the order; but Francis refused it because he wished the Portiuncula to act as a model for all other settlements in the order, in the matter of poverty. The story is barely alluded to in *II Celano* but is given in detail in the *Speculum*. There is some support for the story in the fact that as late as 1244 a Bull of Innocent IV includes the chapel of the Portiuncula among the properties of Monte Subasio.[3]

Two other stories, narrated fully both in the *Speculum* and in

---

[1] E.g. *II Cel.*, 59; *AF* X, p. 167, lines 11–12.   [2] *I Cel.*, 44; *AF* X, 35.
[3] *II Cel.*, 18; *AF* X, p. 142, lines 13–16. *Speculum*, ed. Sabatier (1928), lv, 142–51. On the rent, ibid., p. 144, n.h.

II Celano, are valuable to us rather for the light they throw on the influence of parties outside the order than for any elucidation of Francis's attitude to property-owning. At Assisi the municipality decided, in Francis's absence and without his consent, to erect a new building close by the Portiuncula to house the brothers who came there for the chapters. When Francis returned to Assisi and saw the new building, which according to the *Speculum* was made of stone, he set to with the brothers to pull it down there and then. He and his followers were actually on the roof tearing off the tiles when soldiers on guard for the municipality stopped the demolition by declaring that the building did not belong to the friars but to the municipality.[1]

In the second story a similar violent reaction is unleashed by the founder's chancing to hear that a newly-constructed house at Bologna was "the house of the brothers". He ordered all the brothers living in it to leave at once, even including a sick man among them, and would only allow them to return after Ugolino had publicly stated that the house was his and not the brothers'.[2]

What seems to emerge from these stories is another illustration of Francis's horror of the order owning valuable property, and, in addition, a picture of Ugolino and the municipality apparently groping their way towards the later distinction between goods owned and goods used by the Franciscans. As far as Francis is concerned one can discern in all the stories a common line of principle about the poverty of the settlements of the order, which should reflect the position of the brothers as "strangers and pilgrims" in this world.

But if the evidence is treated chronologically, indications appear that there has been a development in the attitude of Francis to the detailed working out of this principle.

At the earliest stage of all, when he was alone after his conversion and when he gained his first adherents, his dwellings were entirely public places, either churches or, especially when on journeys, caves and holes in the ground. He says himself of this time in the Testament: "And willingly enough we remained in the churches."[3]

---

[1] *Speculum*, ed. Sabatier (1928), vii, 21–3. *II Cel.*, 57; *AF* X, 166.
[2] *Speculum*, ed. Sabatier (1928), vi, 20. *II Cel.*, 58; *AF* X, 166.
[3] *Testamentum*, 4.

In the next stage, when the group had increased a little more, and they occupied the shed at Rivo Torto, it is plain that there has been a shift in his views in the direction of a greater privacy for his followers. It is not easy to see who were the owners of the shed, and by what right the Franciscans occupied it; Jörgensen conjectures, without much evidence, that it belonged to the Crucigers of S. Salvatore delle Pareti, who allowed the use of their property to the group.[1] It may quite well have been abandoned, without an owner: it was not a property to attract claimants. If there was an owner, and an arrangement made for the Franciscans to occupy it, then probably one should think in terms of a purely oral permission, on the lines of the offer made by Count Orlando in 1213 for the Franciscans to occupy Mount Alverna. In that instance, according to the declaration of the Count's sons in 1274,[2] all rights over Alverna were made over to Francis and his companions, but the transaction was purely oral and nothing was ever set down in writing.

At the third stage of development, when Francis made the move from Rivo Torto to the Portiuncula, the group exchanged a casual and undefined position for the regular relation of a lessee or tenant. The lease was no ordinary one, since the friars were obviously expected to remain in permanent occupation; at the same time Francis had been strict in observing the forms of paying rent. There is a choice of explanations of Francis's actions at this juncture. If the witness of the *Speculum* is taken, the action at the Portiuncula was a symbolic one, by which Francis intended to teach his followers never to accept property rights, even in instances such as these where the Franciscans had to all intents and purposes taken the place of a property-owner.[3]

One could go on to say that a more regular system of occupation had been forced on Francis by the growth of the order and his experience of the arrangement at Rivo Torto. We know from *I Celano* that the Rivo Torto shed was so cramped that Francis had to write the names of the brothers on various beams in order to avoid confusion.[4] The *Speculum* describes the move to the

---

[1] Jörgensen-Sloane, p. 162, n. 1.
[2] *BF* IV, p. 156, n.h; Jörgensen-Sloane, loc. cit.
[3] *Speculum*, ed. Sabatier (1928), lv, 147.
[4] *I Cel.*, 44; *AF* X, pp. 34-5, lines 2-4.

Portiuncula as a considered step, undertaken because of the deficiencies of their previous home, which was not big enough for the common life of the brothers and had no church in which they could say their hours. In their account Francis goes round to the local Church authorities in turn, first to the Bishop of Assisi, then to the canons of S. Rufino, making known his requirements before the Benedictines of Monte Subasio were able to satisfy him.[1]

Alternatively, the Portiuncula arrangement could be interpreted as an *ad hoc* one, carrying no special significance for the order at large, in which Francis decided to pay rent because of the fact that he was taking over from the monks a consecrated building.[2]

In the final stage, represented by the stories of the house at Bologna and the municipality's building at Assisi, there is no sign of any further development in the attitude of Francis; on the contrary, both episodes give the impression that he is no longer fully master of the situation. In time-sequence these events must be placed well after the move to the Portiuncula; Bihl and the Quaracchi editors on the evidence of Ugolino's movements place the Bologna affair in either 1219, or, more probably 1221,[3] and the Assisi dispute must be placed at a time when the order had grown sufficiently to make it worthwhile for the city to put up a building for the reception of brothers coming to the chapters.

There is no clear indication of the nature of Francis's response to the solution of the problem of property-owning as put forward at Bologna and Assisi. If we can trust the *Speculum*, his attitude at Assisi was a grudging recognition of the logic of the soldiers: "All right, if the house is yours, I won't touch it."[4] A rent-paying system, like that obtaining at the Portiuncula, maintained the principle of impermanence in settlements to this extent, that it took away from the Franciscans the right to alienate the property at will. But in the solution proposed by Ugolino for Bologna even this restriction on the use of the Franciscans has been reduced almost to vanishing point.

A plausible theory could be made out, on the basis of these

---

[1] *Speculum*, ed. Sabatier (1928), lv, 142–5.
[2] I owe this suggestion to the Reverend Dr T. M. Parker.
[3] *AF* X, p. 166, n. 7.
[4] "Ergo, si vestra est domus, nolo tangere eam", *Speculum*, ed. Sabatier (1928), vii, 23.

stories in the biographical sources, assimilating the development
of Francis's view on property-owning to the general growth of the
ideal between 1209 and 1226. Here, one could say, as on other
questions, Francis was able to adapt his ideal to circumstances so
long as the rate of growth of his community was slow and steady;
when the rate of growth took its dramatic upward curve, at a
point lying somewhere in time between the move to the Portiuncula and the Bologna and Assisi episodes, he ceased to be able to
continue the process of adaptation.

We may now turn from the biographical sources to the writings
of Francis. The outline of an original method of treating these
sources appeared in 1951 under the names of Esser and a fellow-
Franciscan, Lothar Hardick.[1] To their German translation of the
writings of Francis, a work of devotion intended for members of
the third order and others particularly interested in Franciscan
life, they added a study of certain key-words and concepts used
by the founder.[2] By examining one by one the contexts in which
Francis used these words and concepts, they claimed that they
were able to discover the actual meaning which the words carried
for Francis. The method was applied to words and ideas, like
spiritus, *penitentia*, or the practice of confession to laymen, which
assist the understanding of Francis's spirituality as a whole; it was
not applied to the words which he employed to express in detail
his ideal of poverty. For the latter the task of analysis is more
difficult because these "poverty-terms" are often employed only
in the Rules, where differences in the context are small. Where the
terms do overlap, however, and are used over again in other
writings of Francis, there is room for some further investigation
on the lines suggested by Esser and Hardick.

The term "sibi appropriare", which Francis uses in both the
Rules about the goods of the order, is put to work again in the
title of the Fourth Admonition. One may now put these two contexts side by side. In the first case the Rule of 1221 says to the
brothers "quod nullum locum sibi approprient", and the Rule of
1223, "Fratres nihil sibi approprient." In the second case the title

---

[1] K. Esser, L. Hardick, *Die Schriften des hl. Franziskus von Assisi*, Werl-i-W.
1951.
[2] Op. cit., part 3, pp. 161–97.

sentence of the Admonition runs: "Ut nemo appropriet sibi prelationem." [1]

The best way of trying to establish what meaning "sibi appropriare" has which is common to each of these instances is to examine the text of the Admonition in detail. This short piece, containing only three sentences of exhortation, was evidently intended to supplement the passages in the Rules which explain the nature of the position of a superior in the Franciscan order. Francis charges those who may be appointed to such a position not to take any more pleasure in it while they have it than in the office of a servant, and not to care any more when they lose it than they would if they had been excused some menial task. So far, so good; but what is the relevance of the use of "sibi appropriare" in this connection? In the Admonition it runs parallel, as a prohibited attitude, to the two verbs expressing personal emotion towards the office of a superior—"gloriari" and "turbari". The whole passage is highly allusive and elliptical in its expressions, but the burden of it seems to be that the brothers should not take as an individual honour what is properly the common duty of all.[2]

Francis is here demanding that the spiritual denudation of the brothers should be as complete and absolute as their material denudation. It is a theme which he treats in greater length in the Fourteenth Admonition, *De paupertate spiritus*, where he contrasts those who inflict on themselves many austerities, and yet are offended if any injury is done them or anything taken from them, with the true poor who hate themselves and love him who strikes them on the cheek.[3] If we invert Francis's process of thought, and argue from the spiritual denudation to the conditions of the material denudation, we may transfer the significance of "sibi appropriare" in the Fourth Admonition to the prohibition contained in the Rules. What is condemned in the discussion of the

---

[1] *Verba admonitionis*, 4; *Analekten*, ed. Boehmer, p. 43. Of the series of Admonitions, Moorman speaks as follows: "Whether they are actually 'writings' of S. Francis which he read to the Chapter, or whether they are really spoken words which his hearers afterwards wrote down, it is impossible to say. But one thing is certain, and that is that they clearly represent the thought and the spirit of S. Francis." *Sources*, p. 21. I have assumed that the title of this Admonition is primitive, and represents, at the least, the usage of the founder.

[2] For further details on this Admonition, see below, pp. 62–3, where the full text is given, with a translation.

[3] *Analekten*, ed. Boehmer, p. 46.

material goods of the order is the action of the brothers in arro-
gating to themselves as an individual corporation goods which
should be the common property of all men.

The spiritual significance of "sibi appropriare" for St Francis
is confirmed by one other passage, in the Rule of 1221. "And no
minister or preacher should appropriate to himself the office of
being minister for the brothers or the office of being preacher, but
at whatever hour the command may be given him, he should lay
down his office without any contradiction." [1] Here, again, there
is a meaning analogous to that of the Fourth Admonition.

Making anything one's own involves excluding somebody else
from it, and therefore Francis, in the Rule of 1221, immediately
he has spoken of the property of the order, goes on to instruct the
brothers as to how they should receive visitors. The complete
passage reads:

> Let the brothers be careful wherever they may be, in hermitages
> or in other settlements, not to appropriate a settlement to themselves
> or maintain it against anyone. And whoever may come to them,
> friend or foe, thief or robber, let him be kindly received. [2]

We can see a similar thought in Francis when he replied to the
companion who remonstrated with him for giving away his cloak
to a beggar. [3] He felt that he could only hold material goods so
long as he was not depriving others who needed them more.

The objection which Francis makes, it seems, to the exercise of
property rights is to the idea of exclusion which is implicit in them.

Money he abominated as an object in itself. To ensure that the
brothers were banned from even the most harmless contacts with
it, he devoted an entire chapter of the Rule of 1221 to blocking
every possibility of their evading his command to them. [4] It is clear
that he regarded it as something unnatural, inextricably associated
with the avarice of the world. It is a view which has affinities with
Aristotelian thought, comprehensible in the circumstances of the
contemporary economic system.

The case of property is quite different. Francis nowhere in his
own writings so much as mentions the words *dominium* or *proprietas*,

---

[1] *Regula prima*, 7; *Analekten*, ed. Boehmer, p. 16, lines 2–5.
[2] *Regula prima*, 7; *Analekten*, ed. Boehmer, p. 8, lines 5–8.
[3] *II Cel.*, 87; *AF* X, 182. See above, p. 39, n. 4.
[4] *Regula prima*, 8; *Analekten*, ed. Boehmer, pp. 8–9.

which were to loom so large in later Franciscan history. He gives
one sentence alone to the question of the common goods of the
order in each of the two Rules. This fact, taken in isolation, does
not prove that he attached scant importance to the question of
property-owning in the order: as we have seen, the total denudation of the brothers was a point of great spiritual significance, and
breaches of his prohibition aroused in him the most violent reactions. At the same time, it is not apparently property as a legal
concept which arouses his hostility. At Mount Alverna he was
apparently prepared to accept full property rights from Count
Orlando so long as they were held in a remote and mountainous
area where the occupation of the friars would not reasonably
involve the exclusion of others from the enjoyment of the land.
At Rivo Torto he occupied the shed only so long as it remained
unclaimed by anybody else; as soon as the peasant drove in his ass,
he went away and left the building to him.

What, then, has this investigation revealed as the distinguishing
marks of Franciscan poverty, in the intention of the founder? The
friars are to be on terms of equality with the poorest of the poor.
Their means of maintenance are to be of a transient and uncertain
kind. Their labour is to be casual. They are to beg, and their
begging is to be taken from door to door, without discrimination,
ostiatim. They are to be withdrawn entirely from the ordinary
economic framework of society. Even the handling of money
tokens is forbidden them, and they are not allowed to use money
substitutes.

This prohibition of money is absolute; the prohibition of common property is not. Coins may not even be handled; but property,
as a legal concept, is not totally forbidden—or so it would seem.
What St Francis wishes to condemn is the property-owning mind.
The term "sibi appropriare" has a spiritual, as well as a purely
economic, connotation. In practice, one may trace a development
in his attitude towards the common dwelling-places of the order;
and then, towards the end, a sharp reaction. What was his final
attitude? Most likely, he was simply uncertain. What does seem
clear is that the legal issue of common property, the *dominium* or
proprietas of the order, played scant part in Francis's lifetime. So
long as the means of maintenance of the order are genuinely
transient and insecure, then the legal issue of *dominium* remains

unimportant; it is only when the order no longer has the same economic insecurity that the issue of *dominium* comes to the fore. This development we shall be discussing in our third chapter.

3. THE ORIGINS OF FRANCISCAN POVERTY

We have seen the nature of the poverty which Francis desired for his friars. We should now ask: What was its source? Where did Francis get this idea of absolute poverty?

On some topics Francis gave uncertain judgements to his followers, oscillating between different views on different occasions. On the question of Papal privileges, for example, he at one time, in the Testament, gave an absolute prohibition to the friars;[1] but it can be shown that his own practice was not as uncompromising as this.[2]

On learning, he showed a similar inconsistency. Sometimes he appeared to wish to prohibit it altogether, as when he refused a novice a psalter,[3] or spoke of the postulant from the clergy renouncing his learning in order to cast himself naked into the arms of the Crucified;[4] yet on one occasion he gave a clear written permission for a friar to teach theology in the order.[5]

But on poverty he is far more certain. Where breaches of the rule of poverty are concerned, we see him proceed decisively against offenders. A postulant in the March of Ancona who tried to evade the conditions of entry, and gave his goods to relatives instead of the poor was immediately expelled.[6] A friar who quite accidentally touched money was made to put it on a dung heap for his penance.[7] Peter Catanii, when he wanted to reserve something from the goods of postulants for the needs of friars coming

---

[1] *Testamentum*, 8.

[2] A. Callebaut, "Saint François et les privilèges, surtout celui de la pauvreté concédé à sainte Claire par Innocent III", *AFH* xx (1927), 182–93.

[3] *II Cel.*, 195; *AF* X, p. 242, lines 12–14.

[4] *II Cel.*, 194; *AF* X, p. 241.

[5] "Placet mihi, quod sacram theologiam fratribus legas, dummodo propter huius studium sanctae orationis et devotionis spiritum non extinguant. . . ." *Epistola ad S. Antonium de Padua, Analekten*, ed. Boehmer, p. 71. The authenticity of this letter, formerly suspect, has been demonstrated by Esser in his article, "Der Brief des hl. Franziskus an den hl. Antonius von Padua", *FS* xxxi (1949), 135–51.

[6] *II Cel.*, 80; *AF* X, 178–9.

[7] *II Cel.*, 65; *AF* X, 170.

to the chapters, was told that rather than violate the Rule in such a way he should strip the altar of our Lady.[1]

Why this severity? The reason which Francis gave for his actions was that Franciscan poverty represented the poverty of the gospels. To evade the precepts of the Rule in this matter meant disobeying the gospel. He told Peter Catanii this: Mary, he said, would rather see her altar bare than the gospel of her Son disregarded. He gave a similar answer to a minister who asked permission to keep valuable books: he told him he could not give it to him because he had promised to keep the gospel.[2]

The most strongly Spiritual sources, the *Speculum* literature, and the *Intentio*, treated his conception of Franciscan poverty, as representing evangelical poverty, as the prime cause of the conflict between the founder and the ministers. Francis, in their interpretation, would not consent freely to modifications of poverty in the Rules because this would mean rejecting the commands of the gospel.[3]

There is no doubt that Francis saw his way of life as a reproduction of the way of living of Christ and the apostles described in the gospels.

Throughout his life his response is to the texts of Scripture before anything else. When he left the world, he did not join one of the established orders, although he was more than once advised to do so. Instead he remained near Assisi living for a long time, perhaps a year or two, as a hermit without any clear plan of life. His next step came as the result of hearing texts of Scripture, on the day that the Gospel for St Matthias's day was read at the Portiuncula, giving the instructions for the missionary tour in Matthew.[4] No doubt there were good contemporary reasons why it should have been this passage of Scripture that should have aroused him in preference to some other: surely it was no accident that the instructions at the sending of the disciples had been the favourite texts of the lesser-known poverty movements of the twelfth century.

Yet his own response, however it was unconsciously conditioned,

---

[1] *II Cel.*, 67; *AF* X, 171.
[2] *II Cel.*, 62; *AF* X, 168. *Speculum*, ed. Sabatier (1928), iii, 7–8.
[3] See below, pp. 81–2.
[4] Matt. 10.7–13. *I Cel.*, 22; *AF* X, 19. Jörgensen-Sloane, p. 56, n. 1.

was still direct to the words of Scripture. He can be shown consciously rejecting contemporary regulations in favour of Scripture.
No better instance of this could be found than his adopting for the
Rule the instructions of Jesus to the missionaries, "Eat what is set
before you", and thus flouting all contemporary opinion, which
regarded fasting as an essential mark of the religious life.[1]

Much of the language which Francis used suggests a very close
relation between the way of living of his order and the life of
Christ and the apostles. The Rule of 1221, less cautious than the
later redaction, introduces itself by saying:

> This is the life of the gospel of Jesus Christ which brother Francis
> asked to be permitted to him by the lord pope Innocent. . . .[2]

I Celano, describing how Francis wrote his first Rule before the
journey to Rome to seek Innocent III's confirmation, seems to
imply that it consisted almost exclusively of passages of Scripture.
He said that he wrote "simply and in few words . . . using particularly the words of the holy gospel", and then, "He inserted,
however, a few other things which had become absolutely necessary to the practice of holy life."[3] As late as 1223, when much new
legislation had been added in the interim to the early form of
1210, Francis still concluded his account of the Franciscan life
with words which could be taken to mean that the gospel itself
was the Rule for his followers.[4]

It does seem that he wanted to observe the gospel way of living,
not only on the major issues, like renouncing money or eating
meat rather than fasting, but on minor points of detail as well. The
use by the early friars of the greeting "Peace be to this house",
borrowed, again, from the instructions to the missionaries, at once
springs to mind.[5] No detail from the gospels was too unimportant
to be incorporated into Francis's imitation. Having seen, for
example, that Christ fasted forty days after his baptism, Francis

---

[1] Luke 10.8. *Regula prima*, 3; *Analekten*, ed. Boehmer, p. 4, lines 21–2. *Regula
bullata*, 3; *Analekten*, p. 31, lines 30–2. Esser and Hardick, *Schriften*, p. 178.

[2] *Regula prima*, prologus; *Analekten*, ed. Boehmer, p. 1.

[3] *I Cel.*, 32; *AF* X, 25.

[4] "ut . . . paupertatem et humilitatem et sanctum Evangelium Domini
nostri Iesu Christi, quod firmiter promisimus, observemus." *Regula bullata*,
epilogus; *Analekten*, ed. Boehmer, p. 35.

[5] Luke 10.5. *Regula prima*, 14; *Analekten*, ed. Boehmer, p. 13, lines 21–2.
Regula bullata, 3; *Analekten*, p. 31, lines 29–30.

wrote into the Rules a recommendation to the brothers that they, too, should fast from Epiphany to Easter.[1] He customarily related the events of his own life to those of Christ's: a final meal with his brothers is transformed in this way into a commemoration of the Last Supper.[2] Whenever possible the minor regulations of Franciscan life were modelled on the life of Christ. Because Christ called himself a servant, the titles of the officials of the order, *minister, custos, guardianus* were deliberately chosen so as to suggest a position of humility.[3]

Francis was prepared to run the brothers into discomfort and even into danger in his desire to observe completely the gospel maxims. In the early days, when he had only eight followers and when dispersing them might mean the collapse of the community, he still insisted on sending them out in pairs to preach as Christ had sent the disciples.[4] Later on, in 1217, he risked the brothers' safety in foreign countries by sending them out without any preparation, either in knowledge of the language or holding safe conducts, so that they would literally as well as metaphorically be carrying nothing for their journey.[5]

The response which best pleased him in his brothers was a total and unqualified imitation, down to the last detail. *II Celano* gives a story where Francis is seen holding up as an example to the rest the attitude of Brother John the Simple. He says:

> So when St Francis stopped somewhere to meditate, whatever the gestures or movements he made, simple John at once repeated and imitated them. When Francis spat, he spat; when Francis coughed, he coughed, joining his sighs to those of Francis, and his weeping to the weeping of the saint. When the saint lifted up his hand to heaven, he did the same, watching him carefully, as his pattern of behaviour, and imitating all.[6]

[1] "Et similiter omnes fratres ieiunent . . . ab Epiphania, quando Dominus noster Iesus Christus incepit ieiunare, usque ad Pascha." *Regula prima*, 3; *Analekten*, ed. Boehmer, p. 4, lines 17–20. In the Rule of 1223 the instruction is given as a counsel only: "Sanctam vero Quadragesimam . . . qui voluntarie eam ieiunant benedicti sint a Domino, et qui nolunt non sint astricti." *Regula bullata*, 3; *Analekten*, p. 31, lines 16–19.   [2] *II Cel.*, 217; *AF* X, 255.
[3] See *Regula prima*, 4; *Analekten*, ed. Boehmer, p. 5, lines 4–9. Again, *Regula prima*, 5; *Analekten*, p. 6, lines 8–14. *Regula bullata*, 10; *Analekten*, p. 34, lines 6–10.
[4] Luke 10.1. *I Cel.*, 29; *AF* X, 23–4.
[5] For the results, in France, Germany, and Hungary, see Jordan of Giano's account: *Chronica Fratris Jordani*, ed. H. Boehmer, Paris, 1908, pp. 4–7.
[6] *II Cel.*, 190; *AF* X, p. 239, lines 15–19.

This was to outdo Francis himself, and even he felt obliged gently
to restrain Brother John. The general idea he praised and recommended to the other brothers. It was the attitude he strove for
himself in his own imitation of the life of the gospel: he was to
follow the words of the gospel in the same unqualified way he
expected the brothers to follow him.

Evidently he wished the brothers' way of living to be an exact
replica of the way of life of Christ and the apostles. Will he expect
the same response to the example of the poverty of Christ and the
apostles, as it is reflected in the gospels?

No aspect of the religious life more frequently requires the use
of dispensation and accommodation to circumstances than the
practice of poverty. All the testimony, in the *Speculum* sources and
in the writings and other biographies as well, suggests that for
Francis this was quite untrue: he seems to have been less willing
to modify poverty than any other feature of the life of his followers.

Even where there were good grounds for dispensation he went
to great lengths to avoid any breach of his rule of poverty. Once
in Slavonia he needed to travel on shipboard to make his return
to Italy, and the owners demanded a money fare. It was a legitimate occasion for dispensation from the Franciscan and evangelical prohibition of money; but rather than do this Francis stowed
away, and emerged on the voyage to pay his fare by service.[1]

To cite the example of the founder alone is, of course, not
enough. Many saints have asked less of their followers than they
have of themselves, and it might be that while he required a complete imitation of his austerities from the *élite* group under his
personal supervision, he intended to set a lesser standard for the
order at large. It might be that he accepted the possibility of
different levels of observance within his order.

But can we say that this is true of poverty, or only of other
aspects of Franciscan life? There were a number of points on
which Francis was intransigent. As we have seen, he would not
allow any mitigation of the gospel counsel to sell all and give to
the poor. He would not allow any friars to be excused from the
duty of begging: a friar who would not beg was expelled from the
order.[2] Clearly he was not prepared to allow exceptions to the
prohibition of money, for he told the friars to treat any of their

[1] *I Cel.*, 55; *AF* X, 42.   [2] *II Cel.*, 75; *AF* X, 176.

number who had money as an apostate.[1] Already, with disappropriation, begging, and the renunciation of money, we have covered three of the headings under which Franciscan poverty may be comprised.

One may do more than point to individual instances in which Francis refused deviations from the standard of poverty he had set for the brothers; the example of his treatment of the Clares might be adduced to show that he took this standard of poverty to be the distinguishing mark of the apostolic life. The Clares, who were debarred by their sex from the active, missionary life that the Franciscans of the first order undertook in imitation of Christ's instructions to the first missionaries, were nevertheless treated by Francis as if they were observing the life of the gospels on terms of equality with his friars. In the *Forma vivendi* given to them in 1213 he told them that they had chosen to live "secundum perfectionem sancti Evangelii", so applying to them a term which he used of his own brothers.[2] In his last will to them he was even more specific, calling his own way of living an attempt to follow the life and poverty of Christ and Mary, then encouraging them always to live in that same most holy life and poverty.[3] Poverty was the one feature which the life of the Clares had in common with that of the first order; apart from that they led the stable, enclosed life of other nuns. Indeed those houses outside Assisi which ignored St Clare's own observance of poverty, and followed Rules written for them by others, became in the end hardly distinguishable from ordinary Benedictine nunneries. Therefore, we may say, for Francis the mark of an apostolic life was the observance of poverty in accordance with the invitation of Christ to the rich young ruler, and with those of the instructions to the first missionaries which related to the practice of poverty. If this is so, one can understand why Francis demanded a more rigid observance in poverty than in anything else: it was poverty alone which gave the friars the right to call themselves followers of the apostolic life.

[1] *Regula prima*, 8; *Analekten*, ed. Boehmer, p. 9, lines 6–9.
[2] *Analekten*, ed. Boehmer, p. 35.
[3] "Ego frater Franciscus parvulus volo sequi vitam et paupertatem altissimi Domini nostri Iesu Christi et eius sanctissimae matris. . . . Et rogo vos, dominas meas, et consilium do vobis, ut in ista sanctissima vita et paupertate semper vivatis." Ibid., pp. 35–6.

Francis's own practice supports the opinion that it was the precepts of poverty, and not the rest of the instructions to the missionaries, which he regarded as the essentials of the apostolic life. There was a time, if we can trust our source, when he was in doubt whether he should give up all missionary work and retire from the world. The argument by which Silvester and Clare persuaded him to continue his active work was not that he should do this because leading the apostolic life demanded it but because he should heed the cry of the Church.[1] His attitude to Silvester points in the same direction. Silvester seems to have led a purely contemplative life; yet we never hear of Francis rebuking him for taking no part in the missionary work of the friars. Provided that evangelical poverty was observed, Francis was prepared to allow wide variations, swinging the balance to one extreme or the other, in the alternation between missionary work in the towns and contemplation in the hermitages.

St Francis's idea of poverty, then, was derived from his imitation of the apostolic life. This conclusion leads us on naturally to what was, of course, the determining influence in Francis's idea of poverty: the imitation of Christ.

4. THE ABSOLUTE POVERTY OF CHRIST AND THE APOSTLES

St Francis had a definite idea of the nature of the poverty of Christ; but he never explained it concisely or explicitly, because he had assumed that everybody knew already what it was.

There can be no doubt of the vital importance of the poverty of Christ. We have seen how the observance of poverty was, for Francis, the essential constituent of the apostolic life. But, in his outlook, this imitation of the apostles was, so to speak, summed up and comprehended in the imitation of Christ. A stress on the imitation of the life of the apostles was a feature of a number of popular movements of the twelfth century. *Apostolica vita* was a popular concept which surely influenced Francis. Nevertheless, there is this difference between the ideas of Francis and those of

---

[1] *I Cel.*, 35; *AF* X, p. 28, lines 10–15. Bonav. *Leg. Maj.*, xii, 2, 611. *Actus Beati Francisci et Sociorum Eius*, ed. P. Sabatier, Paris, 1902, chap. vi, pp. 55–6.

his twelfth-century predecessors: they put first the following of
the life of the apostles, he the following of the life of Christ.[1]

If this imitation of Christ was intended to be a total one, yet
there is one principle of Christ's life which has a peculiarly com-
pelling force for Francis: his poverty. It has a unique emotional
significance for him. When he was at table with the brothers, a
friar on one occasion had only to speak of the poverty of Christ
and of Mary, to send him sobbing from the meal, to eat the rest
of his bread in tears on the bare ground.[2] So much importance
did he attach to the principle of poverty that he made it a particular sign of Christ. When a friar was abusing some idle beggar
who had asked him for alms, he rebuked him on the grounds that
any poor man stood in the place of Christ. He said, in *I Celano's*
version: "He who curses a poor man, does an injury to Christ,
because he bears the noble sign of him, 'who made himself poor
for us in this world'."[3] He used the example of Christ's poverty
as a justification of the poverty, both of his own life, and that of
his followers. Once, leaving the cell he occupied at the hermitage
of Sartiano, he heard a brother calling it "Brother Francis's
cell". He stopped immediately, told the brother that because he
had given his name to the cell, he would never use it again, and
appealed to the example of the Lord. Christ, he said, when he was
fasting forty days in the desert, had no cell made for him, nor
any house, but used a stone as shelter.[4] Again, when in the Rule
of 1221 he wished to urge his brothers not to be ashamed to go out
begging, he did so by setting before them the example of Christ
"who lived on alms".[5]

It is hardly too much to say that the poverty of Christ was the
key idea of the whole Franciscan movement.

There are many occasions on which Francis refers in general
terms to "the poverty of Christ". Yet nowhere does he clearly
explain its meaning in material terms. Why is this so?

[1] Esser and Hardick, *Schriften*, p. 175. On Francis's view of the following of
Christ, see Esser and Hardick's whole discussion, op. cit., pp. 174–9; and on the
earlier precedents, W. Völker, "Nachfolge Christi", *Die Religion in Geschichte
und Gegenwart*, 2nd edn., IV, Tübingen, 1930, coll. 396–401.

[2] *II Cel.*, 200; *AF* X, 244. On the companions' use of the ground as a table,
see also *Speculum*, ed. Sabatier (1928), xxi, 56.

[3] *I Cel.*, 76; *AF* X, p. 57, lines 20–1.

[4] *II Cel.*, 59; *AF* X, 167.

[5] *Regula prima*, 9; *Analekten*, ed. Boehmer, p. 10.

In untrained minds the deepest assumptions are often those which are never made explicit. A tendency to assume, without defining, some fact or premiss was quite usual with Francis. It was at the same time a source both of strength and of weakness. On the one hand it can be seen as part of his sublime confidence in the providence of God, which, he believed, would see the friars through any transient difficulties of living or organization. On the other, in the writing of the Rules it led to endless difficulties of interpretation. When reading the Rule of 1221 it soon becomes apparent why it was necessary for some outside hand to take up Francis's work and put it, at least roughly, into the form of legal regulations. A minor detail will suffice as an illustration. In the later, far more concise form of 1223, the order is given in a sentence, that only provincials should receive postulants.[1] On re-reading the text of the second chapter in the Rule of 1221, it becomes apparent that this had been Francis's intention from the first; but instead of saying so, he assumes from the start that this would be the natural arrangement and proceeds to explain the reception of postulants with this unspoken assumption in mind.[2]

We cannot therefore expect any definition of the nature of the poverty of Christ from Francis's own lips. We must approach the problem by a more roundabout method.

First, let us examine the implications behind Francis's statements. These show that, for Francis, the poverty of Christ and the apostles was an indivisible concept. Throughout his writings and reported sayings he appeals to it confidently as a unified and coherent example for the imitation of the friars. There is no hint that he made any distinction either of time or person in this respect.

All that we otherwise know of Francis's way of thinking makes it unlikely that he would have doubted whether the poverty of Christ and the apostles was the same at all times. He would not have made a distinction between, for example, the poverty of the apostles on the preaching tour, and the poverty of the apostles in the early Church at Jerusalem. Anything like a collation and comparison of texts was quite foreign to his ideas; what he desired

---

[1] "Si qui voluerint hanc vitam accipere et venerint ad fratres nostros, mittant eos ad suos ministros provinciales, quibus solummodo et non aliis recipiendi fratres licentia concedatur." *Regula bullata*, 2; *Analekten*, ed. Boehmer, p. 30, lines 4–7.

[2] *Regula prima*, 2; *Analekten*, ed. Boehmer, p. 2.

for his brothers was the kind of wisdom which is placed as sister next to simplicity in the *Laudes de Virtutibus*.[1]

There is in his mind a standard of poverty common to Christ and the disciples and even to Mary. In his last will to the Clares, as we have seen, he referred indiscriminately to the life and poverty of Christ and Mary. In the Rule of 1221, in the chapter mentioned above, *De petenda elemosina*, he juxtaposed the poverty of all three as an example which the friars ought to follow. He said:

> And let them not be ashamed, but rather remember that our Lord Jesus Christ, the Son of the living omnipotent God, set his face as the hardest flint, and was not ashamed to be made a poor man and a stranger for us and lived on alms, himself and the blessed Virgin and his disciples.[2]

Secondly, following the general principle laid down at the beginning of the chapter, let us turn away from words alone to the symbols which, we saw, form the basis of Francis's thought. If we are to re-create his view of the poverty of Christ, it must be in the terms in which he was accustomed to think—in the primary visual images which are the key to the understanding of his thought.

The key figure in Francis's mind, we may suggest, is the image of the naked Christ.

Nakedness was a symbol of great importance for Francis. He used it to mark the beginning and the end of his converted life. When he wished to repudiate his father's goods and enter religion, he did so by stripping himself naked in the bishop's palace at Assisi.[3] At the end, dying in the Portiuncula, he forced the companions to strip him, so that he could face death unclothed on the floor of the hut.[4] It was associated with quite commonplace actions. When he slept, for example, it had to be on the naked ground; on one occasion that he was given a pillow, at Greccio in illness, he insisted that the devil had got into it, and would not sleep till he had thrown it out.[5] Twice he even chose to abandon the table of the friars, to sit on the naked ground to eat his meal, impelled on each occasion by the thought of Christ's poverty. Once, as we have

---

[1] *Analekten*, ed. Boehmer, p. 65, lines 4–6.
[2] *Regula prima*, 9; *Analekten*, ed. Boehmer, p. 10, lines 6–10.
[3] *I Cel.*, 15; *AF* X, 14–15. See also Bonav., *Leg. Maj.*, xiv, 4, 622.
[4] *II Cel.*, 214; *AF* X, p. 253, lines 13–16. *II Cel.*, 217; *AF* X, p. 255, lines 18–21. Either two such strippings or, as seems more likely, repetition by Celano.
[5] *II Cel.*, 64; *AF* X, 169–70.

seen, it was a chance reference to the poverty of Christ and Mary;
on the other occasion he made a conscious parable of his action.
It was the episode in which he appeared disguised as a beggar to
reproach the brothers at Greccio for the luxury of their table.
After he had revealed himself, he sat down by himself on the
ground, and put his dish into the cinders. "Now", he said, "I sit
like a friar minor"; and, to the brothers, "The examples of the
poverty of the Son of God ought to constrain us more than other
religious." [1] Again, on another occasion, he linked nakedness with
the name of Christ when he spoke of a learned postulant in a certain fashion resigning his learning so that he may "offer himself
naked to the arms of the Crucified One".[2]

In fact we may detect in these stories an echo of the well-known
saying of Jerome: "Naked to follow the naked Christ." [3]

The obvious example of the nakedness of Christ in Scripture is
the Crucifixion. This was a central theme for the meditation of
St Francis, a meditation which culminated in the reception of the
stigmata. But there is another, perhaps less well-known scene, in
which Christ is found stripping off his garments. It is the description of the Last Supper, when Christ began to wash the disciples'
feet. That Francis was imbued with the symbolism of this scene,
and used it in explanation of the Franciscan way of living, will
emerge from the wording of his Fourth Admonition. This short
piece, describing the position of a superior in the order, has
already been cited; now we may quote it in full.

> That no one should appropriate to himself the office of prelate.
> "I came not to be ministered unto, but to minister", says the Lord.
> Those who are set over others should glory no more in that office of
> a prelate, than if they were given the office of washing the brothers'
> feet. And if they are more disturbed at the office of prelate being
> taken away from them, than at the taking away of the office of
> washing feet, so much the more they make a bag to the peril of their
> soul.[4]

[1] II Cel., 61; AF X, p. 168, lines 14–18.
[2] II Cel., 194; AF X, 241.
[3] Hieronymus, Epistolae, cxxv, 20; PL XXII, 1085.
[4] " 'Non veni ministrari, sed ministrare', dicit Dominus. Illi qui sunt super
alios constituti, tantum de illa prelatione glorientur, quantum si essent in
abluendi fratrum pedes offitio deputati. Et quanto magis turbantur de ablata
sibi prelatione quam de pedum offitio, tanto magis sibi loculos ad periculum
anime componunt." Verba admonitionis, 4; Analekten, ed. Boehmer, p. 43.

The Admonition is giving a symbol-picture of the Last Supper. The washing of feet is the work of Christ. It is the sign of the true disciple. Christ says: "If I then, your Lord and Master, have washed your feet; ye also ought to wash one another's feet." [1] So, in the text of the Admonition, Francis adopts this washing of feet as the sign of a true follower of the Rule.

On the other side of the picture is the symbol of the bad disciple. As Christ washed the disciples' feet, he said: ". . . and ye are clean, but not all. For he knew who should betray him. . . ." [2] Later he said to the betrayer: "That thou doest, do quickly." The narrative continues: "Now no man at the table knew for what intent he spake this unto him. For some of them thought, because Judas had the bag, that Jesus had said unto him, Buy those things that we have need of against the feast; or, that he should give something to the poor." [3] In the Vulgate of this passage the term for bag is *loculi*. That term is never used in the gospels except in reference to the bag which Judas carried. [4] When Francis in the Admonition says of the bad brothers, that they "make a bag for themselves to the peril of their soul", the term which he uses for bag is also *loculi*. He says, ". . . . tanto magis sibi loculos ad periculum anime componunt". It is clear from this elliptical phrase, "loculos componunt", that an allusion is intended; it is clear from the conjunction of terms that it is an allusion to the text of the Vulgate where it refers to Judas's bag.

In the gospels, the bag and the betrayal of Christ are always associated. That is true in the text we have quoted from the account of the Last Supper; it is true also of the text which gives Judas's criticism of Mary's anointing Christ's feet with spikenard: "Then saith one of his disciples, Judas Iscariot, Simon's son, which should betray him, Why was not this ointment sold for three hundred pence, and given to the poor? This he said, not that he cared for the poor; but because he was a thief, and had the bag,

[1] John 13.14.
[2] Ibid., 10–11.
[3] Ibid., 27–9.
[4] *Loculi* appears twice in the gospels, as a translation for γλωσσόκομον: John 12.6 (*Novum Testamentum Latine, Evangelia*, ed. J. Wordsworth, H. White, Oxonii, 1889–98, p. 592); John 13.29 (ed. cit., p. 604). In each case it is used of the bag which Judas carried. The singular, *loculus*, appears once. The meaning is different: it is a translation of σορός, and is taken for the bier of the widow's son at Nain, Luke 7.14 (ed. cit., p. 349). See the *Index verborum*, p. 759.

and bare what was put therein." [1] With these gospel texts in mind, Francis therefore uses the bag in the Admonition as a symbol of the bad brother who betrays the Rule.

The symbol of the bag is used in exactly the same sense else-where in St Francis's writings. In the Rule of 1221 he says that a brother who breaks the Rule by keeping money should be treated as an apostate: ". . . we should all hold him for a false brother and an apostate and a thief and a robber and a bag-haver . . .". Again the term used is *loculi*: ". . . omnes fratres teneamus eum pro falso fratre et pro apostata et fure et latrone et loculos hab-ente . . .".[2] Again it is plain that an allusion is intended to Judas in the Vulgate.

The bag and the betrayal are one, for Francis. To have a bag is to associate with the betrayer. Conversely, to renounce the bag is to associate with Christ. Here are two images. On the one side, as we have suggested, is the naked Christ. On the other, standing in opposition to him, is the "bag-haver".[3] Disciples join one or the other: true disciples renounce their bag and follow Christ, while false ones retain theirs, and follow Judas. The bag marks their division: it stands for the material reserves of wealth, which the true disciples renounce and the false retain. In Francis's view, Christ and the apostles, the pattern of imitation, have no reserves at all. Their absolute poverty consists in the renunciation of all reserves of material goods, both individual and common.

This interpretation of the bag is remarkable. Later in the thir-teenth century anti-Franciscan controversialists used the case of the bag which Judas carried to disprove the friars' view of the poverty of Christ. To them the bag showed that Christ and the apostles had reserves of goods in common. They cited Scripture in support.[4] The Fathers and traditional commentaries took it that this meant that Christ and the apostles had common reserves. Franciscan apologists, for their part, were content to argue that this case of the bag showed Christ and the apostles having common

---

[1] John 12.4–6.

[2] *Regula prima*, 8; *Analekten*, ed. Boehmer, p. 9. Compare John 12.6, in the Vulgate, ed. cit., p. 592: "dixit autem hoc non quia de egenis pertinebat ad eum sed quia fur erat et loculos habens ea quae mittebantur portabat."

[3] The phrase "loculos habens" of the Vulgate (John 12.6) has been in some way transmuted by Francis.

[4] I.e., John 13.29.

goods only as an exception, at a special time, and not as part of their regular way of life.[1] But all were agreed in admitting that the bag held the reserves of the whole college of apostles—of Christ and the apostles together.

Yet, if we are right in our hypothesis, this was not true for Francis. The bag was held, if we follow the language of the Admonition, "ad periculum anime". It was an exception to the common way of life of Christ and the other, true disciples. It represented a personal breach by Judas.

In this respect Francis ran against tradition. But the fact that he did so need occasion neither surprise nor dismay. It is in accord with his customary way of thinking. While it is possible to exaggerate the extent of his unworldly ignorance, nevertheless it remains true that he forswore formal learning. He was not given to the use of commentaries. As we have seen, he wished to learn the whole tenor of a passage, rather than concern himself with the precise details contained in it. What lay behind his treatment of the bag is the total picture of the life of Christ and the apostles wandering naked, without any common reserves, living on alms. The Franciscan order was an attempt to re-create this way of life. They had no reserves, in just the same way. They had no regular supporters—they begged from door to door. They had no money—which is, *ipso facto*, a form of reserve. With the material state went a spiritual one—and this was realized by later Franciscan biographers. Bonaventura altered *II Celano* in order to introduce the symbol of the bag. Of the learned man who will not, in a fashion, renounce his learning, he makes this comment: "For in no way does a man perfectly renounce the world who keeps the bag of his own interpretation in the secret places of his heart."[2] The author of the *Speculum*, similarly, attributes the use of the symbol of the bag to Francis in his reply to the learned man who wished to keep his books. St Francis, in this account, says: "You wish to be seen by men as Friars minor and to be called observers of the gospel, yet in works you wish to have a bag."[3] It is interesting to see both Spiritual and more orthodox interpretations of Francis aware of the significance of the symbol of the bag. The idea of the

[1] See below, pp. 135–8.
[2] *Leg. Maj.*, vii, 2, 587; contrast *II Cel.*, 194; *AF* X, 241.
[3] *Speculum*, ed. Sabatier (1928), cap. vi, p. 8, para. 6.

6

total renunciation of reserves, with which the symbol of the bag is linked, is, we would say, the clue to the Franciscan observance of poverty, at both the material and spiritual level.[1]

The doctrine of the absolute poverty of Christ and the apostles lay at the heart of the Franciscan observance. In Francis's intention, the friars' poverty was to be a perfect imitation of the poverty of Christ and the apostles. This poverty consisted essentially in the renunciation of all reserves of material goods, whether those of the individual or the group. Christ and the apostles renounced material goods in order to cast themselves on providence, and live on alms. The one apostle who did not do this, and who kept a reserve in his bag, was the betrayer, Judas.

Poverty in this context, it should be noted, means the renunciation of goods rather than the renunciation of rights. We found it extraordinarily difficult to discover St Francis's views about the common goods of the order. We found that it was, at the least, doubtful whether he ever intended that the order should be divested totally of property rights. The issue of common *dominium* had scarcely any importance in his lifetime; and we should probably not be in error if we said that Francis never seriously thought about it. What he fought for all his life was the actual denudation of material goods of his followers, both as individuals and as a community. When, therefore, he spoke of the poverty of Christ and the apostles, he had in mind their renunciation of reserves of actual goods. We may say that Francis believed Christ and the apostles had no reserves of material goods; but we are on no secure ground if we say that he believed that they renounced all property rights.

The aim of the first part of this book is to trace the development of the scholastic doctrine of the absolute poverty of Christ and the

---

[1] The following contributions may be mentioned as bearing on St Francis's view of poverty and the poverty of Christ. I received a reference to them in a personal communication from Dr Esser, after the body of my text had been completed. Regrettably, pressure of business has since prevented me from so much as reading them, but they may be mentioned to the reader in the confidence of Dr Esser's name. They are: K. Esser, "Mysterium paupertatis. Die Armutsauffassung des hl. Franziskus von Assisi", *Wissenschaft und Weisheit* (Jahrg. 1951), 177–89; "Armut als Darstellung des Reiches Gottes", in K. Esser, *Antwort der Liebe*, Werl.-i.-W., 1958, pp. 141–64; W. Hillman, "Perfectio evangelica. Neutestamentlichtheologische Grundlagen des Ordenslebens", *Wissenschaft und Weisheit* (Jahrg. 1956), 161–72.

apostles. The starting-point of this doctrine, we now see, lies in the mind of St Francis. The poverty of Christ had immense emotional significance for him: hence the vital importance of the doctrine for his later followers. He left to them the belief in the poverty of Christ as a definite, unified concept. He built the observance of the order on this doctrine. They had the task of working out the doctrine in scholastic form and defending it against the attacks of enemies.

The further development and elaboration of the doctrine forms the subject of the following chapters.

The third chapter will be almost solely concerned with the practice of poverty within the order in the twenty years after St Francis's death; and for a good reason. Francis bequeathed to his order a quite extraordinarily austere standard of poverty. The needs of the life of the order forced this poverty out of the shape which the founder had intended. While in no way abating their reverence for him, or their genuine zeal for poverty, the Franciscan leaders found themselves compelled by subtle, often unconscious, shifts to alter their observance. In the process the theory of poverty was also altered, in the same subtle way. Later, when the scholastic doctrine of absolute poverty was formed, in the writings of Bonaventura, it contained two elements. One was the doctrine of the absolute poverty of Christ as it existed in the mind of Francis. This we have now described. The other was the new theory of poverty, developed out of the exigencies of the order's life in the period 1226–47. The two coalesced, under the pressure of attack from outside, in the mid-thirteenth century, to form the orthodox Bonaventuran doctrine of absolute poverty.

To describe how the new theory of poverty made its appearance in the order, it will be necessary to describe, at length and in detail, the development of the life of the order in those crucial twenty years after the founder's death. Almost all the changes in the way of life of the order necessarily affect the observance of poverty. If the formation of the doctrine of absolute poverty is to be understood, then these changes must be set out, and their effects on the practice of poverty detailed.

3

THE DEVELOPMENT OF THE
OBSERVANCE

WE HAVE now established the idea of the poverty of
the friars in the mind of St Francis. It is almost too
obvious to say that this idea of poverty is so extreme as
to cause immense difficulties as soon as it has to be applied, not to
a band of wandering friars, but to a developing order with its
problems of dwelling places, learning, sick friars, and the like.
And in fact that is precisely what happened. The ideal was impossible,[1] and the story of the twenty succeeding years, to which we
now address ourselves, was to make this tragically clear. Adaptation of the ideal of poverty was forced, consciously or unconsciously, on the friars or on those responsible for their order.

And here at once we encounter the heart of the matter of the
doctrine of the poverty of Christ in the thirteenth and early
fourteenth centuries—the nature of property, and the possibility of
its use divorced from its ownership. Is it possible, in the world as it
is, to have the use of material things without owning them? Can
the friars inhabit a building which does not belong to them?
Can they have MSS. for their learning and yet own none of them?
And if they do so, are they in fact complying with the strict ideal
of poverty which St Francis laid down? Theoretical discussion of
this problem was not to come to the fore until controversy, bitter
and prolonged, compelled it. It is when we reach the time of the
great controversies that we shall have to discuss in much greater

[1] In this sense. The standard of poverty intended by St Francis, if appallingly
severe, was coherent and, just, observable. It could stand with a moral exhortation, "annuntiando eis vitia et virtutes, poenam et gloriam cum brevitate
sermonis" (*Regula bullata*, 9; *Analekten*, ed. Boehmer, p. 34), because this did
not demand learning. But, as I see it, it is incompatible with the regular pursuit
of learning. The new entrants to the order were bound to desire the practice
of preaching, in the full, learned sense. If learning be adopted, then the full
poverty must be mitigated.

detail the concepts involved in the whole question of ownership, or dominion, and of use. In the meantime we have to address ourselves to the story of the years immediately succeeding the death of Francis, and to trace through them the early process of adaptation which was forced upon the order, and which in turn produced new interpretations of the theory of poverty. We may now turn to examine the forces which pressed upon the friars and imposed these changes.

In the eighteenth century, a period marked by exceptional bitterness in the controversy about the Franciscan ideal, the Conventual, Sbaralea, brought out an edition of Papal Bulls of the early centuries relating to the Franciscan order.[1] It was not a pure historical work, but had a secondary polemical purpose, of demonstrating the legitimacy of the way of life of his own branch of the order and, conversely, the illegitimacy of that of its opponents, the Observants. As a counterblast Annibali da Latere, with some official backing, published a supplementary volume to Sbaralea, putting forward the historical arguments for the Observant position.[2] Each of these works carried a wood-cut for its frontispiece. The Conventuals chose to depict the dream which Innocent III had on the night after his meeting with Francis, when he saw him holding up single-handed a collapsing wall of the Lateran; the Observants the little group of Francis and the companions kneeling before the Pope and holding up the primitive Rule of 1210 for his confirmation.

In the pictures the two branches of the order, which to a great extent identified themselves with the party groups of the late thirteenth century, had neatly summarized their respective viewpoints. One puts the emphasis on the apostolic work of the brothers, supporting the tottering structure of the Church; the other on a strict adherence to the original poverty intended by Francis for his order. In so far as the disputes within the order in the thirteenth century are disputes of principle, and not merely contests between the virtuous and the lazy, they may be summarized in terms of the clash of these two viewpoints. For one group, the requirements of the apostolate were so important that

---

[1] *Bullarium Franciscanum*, ed. J. H. Sbaralea, I–III, Romae, 1759–65.
[2] F. Annibali de Latera, *Supplementum ad Bullarium Franciscanum*, Romae, 1780.

it was felt they should condition the observance of poverty; for the other, the observance of a certain standard of poverty was the overriding necessity, which, it was thought, should determine the forms of the apostolate.

At first, and for a long time after the death of Francis, all the circumstances favoured development away from the poverty of early times. The influence of successive Popes was naturally enough directed towards making the Franciscans, like the rival order of Dominicans, a fitting instrument of policy, both spiritual and political. For that purpose an extreme poverty tended generally to be an encumbrance. Benefactors from the outside world, who were attracted by the austerity of Franciscan poverty, played their part in weakening it by donations often difficult to refuse. The friars themselves, the only true guardians of their own observance, too often were not sufficiently concerned to protect their poverty against those outside who for the highest motives wished to lighten their burden. Indeed it was the members of the order above all, and not any figures, however exalted, from the outside world, who were responsible for the evolution of the Franciscan ideal which in the first twenty years carried the brothers so far and so fast from the primitive life of Francis and his companions.

The death of Francis had no very great effect on the life of the order. He had long relinquished the government of the order and after his return from the East made no more missionary journeys outside Italy. His last years were spent largely in the company of a small circle of companions in various hermitages of Umbria and Tuscany. The majority of the brothers at the time could have had no detailed knowledge either of his own way of living or any of his intentions about poverty which were not expressed in the Rule. Many had been received as postulants and professed in the ultramontane provinces without having any direct contact with the founder at all.

This withdrawal of Francis helps to explain how it was possible for such divergent interpretations of his wishes to spring up among the brothers even in his own lifetime. The companions, or their later followers through the Spiritual sources on Francis, accused the ministers of the day of deliberate bad faith in distorting Francis's ideal. It is not necessary to do this, even if we wish to accept the Spiritual presentation of the ideal as substantially correct.

Between the time of his return from the East and his death in 1226, many of the ministers would only meet Francis face to face to hear his views on one or two isolated occasions. If they were to ask for guidance, they might well expect to receive one of those sweeping, dramatic statements which the biographical sources introduce with the phrase: "Dixit cum magno fervore spiritus." In them they would find an exposition of the spiritual realities of a situation, but not the clarification of points of detail in day-to-day administration which they required.

Francis preferred to instruct his followers closely in his ideal in a small group of his own, bringing out this or that aspect of it as circumstances demanded.[1] In the early period leaders who went out to missions or to distant provinces generally received their training in Francis's immediate circle. But after the return from the East, it seems, no one left the group around Francis to serve in the offices of the order. There was therefore a check in the transmission of the original tradition. No amount of written testimony from the companions in later years was able to make up for the loss to the development of the Franciscan ideal represented by the years which the founder spent in semi-isolation among the humblest of his followers.

For the minister-general himself during these years no pleas of ignorance can be made. Brother Elias[2] was a recruit from early days. He must have been in favour with Francis because he appointed him provincial of Syria.[3] He was in the party which came back with Francis when the news of dissension among the brothers reached the East. Francis made one of the party, Peter Catanii, minister-general in his place; then, when he died prematurely, it was natural for his choice to fall on Elias. Some modern writers, with an eye on later history, have concluded that his appointment was made as a result of pressure imposed by Ugolino, but there is no evidence that the selection was anything but a free choice on the part of Francis. In many ways Elias was well suited to the task. He had experience of command and was a man of some learning; at the same time he was a lay brother, he had worked

---

[1] E.g., see Gratien, *Évolution*, pp. 30–1.

[2] The following account of Elias was written before the publication of Brooke, *Early Franciscan Government*, which gives a thorough discussion of the place of Elias in the history of the order. To this the reader may be referred.

[3] Gratien, *Évolution*, p. 15, n. 22.

in the mission field, and, perhaps most important of all, he had seen the fraternity in its primitive state before the time of rapid expansion. The marked hostility of the companions to him, which is reflected in the Leo-sources, partly springs from their feeling that he had at one time been one of themselves, and yet had deviated from Francis's own standard.

Among all the sources, only *I Celano*, which was written well before his fall, about 1228,[1] has a good word to say for Elias. *II Celano* and Bonaventura avoid mentioning him by name. Of the early chronicles, Jordan of Giano gives a hostile account of his second generalate,[2] while Salimbene devotes a special section to his misdeeds,[3] and Eccleston treats at length of the disordered scenes which accompanied his predominance in the order.[4] For them all Elias was the betrayer, who played Judas to St Francis and led his order into evil ways.

What does emerge from all contemporary accounts is that he was a man of great personality. All his actions are on the grand scale. He made a remarkable rise from the position of a casual schoolmaster teaching the children of Assisi the psalter to that of minister-general of the Franciscans, the confidant of both Gregory IX and Frederick II. He was the driving-force behind the building of the basilica at Assisi to house the body of Francis. Not only was this large church built so quickly that three years after the start of work, in 1230, it was ready to receive the body in a shrine in the crypt, and nine years after that, at the time of Elias's fall, for the

---

[1] *AF* X, p. iv, and n. 9; on Elias's place in *I Celano*, see Moorman, *Sources*, pp. 65–6.

[2] *Chronica Fratris Jordani*, ed. H. Boehmer, Paris, 1908, pp. 54–8.

[3] *Cronica*, ed. O. Holder-Egger, *MGH, Scriptores* XXXII, Hannoverae et Lipsiae, 1905–13; *Liber de Prelato* "quem feci occasione fratris Helye", pp. 96–163.

[4] *Fratris Thomae vulgo dicti de Eccleston tractatus De Adventu Fratrum Minorum in Angliam*, ed. A. G. Little, Manchester, 1951, coll. xiii, pp. 65–9. The 1951 edition has generally been used here. Little changed his mind about the value of Eccleston's account. In the 1909 edition, published at Paris, p. xxiv, he said: "What he says about Elias is confused: he mixes up the events of 1230, 1232 and 1239. Here he is no doubt using a lost source which is also used by the *Speculum Vitae* and the *Chron. XXIV Generalium*. From the point of view of clarity, there is scarcely anything to choose between these three documents." In the 1951 edition, p. xxv, he says: "His account of Elias and the events of 1230, 1232 and 1239 is clearer and more chronologically accurate than the accounts given in the *Speculum Vitae* and the *Chron. XXIV Gen.*" In the 1951 edition Little stresses the value of the verbal information Eccleston would receive from participants.

bells to be put in the tower, but also, as Gratien says, the entire plan was conceived "at a time when the Friars Minor were often up against the distrust of the secular clergy, and had the greatest difficulty in obtaining so much as an oratory with a portable altar".[1]

There was about his career an air of high drama which made him an irresistible subject for the Spiritual writers, and for Eccleston and Salimbene, who shared a liking for striking anecdotes. He was the only general in Franciscan history to have served two terms of office, once from 1221 to 1227 and again from 1232 to 1239. There was a mysterious episode at the translation of Francis, when Elias and his supporters apparently moved the body secretly without the knowledge of their colleagues,[2] another unusual scene when he was carried in by his followers in an attempt to coerce the chapter into re-electing him,[3] and a conflict at the chapter-general of Rome in 1239 when his enemies combined against him and had him deposed by Gregory IX.[4] His end, presiding as an excommunicate over a tiny schism in his native place of Cortona, was as dramatic as the rest of his life in the order. It was hardly surprising that contemporaries should have regarded him as the man chiefly responsible for the brothers' loss of the purity of observance of Francis's day. They could point to obvious deviations from Francis's wishes in his money collections for the basilica and in his abusing the powers of the general in order to buttress his personal position.

Yet in some points Elias's actions, whatever his motives may have been, show him standing closer than his successors to the original ideal of Francis. His predilection for appointing laymen to office, criticized by his enemies as an instrument of his despotism, at least tended to preserve the mixed character of the fraternity, which Francis had desired. To the end of his life he retained the regard of St Clare, always a determined defender of Franciscan poverty. How can one reconcile his continued friendship with her with the black picture of his character given by the Spiritual sources? Clare was particularly close to the companions, and Leo

[1] *Évolution*, p. 140.
[2] Gratien, *Évolution*, pp. 23–7; *Eccleston*, ed. Little (1951), coll. xiii, p. 65, and n. f.
[3] *Eccleston*, loc. cit., and n. e.
[4] See below pp. 88–9.

used her convent as a safe place for keeping his rolls of reminiscences, the primary sources for *II Celano*.[1]

This contradiction is the crux of the problem of Elias. No modern writer has succeeded in solving it. Lempp, in his biography of Elias, spoils his work by relying on a late and untrustworthy compilation, the *Speculum vitae*.[2] Salvatore Attal has done no more than speculate about the problem,[3] and H. E. Goad, in an article written for a volume of Franciscan essays, has to deny the authenticity of all the evidence of hostility between Elias and the companions in order to support his hypothesis that Elias led a party of the "Assisi laymen" in the order, devoted to Francis's primitive ideal.[4]

A better way of viewing the career of Elias is to regard it, not so much as a source of positive good or evil for the Franciscans, as a great opportunity missed. After the death of Peter Catanii, Elias was one of the very few who was in a position to act as a bridge between the early companions and the ministers. His early entry and the favour of Francis could have recommended him to one group, his power to command and his zeal for the apostolate to the other. It was open to him to take the position of the essential organizing figure, which in so many religious societies has translated the lofty ideals of their founders into terms acceptable to later followers. His personality quite overshadowed that of John Parenti, his successor in 1227, as the sources show. Elias dominated the time after Francis's death, which was the moment when the situation was still fluid and patterns of conduct were not yet formed in the provinces. But, seduced by the vision of the basilica at Assisi, he refused his destiny. It was appropriate that it should have been the municipality of Assisi which in 1937 put up a memorial to him, because he made a more lasting contribution to the development of the city than ever he did to the evolution of the Franciscan ideal.

---

[1] On the witness of Ubertino da Casale, *Arbor vitae crucifixae Jesus*, Venetiis, 1485, fol. 222a1; cited, Jorgensen-Sloane, p. 383, n. 1.

[2] E. Lempp, *Frère Élie de Cortone*, Paris, 1901; O. Holder-Egger and B. Schmeidler, "Zur Kritik minoritischer Geschichtsquellen" Part II, "Der Bericht des Speculum Vitae S. Francisci über den Generalminister Elias", *Neues Archiv der Gesellschaft für altere deutsche Geschichtskunde*, xxxviii (1913), 493–502.

[3] S. Attal, *Frate Elia, compagno di S. Francesco*, Roma, 1936.

[4] H. E. Goad, "Brother Elias as the leader of the Assisan party in the order", *Franciscan Essays* II, BSFS Extra Ser. III, Manchester, 1932, pp. 67–83.

The factors which made for a development in Franciscan life continued to operate independently of the personalities occupying the place of minister-general. Development by means of Papal privileges, which began in the period of Francis's withdrawal from active life in the order, continued if anything more quickly in the rule of Parenti than it did in the generalates of Elias. This is not to say, of course, that the process could not have been halted at the will of a minister-general; the fact was that at this time no general appeared who had either the wish or the strength of will to do so, and so one cannot tell whether it would have been possible for an individual personality to prevail against the train of events.

Most likely the majority of the brothers at this time shared John Parenti's view, that there was no real conflict between the reception of the Papal privileges and the literal observance of the Rule. In Parenti's generalate we have the first mention of the appointment of a *lector* to teach the Franciscans theology, inserted casually by Jordan of Giano in his account of events in the province of Germany.[1] Evidently Parenti, himself a doctor of law of Bologna,[2] favoured the development of learning. He headed the delegation to Gregory IX, which obtained the first major Papal declaration modifying the practice of poverty. On the other side, the Chronicle of the Twenty-Four Generals, a source far from Spiritual in tone, describes him coming into the chapter when the difficulties of the Rule were being discussed, and holding the Rule in his hands, "saying that it was clear and observable and should be observed by all to the letter".[3]

Parenti, with his real humility[4] and his gift of tears,[5] belonged to the first generation of Franciscans who, like many of their successors in later centuries, viewed their practice of poverty with the heart rather than the head. The whole question of Franciscan

---

[1] *Chronica*, ed. Boehmer, p. 47.

[2] Gratien, *Évolution*, p. 112; and refs. given ibid., n. 1.

[3] *Chronica XXIV Generalium*, *AF* III, Ad Claras Aquas, 1897, p. 213. The same source says that he resigned office because he had been saddened by these doubts over the observance: ed. cit., pp. 213–14.

[4] According to Eccleston, his humility abashed Elias's supporters who had broken into the chapter to supplant him. Parenti's response was to start taking off his habit, as a sign of resignation. *Eccleston*, ed. Little (1951), coll. xiii, p. 65.

[5] *Chronica XXIV Generalium*, *AF* III, p. 211. Here again, on Parenti as minister-general, ref. should be made to Brooke, *Early Franciscan Government*.

poverty in the thirteenth century is one in which a logical analysis was far more difficult for friars at the time than it is now for historians who can assess the situation in the light of subsequent events. We can see now that the provisions of the Rule of 1223 are incompatible with a fully developed apostolate. The poverty required by the Rule does not allow the order to devote itself as a regular part of its activity to the pursuit of learning, for it cannot permit the brothers the necessary security of economic life. The regulations about poverty taken individually—more than all, the absolute prohibition of money—prevent them from undertaking the expense of building and maintaining the large churches necessary if they are to serve adequately the needs of the population. Either the literal observance of the poverty of the Rule must go, or the apostolate of the friars must be kept permanently on the simple lines of Francis and his early companions.

This dilemma was almost certainly never made plain to the friars who went to ask for a decision about the difficulties of the Rule from the Pope in 1230. At that time the process of extending the apostolate of the friars was already under way. Jordan of Giano's casual mention of the appointment of a *lector* in 1228 implies that at least in his own province a regular system of teaching for the friars was in operation. Franciscans, installed at the European centres of learning at Paris, Bologna, and Oxford, were well on the way to making study, and consequently the preaching of dogma, a regular part of the activity of the order.

Meanwhile two privileges of Honorius III, issued in 1222 and 1224, and subsequently renewed by Gregory IX, by allowing the friars the right to ignore interdicts and to have portable altars in their oratories, began the process of exempting the order from the control of local ecclesiastics.[1] In the long run privileges of this type were to open to the brothers the full field of labour previously occupied by the secular clergy alone; but at the same time they were to place upon the backs of the friars the attendant material cares and expenses of the apostolate of parish clergy. There is no indication that the friars of the time realized the ultimate effects which such privileges would have on their practice of poverty; they would regard them as conveniences in their ministry, or

---

[1] *Devotionis vestrae, Bullarii Franciscani Epitome*, ed. C. Eubel, Apud Claras Aquas, 1908, no. 9, p. 2; *Quia populares*, ed. cit., no. 16, p. 3.

barriers against the molestation of the secular clergy. Even Francis, who in the Testament completely prohibited the reception of Papal privileges, did so not because he considered that they would endanger the observance of poverty, but because he regarded the possession of them as incompatible with the humble and subordinate place he desired for his order.[1]

The process of exempting the Franciscans from the control of the secular clergy by means of Papal privileges affected the observance of poverty in the order in two ways. The indirect result, as we have seen, was to subject the friars' standard of poverty to intolerable pressures. More directly, exemption accustomed them to depend on the Papacy for support against their enemies among the secular clergy, and so made them more ready to turn to the Papacy when they encountered difficulties in the practice of poverty. This was not necessarily a disadvantage so long as the pontificate was in the hands of a man like Gregory IX, who had understanding of Franciscan poverty; it could be a source of weakness if the position was occupied by those such as Innocent IV or Martin IV, who lacked any insight into the Franciscan position.

Although the office of cardinal protector of the order acted more than once in this century as a stepping-stone to the Papacy itself, Gregory IX's experience of the affairs of the order was in the nature of things bound to be unique. The fact that he had worked with Francis on the composition of the Rule of 1223 gave him the title to speak with authority about the intentions of the founder.

Sabatier and his followers doubted the sincerity of Gregory in putting forward his claim to know the intentions which the founder had in making his Rule; to them he appears as a politician who for unworthy ends deceived the order about the true wishes of Francis. Their view has no support in contemporary expressions of opinion. The companions, who certainly did not approve of the modifications introduced in the life of the order, and who were hostile to Elias, never represent Ugolino as a betrayer of Francis. In the evidence based on their testimony, *II Celano* and the Leo-sources, he appears as a friend who admires at a distance, even

---

[1] This seems a fair deduction from Esser, *Testament*, pp. 174–82.

where he cannot fully share the enthusiasm of the primitive period.[1]

Apart from the personal link between Gregory IX and Francis, there were other reasons why the brothers should have wished to have recourse to the Papacy in 1230 for the settlement of their difficulties about the Rule. Francis by his prohibition of all privileges in the Testament made a demand which the order would have been unable to fulfil in its literal sense under any circumstances. In his request that they should regularly do manual labour, and in fact in the whole implied appeal in the Testament to follow the way of living of himself and his companions, Francis was asking the ministers, even as early as 1230, to do a considerable *volte-face*. His request was all the more embarrassing because there was room for doubt whether Francis in 1226 still had the legislative authority required to impose his wishes on the order "per obedientiam". The Rule of 1223, issued two years after Francis's resignation from office, nevertheless included the ambiguous phrase "and let the other brothers be bound to obey brother Francis and his successors".[2]

The only authority with sufficient weight to settle this delicate matter, which concerned all the future life of the Franciscans, was the Papacy. The Bull *Quo elongati*, in which Gregory answered the queries of the chapter-general, was of the first importance for later history, both because of the intrinsic significance of the decisions taken in it, and because of the precedent which it afforded of arbitration by the Holy See on the details of Franciscan observance. It not only dealt with the question of the Testament and with matters of principle such as the prohibition of money, but gave decisions on the *minutiae* of their observance. Gregory devoted sections of the Bull to settling queries as to whether the minister-general can depute the duty of examining preachers in the order, or whether all the custodians from the provinces need attend the chapter-general in order to vote for a new minister-general.[3]

In part, such exhaustive discussion was made necessary by the Rule, which oscillates between a too great imprecision and an

---

[1] *II Cel.*, 73, *AF* X, 175; *Speculum*, ed. Sabatier (1928), xxiii, 61–7. *II Cel.*, 63, *AF* X, 168–9; *Speculum*, ed. Sabatier (1928), xxi, 56.

[2] *Regula bullata*, 1; *Analekten*, ed. Boehmer, p. 30.

[3] *Epitome*, ed. Eubel, no. iv, pp. 229a–31b.

equally excessive rigidity on points of detail. An examination of the text of the Rule shows that there is a place both for Parenti's judgement, that it was clear and observable, and the words of the preamble to *Quo elongati*, describing it as containing "certain things doubtful and obscure and certain things difficult to understand". The general meaning of Francis comes across well enough in the version of 1223; it is only when it is treated as a legal document imposing obligations under the vow that serious difficulties begin to appear.

But—and this was the misfortune of Francis's later followers— it was in just this juridical way that the Rule had to be treated. Ordinary brothers, who had promised to observe the Rule, required to know, for their consciences' sake, exactly where their obligations ended. Ministers, grappling with the problems of an expanding community, needed to see at what points the Rule obliged them under sin and at what points they were allowed discretionary powers.

On the whole, modern scholarship has been inclined to regard the position of the followers of Francis in the first generation after his death with a more sympathetic eye than was formerly the case. The problems of casuistry which were involved are no longer considered as mere pretexts of the lukewarm for evasion of the Rule. Even Moorman, a member of the Sabatier school, whose sympathies are definitely with the rigorists in the order, has this to say about the development of the Franciscan observance in the thirteenth century:

> The problem as to whether the absolute Poverty of Francis and his first disciples could ever have become the standard for an Order of world-wide extent is one which will never be solved. It is easy for students who themselves have never had to face the problem of complete renunciation to lament all that occurred from 1221 onwards, and it is perhaps not unnatural that writers who themselves belong to the Order of St Francis should have been more lenient towards the relaxing party than those who see the problems only on paper.[1]

At the end of the last century, when Sabatier's influence was at its height, much support was given to a theory of Franciscan origins which, by denying that Francis ever intended to found an

[1] Moorman, *Sources*, p. 153.

order in the medieval sense, removed all force from arguments based on the requirements of religious orders. According to this theory, Francis, when he first received followers, intended only a free fellowship preaching and doing penance; the technical apparatus of vows and superiors as well as the division between the two orders of professed men and women and the third order of lay people was thrust upon him later by the Papal court. In the hands of Karl Müller the hypothesis formed the basis of the first scientific account of the development of the Franciscan ideal;[1] later it was taken up and popularized by Sabatier, and finally put forward in a modified version, stripped of its anti-papal bias, by Mandonnet in 1897.[2]

Since then opinion has turned decisively against the "spontaneous fellowship" theory: a number of refutations appeared soon after Mandonnet's work was published;[3] and standard authorities, like Balthasar, Gratien, or Douie, either dismiss it in a few lines or ignore it altogether. If any lingering attachments to it remained, they should have been given the death-blow by a summary article of Esser's published in 1957.[4] The general conclusion is that however novel Francis's foundation may have been in some respects, in certain vital particulars, such as the wearing of common clothing and the inculcating of obedience to common superiors, it conformed to the definitions of a religious order.

Older writers who accepted the Müller theory were, perhaps not entirely logically, disposed to condemn out of hand the brothers who asked for Papal arbitration on the Rule. All their sympathies lay with brothers of the stamp of Leo and the companions, who desired no further defining of their obligations and would be content to regard the whole gospel as their Rule. To-day, with Müller's theory discredited, those who set greatest store by the intentions of Francis will see that some form of development of Franciscan life can be justified from the wishes of the founder. He

---

[1] *Die Anfänge des Minoritenordens und der Bussbruderschaften*, Freiburg-i-B., 1885.
[2] P. Mandonnet, *Les origines de l'Ordo de Poenitentia*, Fribourg, 1898. The view was originally stated in a congress of the previous year.
[3] For example, F. Van Ortroy, *Analecta Bollandiana*, xviii (1899), 294–6; L. Lemmens, *Römische Quartalschrift*, xvi (1902), 98–101.
[4] K. Esser, "Gestalt und Ideal des Minderbrüderordens in seinen Anfängen", *FS* xxxix (1957), 1–22.

who wills the end wills the means also. If Francis wished to found a religious order in the true sense, his followers should be prepared to accept modifications made necessary by the conditions of life in a religious order. The vow, for example, must relate to some definite obligations, which can be set out in a written rule.

Clearly such a process is likely to extend over a period of time. According to the Leo-sources, it began in the lifetime of the founder. Francis, in their account, wished his brothers simply to observe the form of life of the gospels. The ministers, on the other hand, were unable to support the weight of such an obligation, and forced Francis to put in hand alterations in order to make it plain that the Rule and the gospel were two distinct entities. The text, "Take nothing for the journey", from the instructions to the first missionaries, which had been included in the Rule of 1221, was dropped from the version of 1223, they said, purely on these ideological grounds.[1]

Disputes about the obligation of the evangelical counsels for the friars continued for the rest of the century; all the major Papal declarations on the Rule, up to and including *Exivi de paradiso* in 1312, found it necessary to include a note of the orthodox distinction between the Rule and the gospel, and the matter was not finally settled until the destruction of the Spirituals in the order by John XXII.[2]

But dissidents on this point were, at most times after 1230, a small minority possessing no power in the order; it is only in the earliest period that one comes across incidents in which the authorities of the order treat evangelical counsels not expressed in the Rule as if they were as binding on the friars as the rest of their regulations. In 1224–5 the custodian of Penna refused the judicial oath on the ground that it would infringe Christ's exhortation in the Sermon on the Mount: "Swear not at all",[3] and at Valenciennes in 1225 the Franciscans refused a new site for their convent because they considered that if they moved they would be disobeying Christ's command to the missionaries, "Go not from

---

[1] *Speculum*, ed. Sabatier, iii, 9–10.

[2] *Ordinem vestrum*, 1245, *Epitome*, ed. Eubel, p. 238a; *Exiit qui seminat*, 1279, ed. cit., pp. 291b–2b; *Exivi de paradiso*, 1312, *BF* V, ed. C. Eubel, Romae, 1898, p. 81. On John XXII see below, esp. pp. 213–4.

[3] Matt. 5. 34. *BF* I, no. xviii, p. 21. See Sbaralea's note h, p. 21. The Bull is dated 1 March 1225.

house to house."[1] Later on episodes of this extreme kind occur no more. The vital work had been done in *Quo elongati*.

Until the issue of the Bull the ambiguous wording of the Rule, even in the version of 1223, remained to perplex the conscientious. The Rule began by saying: "The rule and life of the friars minor is this, to observe the holy Gospel of our Lord Jesus Christ living in obedience, without property and in chastity."[2] Was the observance of the gospel comprehended in the threefold vow, or did it go beyond that? In the final injunction of the Rule only the gospel was mentioned. There the founder made his request for a cardinal protector, "that ever submissive and subject at the feet of the same holy Church steadfast in the catholic faith we may observe the poverty and the humility and the holy Gospel of our Lord Jesus Christ, which we have firmly promised".[3] There was thus room for doubt; and the *Speculum*, for example, said that Francis had included such passages in the Rule deliberately after conflict with the ministers, in order that his faithful followers might have a sign of what his true wishes were.[4] *Quo elongati* dispelled notions of this kind, at any rate for the majority of the order, by pronouncing that the brothers were only bound to those evangelical counsels which were expressed as precepts in the text of the Rule.[5] This was a moderate canonist's solution.

The same might be said of Gregory's handling of the problem of the Testament. Without touching the more fundamental question of the moral obligation of the founder's wishes for his order, he declared the Testament void of legal force on the purely technical grounds that it had not been accepted by the ministers, and that the founder had no legal power to bind his successors.[6] He has received some heavy criticism for doing this from the more pro-Spiritual historians. Sabatier, for example, treated himself to a scathing footnote, in which he dismissed Gregory's reasoning

---

[1] Luke 10.7; *Speculum*, ed. Sabatier (1928), iii, 9, note h.

[2] "Regula et vita minorum fratrum haec est, scilicet Domini nostri Iesu Christi sanctum Evangelium observare vivendo in obedientia, sine proprio et in castitate." *Regula bullata*, 1; *Analekten*, ed. Boehmer, p. 29, lines 25–7. I hope to investigate the meaning of "sine proprio" more closely at some later date.

[3] *Regula bullata*, 12; ed. cit., p. 35, lines 17–20.

[4] *Speculum*, ed. Sabatier (1928), iii, 9–11.

[5] *Epitome*, ed. Eubel, p. 229b.

[6] Ed. cit., p. 229.

as a barely specious sophism.[1] But here Sabatier's presuppositions as a theologian distorted his judgement as an historian. He could no more see the necessity for law and organization in the Franciscan order than he could in the Church at large, and so he disqualifies himself as a judge in this matter.

Most historians would concur with Ehrle's verdict, that the invalidating of the Testament "could not have turned out otherwise".[2] Whatever the opinion one may hold about the wisdom of abandoning Francis's way of life as the standard for the order, it is clear that the order could not have accepted the Testament in the form in which it was written. Much of it consisted of simple reminiscence of Francis's early life, and consequently could not be treated as regulations binding on the order. When Francis did issue commands, he contradicted himself. He expressly disclaimed the intention of producing a document which should be binding on the brothers by saying, "And let not the brothers say: 'This is another rule', because this is a remembrance, an admonition, an exhortation and my testament . . ."; and yet, a few lines lower down, we find him giving the brothers his prohibition of glosses on the Rule as a precept under obedience.[3]

What was the effect of the invalidating of the Testament? Looking back, we can see that, in a sense, 1230 represented the last chance for the order to return as a body to the way of living of Francis and the companions; then, *Quo elongati* blocked the way, and ever afterwards the weight of precedent and legislation was too great for it to be possible.

At the same time, Gregory's Bull, carrying a legal decision only, could not do away with the special position which the Testament held among the writings of Francis, because this was a matter of feeling rather than juristic reasoning. The rigorists held to their belief in the Testament as the proper standard of interpretation for the Rule. Although no concerted attempt was made on the other side to suppress all knowledge of it, it became a dangerous document. Authorities who cited it showed a tendency to introduce their quotations with some circumlocution, like the favourite "sicut ipse testatus est", which avoided specific mention of their

---

[1] Sabatier-Houghton, p. 336, n. 1.
[2] F. Ehrle, in *ALKG* III, 572; for full title of article, see below, p. 84, n. 4.
[3] *Testamentum*, 11, 12.

source.[1] Expositors showed themselves aware of the Testament's prohibition of glosses.[2] Here and there, if we can accept the testimony of Ubertino da Casale, the Spiritual leader, ministers took matters into their own hands, and had copies of the Testament burnt.[3] Despite their efforts, the record of Francis's last appeal to the brothers remained as a focus for discontent for the rest of the century.

Gregory's decisions about the Testament and the evangelical counsels acted to clear the ground and to set the Rule of 1223 before the friars as the sole standard of their observance. This done, it was imperative to remedy the weaknesses of the Rule. The decisions about the duties of ministers and the relation to the Clares hardly matter either way. The heart of the matter lies in Gregory's judgements about money and dominion in the order.

In recent times commentators have generally followed Ehrle's example in his article on the development of the Franciscan ideal in the *Archiv für Litteratur und Kirchengeschichte*, and focused their attention on Gregory's treatment of the prohibition of money.[4] As we have seen, Francis forbade the reception of money, either directly or through an interposed person; but in the Rule of 1223 he was induced to allow recourse, exceptionally, to a money-agent of the friars, an *amicus spiritualis*, for the requirements of buying clothes and providing for sick brothers. *Quo elongati* without further discussion extended the functions of the friars' agent by allowing recourse to him for "imminent necessities", and introduced a new official for the reception of money, the *nuntius*, who, it was explained, was the agent of the almsgiver and therefore not an interposed person according to the definition of the Rule. All will agree with Ehrle in considering this decision to be a great modification of the original strictness of poverty.[5] In practice it was made much easier for the brothers to receive money alms. The insecurity of the primitive poverty was greatly diminished.

[1] Esser, *Testament*, pp. 54–5.
[2] See, for example, *Expositio Quatuor Magistrorum super Regulam Fratrum Minorum* (1241–1242), ed. L. Oliger, Roma, 1950, pp. 7–9, 124.
[3] *Declaratio*, ed. Ehrle, *ALKG* III, 168.
[4] F. Ehrle, "Die Spiritualen, ihr Verhältniss zum Franciscanerorden und zu den Fraticellen", Section 1, "Die Spaltung des Franciscanerordens in die Communität und die Spiritualen", *ALKG* III, 564–614; *Quo elongati* discussed, pp. 583–4.
[5] Art. cit., p. 584.

What has not been so generally noticed is how the Bull leaves the safeguarding of poverty in the hands of the brothers. Like most of the Papal arbitrations on the Rule, it did not decide what the brothers ought to do, only what they might be permitted to do. Admitting the validity of Gregory IX's principle, that the *nuntius* was the representative of the almsgiver, the friars walked on a razor's edge: the value of their observance depended on the day-to-day behaviour of the *nuntius* and the constant decisions of superiors as to what did and did not constitute an "imminent necessity". The forms of the Rule have been carefully observed, and if the opportunities for the use of money have been somewhat widened, was it not true that Francis had been the first to make a breach in the absolute prohibition of money, when he saw that charity required it? In the new circumstances of the time, with manual labour outside the convent fallen into disuse, the friars were more than ever dependent on alms, and it must often have been inconvenient for these to be given in kind alone.

On the other hand, under the press of business, the brothers might be tempted to neglect the proper working of the machinery of the *nuntius* and the *amicus spiritualis*, and come to regard the Franciscan renunciation of money as an administrative inconvenience. Once the prohibition ceases to press as a hardship on the individual brother, it is natural for superiors, who control the reception of money, to ask for wider powers for the sake of greater simplicity of government. In the event, the Gregorian system did not last: it was the first of a series of experiments in the administration of goods among the Franciscans.[1]

Important as this judgement on money was, in opening the way to clearly recognizable relaxations later in the century, it did not carry the lasting significance of Gregory's treatment of the problem of holding dominion. Some critics, perhaps from outside the order, had asked who held the dominion over the movable goods of the order, if it was true that the order had no corporate possessions. It was an awkward question. Gregory in his answer seemed to apply the usual legal test of ownership: who had the

---

[1] For the subject generally, M.-M. Clément, "L'administration des biens chez les Frères mineurs des origines au milieu du XVIe siècle", *Positions des Thèses de l'École Nationale des Chartes*, Paris, 1943, pp. 41-7. I am indebted to the writer, now Mme. Le Clerc, for her efforts, unfortunately in vain, to locate a copy of her thesis.

right to alienate the goods under discussion? In this instance, not the friars—they had to ask the permission of the cardinal protector before they could sell or exchange movable goods outside the order, or alienate them in any way. This might imply that the cardinal protector was the owner; but, as Gratien says, at the end of Gregory's explanations "the matter was still not very clear".[1]

The answer could not be expected to satisfy a serious critic of the Franciscan position for very long; meanwhile Gregory had been compelled in the course of his reply to give an interpretation of the sentence of the Rule of 1223: "Fratres nihil sibi approprient nec domum nec locum nec aliquam rem."[2] This involved a definite change of terms. The meaning which Francis gave to "sibi appropriare" is not so much legal as spiritual; as we have seen,[3] he does employ it in contexts where it can have no legal significance. Gregory's definition, on the other hand, is given in terms which are solely and exclusively legal. It runs as follows:

> We say therefore that [the friars] ought not to have *proprietas*, either individual or common, but may have the *usus* alone of the utensils and books and movable goods which they are permitted to have, and the friars, as the minister-general and provincial direct, may use them, leaving the dominion of their settlements and houses to those to whom it is known to pertain. . . .[4]

It is a significant moment for the evolution of the Franciscan ideal. Here the brothers by their question to the Papacy showed themselves aware of the theoretical aspects of Franciscan poverty. Gregory in reply gave them a definition which remained essentially unchanged as the basic tenet in discussions about the Rule up to the time of John XXII. His statement includes a number of assumptions. One was that it is legitimate to make a distinction between the dominion and the use of all goods held by the order; this was to be questioned later. Another was that Francis intended his order to be divested of all forms of dominion. Contemporary opinion seems to have believed this to be so, and modern writers have shown no sign of wishing to dispute their verdict. But were

---

[1] *Évolution*, p. 183.
[2] *Regula bullata*, 6; *Analekten*, ed. Boehmer, p. 32.
[3] Above, pp. 48-50.
[4] *Epitome*, ed. Eubel, p. 230a. Here *usus* means simply "use"; it is not differentiated, as it was later, into more precise legal terms, *ius utendi*, *simplex usus facti*, and the like. See below, p. 144.

they right? The earlier Rule only refers to settlements; the all-embracing terms, "nihil", "aliquam rem", only came in in 1223.[1] Clare always believed that the poverty which Francis desired both for her nuns and for the first order consisted especially in a renunciation of common dominion, and she fought hard with Ugolino in order to maintain her right to a complete disappropriation. Nevertheless all her anxieties were in case some landed property should be thrust upon San Damiano and its associated nunneries. We hear no word from her about the ownership of movable goods, for example.[2] Could it be that Gregory has turned a rhetorical flourish in Francis's writing into a permanent condition of his followers' way of living?

Gregory's first recorded application of the legal distinction between dominion and use to the problem of Franciscan ownership dates back to a time before the Rule of 1223 was written, when as cardinal protector he mollified Francis's anger over the house at Bologna by declaring that it was his property and that the friars were only using it with his permission.[3] What Francis's feelings about this solution were, it is difficult to say. He was himself chary of staying in fine houses, even as a passing guest.

A system which kept all property rights in the hands of the benefactor could be a genuine source of insecurity for the friars. At Northampton, the brothers' care in leaving the property-rights over their settlement in the hands of the benefactor resulted in their summary expulsion when he had a fit of pique over the reception of his own son into the order.[4] In the end he relented and allowed the friars to return. The story showed what could happen under

---

[1] *Regula prima*, 7; *Analekten*, ed. Boehmer, p. 8, lines 5–7. *Regula bullata*, 6; *Analekten*, p. 32, lines 17–18.

[2] See Jörgensen-Sloane, pp. 136–7, 185–91. Clare herself seems to have admitted common property over the land which formed the enclosure. In her Rule she orders the sisters to observe the vow of poverty "in non recipiendo vel habendo possessionem vel proprietatem per se neque per interpositam personam. . . . nisi quantum terrae pro honestate et remotione monasterii necessitas requirit . . ." (Jörgensen-Sloane, p. 185, n. 2). Honorius III, referring to projected houses of Clares in Tuscany in 1218, includes a similar exception clause. He says: ". . . quamplures Virgines, & aliae Mulieres . . . desiderant . . . fabricari sibi aliqua domicilia, in quibus vivant nihil possidentes sub Caelo, exceptis Domiciliis ipsis, & construendis Oratoriis in eisdem." *BF* I, no. i, p. 1b. See below, p. 98.

[3] *II Cel.*, 58; *AF* X, 166; *Speculum*, ed. Sabatier (1928), vi, 20. See above, pp. 45, 47.

[4] *Eccleston*, ed. Little (1951), coll. iv, pp. 23–4.

adverse circumstances; at the same time Eccleston's emphasis in telling it suggests that it happened very rarely.

In any case a system which left property rights to the donor was not, and could not be, applied under all circumstances. It was useless for covering cases where an unknown mass of almsgivers had contributed for the site and materials of a convent, and there was no one donor available to hold the property rights. For this reason among others the system recommended by Gregory's Bull seems never to have been put into effect over the whole order. In the English province, for example, it quite early on became the custom for town convents to make their municipality the trustee of the property they used.[1] Elsewhere ecclesiastical authorities were sometimes used for the purpose.[2]

Our verdict on *Quo elongati* as a whole must be that it raised as many questions as it answered. The original problem of the movable goods of the order continued to be a stumbling-block, especially in learned circles: there is clear evidence that this was so in the comments on chapter six of the Rule of the *Expositio quatuor magistrorum*, a collection of notes and queries on the Rule sent in from the province of France at the request of authority in 1241–2.[3]

Whether it was recognized at the time or not, the permanent work of the Bull was to do away with the rigid observance of the Rule to the letter, and replace it with an administrative system which stood close to, but was still not coterminous with, the prescriptions set down by Francis in 1223. The system, such as it was, was adapted to the circumstances under Gregory's eye in 1230; but if a new situation arose which put greater pressure on poverty, then there would be a demand from some sections of the order for easier terms.

Change was not long in coming. Elias's second tenure of the generalate showed signs of becoming a despotism. He governed as he pleased, and never summoned the chapter-general. He sent obnoxious deputies to fulfil his duty of visiting the provinces, and although some of his commands which created indignation, such as

---

[1] A. G. Little, *Studies in English Franciscan History*, Manchester, 1917, pp. 6–7.
[2] See, for example, *BF* I, no. cclii, pp. 144–5; cited, Balthasar, *Armutsstreit*, p. 34.
[3] Ed. Oliger, pp. 152–6.

the order to the brothers to wash their own breeches,[1] were Franciscan in spirit, others, like the demands for money for the basilica, certainly were not. A movement of opposition to him arose, whose motive force came from the ultramontane provinces, especially France, and whose leaders were often men who had never known Francis. They forced a chapter-general on Elias, at Rome in 1239, and in the course of a tense meeting impressed their case sufficiently on Gregory to have Elias deposed, and one of their number, Albert of Pisa, elected in his place. The new minister-general was in priest's orders, and before the members of the chapter dispersed they heard the first Mass said in the order by a minister-general.[2]

It was a revolution, but the most striking changes were made after Elias's fall, in the new legislation whose first aim was to prevent any recurrence of his misrule. By these decrees, which had been prepared by a commission of the rebels against Elias, and then accepted at the chapter, lay brothers, whom he had used as instruments of his despotism, were excluded from office in the order, and their future recruitment more or less completely prohibited.[3] The change was analogous to the development among the Benedictines which transformed them from a mixed to a clerical body and cut down the performance of manual labour to give more time for saying the divine office. Among the Franciscans the depression of the lay brothers meant an increased stress on the active at the expense of the contemplative side of their life. It was not that the laymen were necessarily better representatives of Francis's ideal than the clergy. The "rusticitas" of some Italian lay brothers, who earned Salimbene's scorn, was as far from Francis as the most Conventual minded of the clergy, and it is difficult to imagine any friar with less understanding of the founder than the litigious fourteenth-century lay brother, Bonagratia of Bergamo. What occurred was that the dominance of the clergy, which had long been growing and was now given legislative sanc-

---

[1] *Eccleston*, ed. Little (1951), coll. ix, p. 42.

[2] Ed. cit., coll. xiii, pp. 67–9.

[3] For the substance of these decrees, see the constitutions of Narbonne, 1260. The definitive edition is by M. Bihl, "Statuta generalia Ordinis edita in Capitulis generalibus celebratis Narbonae an. 1260, Assisii an. 1279 atque Parisiis an. 1292", *AFH* xxxiv (1941), 13–94, 284–358. The relationship between the two is discussed, art. cit. pp. 338–9. On the prohibition of lay brothers, see Narbonne, I, 3, art. cit., p. 39, and VI, 11, art. cit., p. 71.

tion, led to a concentration on the apostolate, and a consequent growth of pressure on poverty.

The greatest single cause of pressure on poverty was building. The clergy, who were in the ascendant at this time, wished to exercise a full apostolate, and found that they were unable to do so because of the deficiencies of existing settlements. Some were placed too far away from the centres of population to be accessible to the faithful who wished to receive the sacraments and hear sermons from the friars; others, better placed, still lacked a church big enough for their congregations; others again had been built on narrow sites which prohibited any further expansion. In many cases there was nothing for it, if the brothers were to fulfil these functions, but to take a new site, often an expensive one in the centre of a town, and build afresh.

Nor was this all. The Franciscans since the days of their founder had come to need more elaborate buildings for their own use. All that the early friars had wanted was a place to assemble in and say their office after they had returned from manual labour in the outside world. Now the clergy, who wished to employ the full resources of dogmatic preaching for the work of evangelization, had as a necessary consequence adopted study as a normal activity in the convent; this required space and quiet, and thus imposed the building of larger convents subdivided so as to provide for different activities.

To supply the deficiencies of the Rule, and to give more stability to the internal life of the convent, they had borrowed regulations from traditional monasticism:[1] these, as one would expect, were best put into practice in a monastic type of building, and so had the same effect as academic studies in forcing the erection of larger convents.

What this meant in the building programme was that when the brothers were given buildings already on a suitable site, they could rarely use them, save for the materials they contained. The needs of their life were such that they had to bear the expense of pulling down the old and erecting a new structure expressly designed for the purpose. Thus after 1239 in every province where the foundation, alteration, or transference of convents was being taken in hand, the generosity of the friars' almsgivers was being strained to the uttermost.

[1] I.e., *via* the Dominican constitutions.

The heaviest burden was placed on the resources of the friars at a time when they had made no permanent or regular addition to the means of maintenance employed by Francis and his companions in the first days of the order. Indeed, one major source of livelihood, the practice of manual labour outside the convent, had dropped out of use.[1] As far as begging was concerned, other orders were now in the field, competing, in effect, for a total amount of alms which must somewhere have a limit. The same was true of the unsolicited alms which the brothers obtained, either by bequest or by direct gift.

It could in fact be argued that from the 1240s, when the expenses of building first became an acute problem, the means of subsistence of the friars had ceased to be adequate to cover the drain imposed by their new activities. Various signs of strain begin to make themselves felt about this time. From the time of Innocent IV there is a less restrained use of indulgences to encourage the faithful to contribute to the building of convents.[2] For the first time the brothers obtain permission to supplement their alms by taking restitution money, consisting of fines paid by usurers or sums illicitly gained whose owners were unknown. Significantly enough, the first known grant of this kind was made to meet the expenses of the *studium* at Bologna, in 1236.[3]

Finally, in the third rubric of the constitutions of Narbonne, which are held to contain all the substance of the lost decrees of 1239, condemnations are included of some crude abuses connected with the reception of money, such as the placing of collection boxes in Franciscan churches.[4] These, it may be objected, were abuses liable to make their appearance at any time; we have already heard of their introduction under the reign of Elias, and we shall see them reappear at other times wherever there are relaxed superiors in control. Undoubtedly this is so; at the same time, it should be pointed out that in this time of rapid develop-

---

[1] Narbonne, VI, 1, "Statuta generalia", ed. Bihl, *AFH* xxxiv (1941), 69. "Cum regula dicat, quod 'fratres quibus dedit Dominus gratiam laborandi, laborent fideliter et devote', ordinamus quod fratres tam clerici quam laici compellantur per suos superiores in scribendo, studendo et aliis laboribus sibi competentibus exerceri." There is no mention of manual labour.

[2] Gratien, *Évolution*, p. 177.

[3] *BF*, I, no. cci, pp. 196-7; Gratien, *Évolution*, p. 176.

[4] Narbonne, III, 5; see also 6-9. "Statuta generalia", ed. Bihl. *AFH* xxxiv (1941), 46-7.

ment all the weight of circumstances pressed against superiors who wished to hold rigidly to the Rule, forcing them into minor evasions, and here and there favouring the emergence of extremists who made free with the regulations on poverty.

How much these changes were dictated by consciously held principles, it is impossible to say. We know that many of the new regulations were borrowed from the Dominican constitutions;[1] the question is: Did the superiors of the day, who admired the Dominicans sufficiently to wish to adapt their decrees, take over at the same time their attitude to the practice of poverty? Even as early as this, one would expect Dominican influence to slacken rather than to tighten the Franciscan practice of poverty.

Haymo of Faversham, a principal architect of these changes, is believed to have had some leaning towards the Dominicans.[2] His influence was great. He was a leading figure in the revolt against Elias. At Rome in the chapter-general he made the decisive speech which ended Elias's hopes of riding out the storm and retaining the generalate. On Albert of Pisa's premature death, he succeeded him as minister-general. In a reign of four years he saw to it that the bulk of the new legislation was incorporated permanently into the Franciscan observance. He was, moreover, a man of personal virtues. Eccleston, who knew him when he was provincial of England, described a disposition not unlike Bonaventura's, "benignissimus et dulcissimus", "so pleasing and eloquent, that he was pleasing and acceptable even to those who were hostile to the order".[3] Of his personal poverty there could be no doubt: Eccleston describes him at the provincial chapter, sitting in a humble place in the refectory, with his habit poor and torn.[4]

But there are some indications that his views did not in all respects coincide with those of the founder. One episode recorded by Eccleston appears to show him preferring for his friars in England a greater measure of security in their economic life, on the lines of the Dominican practice. The occasion was the extension

[1] Balthasar, *Armutsstreit*, p. 39. For the latest exact account of this relationship, see Brooke, *Early Franciscan Government*, pp. 293–6.
[2] Gratien, *Évolution*, pp. 151–2.
[3] *Eccleston*, ed. Little (1951), coll. xiv, p. 85; coll. vi, p. 28.
[4] Ed cit., coll. xiv., p. 86. On Haymo, generally, see the forthcoming *The Ordinals by Haymo of Faversham and Related Documents of the Roman Liturgy (1242–1303)*, ed. S. J. P. van Dijk.

intended for the enclosure at the Franciscan house at Gloucester. Generally the Franciscans had been more chary than the Dominicans of taking anything more than a small area of land around their convents, and, in fact, at Gloucester the first provincial, Agnellus of Pisa, very much a superior of the primitive period, had insisted on the brothers giving up a great part of the land they had accepted for their enclosure. This decision Haymo reversed, and justified his action in Eccleston's version in one revealing sentence: ". . . For he said that he would rather the brothers had ample gardens and cultivated them, so that they could have their food at home, rather than beg it from others." [1] It might, of course, have been convenience rather than the principles of the Dominicans which influenced Haymo here; but the story will at any rate remind us that some of the modifications in the practice of poverty after 1239 were put in hand, not by relaxed superiors with private self-indulgences, but by the finest of the Franciscan leaders.

That there were important sections of the order opposed to any modification is demonstrated by the replies which the provinces sent, through their representatives, to the request of the chapter of diffinitors held at Montpellier in 1241 for their comments on difficult points in the text. The province of England made the burden of their reply an earnest request that the Rule should stand, "sicut a sancto Francisco, dictante Spiritu Sancto, tradita fuit". [2] The province of France also made a conservative if less emotional reply in the *Expositio quatuor magistrorum*. Its authors, although they accepted *Quo elongati*, showed themselves anxious that Papal arbitration should not be employed to introduce relaxation. [3] They repudiated any usage which would transform the *nuntius* into a banker for the order. [4] On the question of rents and lands they were firm, and distinguished between the "paupertas imperfecta" of other orders and their own "paupertas perfecta", which excluded such goods, even in cases where the rights of dominion were in the hands of others. [5] On the other hand, their treatment was exclusively juridical and academic. Their arguments were less effective

---

[1] Ed. cit., coll. x, pp. 44–5.
[2] *Eccleston*, ed. Little (1951), coll. xiii, p. 71.
[3] *Expositio Quatuor Magistrorum*, ed. Oliger, chap. ii, pp. 129–31; chap. ix, pp. 163–4.
[4] Ed. cit., chap. iv, pp. 144–5. [5] Ed. cit., chap. vi, pp. 157–8.

because they did not touch on the practical difficulties of reconciling the activities of the Franciscans with their poverty. There
is no word in the *Expositio*, for example, on building, its materials,
and the proper limits of Franciscan construction.

Moreover, modification was often easier. William of Nottingham, the provincial of England, once likened the friars to men
crossing a river, who, if they are to reach the opposite bank, must
strike out for a point higher upstream.[1] Too often, at this time,
the current carried them down. Circumstances worked against
them. The system of granting Papal privileges was frequently
deleterious. Some ran counter to essential Franciscan principles.
One given for the basilica at Assisi in 1240, for example, permitted
the provincial and custodian to appoint a representative to act for
them in law in case of any encroachment on the rights of the
church.[2] This made nonsense of the customary Franciscan claim
to have abandoned all temporal rights. Another, given in 1253,
allowed the friar in charge of building operations to collect money
from alms-boxes in the basilica.[3] It is inconceivable that this
arrangement had the consent of the general then in office, the
zealot John of Parma.

Often the impression given is that measures passed without the
knowledge of the minister-general. Instances can be found in the
Bullarium Franciscanum of cash and property transactions receiving
Papal confirmation which completely by-pass the procedure laid
down in Papal arbitrations on the Rule. These, presumably, after
being completed on the spot by the friars and other interested
parties, were confirmed by the provincial and then sent to the
curia for confirmation. This seems to have been the case at Saint
Jean d'Angely, in Saintonge, in the province of Aquitaine, in
1247, where the friars did not trouble with the *nuntius* or the *amicus
spiritualis*, but appointed a *bourgeois* of the town their representative
in an elaborate contract involving the payment of cash and the
exchange of property rights with the Benedictine house there.[4]

---

[1] "Oportet etiam niti contra fluctus saeculi supra quam necesse est, alioquin
trahet nos inferius quam intendamus; sicut facit aqua volentes transire et
directe tendentes ad ripam oppositam." *Eccleston*, ed. Little (1951), coll. xv,
pp. 99–100.

[2] *BF* I, no. cccxxvii, p. 288; Balthasar, *Armutsstreit*, p. 35.

[3] *BF* I, no. cdlxxxix, p. 666; Balthasar, op. cit., p. 45.

[4] *BF* I, no. ccxix, pp. 470–3; Balthasar, op. cit., pp. 41–2.

An example can be found, even, of the Papacy forcing relaxations on the friars against their express wishes. This happened at Venice, where the provincial of the March of Treviso refused a benefaction which was intended to provide a small convent with permanent revenues, exempt its occupants from begging, and, in effect, turn it into a monastic foundation. Alexander IV, surprisingly enough, for he had been a cardinal protector and understood the Franciscan position, eventually forced the brothers at Venice to ignore their statutes and accept the gift. [1]

The existing dangers to the observance were naturally accentuated when the generalate was in the hands of a weak or an unprincipled friar. Unfortunately, at this juncture, when the pace of development was so hot, the generalate was given to a man who certainly lacked the strength, and probably the will, to struggle against the spread of abuses. Crescenzio da Jesi, who succeeded Haymo in 1244, was an old man when he took office. Probably he was never adequate to the task imposed upon him. Even in the year following his election he pleaded age in refusing the summons to the Council of Lyons, and sent a deputy in his place. [2] In the end, it seems, Innocent IV summoned the chapter-general without him; and they deposed him. Peregrino of Bologna says simply: "He was found to be useless in office. So he lasted no more than a three-year period in office, that is, until the chapter-general." [3]

In one thing he showed energy—the persecution of the zealots. Already, as provincial of the March of Ancona, he had established a reputation for sternness towards them. Angelo da Clareno describes how when he became general he dealt with some sixty-two zealots who wished to appeal against his régime to the Pope, sending them out two by two into exile in distant provinces. Crescenzio, he said, was another Elias in feeling and manner of life. [4]

All the signs are that his preference was for further modification in the practice of poverty. At Breslau, for the sake of doing honour

---

[1] Gratien, *Évolution*, pp. 180–1, and refs. given.

[2] Op. cit., p. 238, and n. 30.

[3] *Eccleston*, ed. Little (1909), Appendice II, "Peregrini de Bononia Chronicon abbreviatum de successione Ministrorum Generalium", p. 143.

[4] Angelo da Clareno, *Historia septem tribulationum ordinis minorum*, ed. F. Ehrle, *ALKG* II, 256–7, and, for the zealot episode, 257–60.

to the Duke of Silesia buried in the Franciscan church, he dispensed the brothers from observing their statutes and permitted them to use rich vestments.[1] Two major relaxing Bulls appeared in his day, one directly under his régime, and the other so soon after as to suggest that he played a part in obtaining it. Gratien, who does his best for him, can only adduce on the other side some conventional words of praise from Eccleston and Bernard of Besse, and the probably fortuitous fact that he authorized the writing of *II Celano*, which turned out to be the most pro-Spiritual of the official biographies of Francis.[2]

It was under these circumstances, with the Papacy under Innocent IV occupied by a man who cared little for Franciscan poverty, and the generalate held by a relaxing Conventual, that the order came to take a formal step down from the standard of observance prescribed by *Quo elongati*. The occasion was the issue of the Bull *Ordinem vestrum*, in November 1245.[3] It claimed for itself the modest function of clarifying still more Gregory's interpretation of the Rule. This was hardly true. Apart from the first section, which removes the ambiguity of language from Gregory's decision on the obligation of evangelical counsels not expressed in the Rule, the Bull is not so much a clarification as a relaxation of *Quo elongati*.

Innocent's treatment of the Franciscan renunciation of money well shows the inferiority of his settlement. Where Gregory had permitted recourse to intermediaries for the sake of buying necessities alone, Innocent allowed such recourse for "commodities" as well, thus giving *carte blanche* to superiors to use agents to take money alms whenever they wished. Gregory had insisted that the new form of intermediary which he introduced, the *nuntius*, was not the agent of the friars but of the almsgivers. To make this claim a reality, he had laid down that the *nuntius* was not to retain any money given to him by benefactors, but use it at once to pay for necessities for the friars, and hand any residue over to the legitimate agent of the friars, the *amicus spiritualis*. Innocent went on repeating Gregory's claim, that the *nuntius* was only the agent of the almsgiver, while omitting the regulation which ensured that he

---

[1] *BF* I, no. dxlv, pp. 722–3; Balthasar, *Armutsstreit*, p. 45.
[2] *Évolution*, p. 233, n. 16, and pp. 235–6.
[3] *Epitome*, ed. Eubel, no. xi, pp. 238–9.

did in practice act solely on behalf of the almsgiver, and not on behalf of the friars.[1]

The effect of Innocent's decision was to take away all cause for the *nuntius* having a separate existence, and to merge his office with that of the *amicus spiritualis*.[2] All that was now required was one official from the outside world, ready to handle all reasonable expenditure, and equally available to the friars as to their almsgivers.

Innocent's settlement of the question of property in the order, although a less flagrant relaxation than his decisions about the use of money, still had the effect of introducing a greater artificiality into the practice of poverty. Under the Gregorian system the rights of dominion were to be retained by the benefactors of the friars; but, as we have seen, the arrangements left some awkward questions unanswered. If the benefactors owned the houses and land used by the friars, who owned the lesser items, the movable goods of the order? Who was the owner of houses and land when a multitude of almsgivers contributed? Innocent's solution of these difficulties was to receive all dominion in goods enjoyed by the Franciscans into the domain of St Peter.[3] Hereafter the Papacy was to be the owner of Franciscan property. The sole exceptions were to be those cases in which donors expressly reserved to themselves the ownership of the goods they presented to the order.

The new system did provide the order's apologists with a comprehensive answer to every attack on their renunciation of property. On the other hand, it still did not provide them with a convincing answer. The Papacy, under this Bull, had received some unusual property. None of it ever figured in lists of Papal

---

[1] In *Quo elongati*: ". . . idem nuntius solvere statim debet, ita quod de pecunia nihil remaneat penes eum. Si vero pro aliis imminentibus necessitatibus praesentetur, eleemosynam sibi commissam potest, sicut et dominus, apud spiritualem amicum fratrum deponere, per ipsum . . . dispensandam . . ." (*Epitome*, ed. Eubel, p. 230a). In *Ordinem vestrum*: ". . . taliter praesentatus a fratribus non est eorum nuntius, licet praesentetur ab ipsis, sed illius potius, cuius auctoritate solutionem facit, seu recipientis eamdem: et ad ipsum, si soluto emptae rei pretio de huiusmodi eleemosyna remaneat aliquid apud eum, possunt etiam fratres pro suis necessitatibus vel commodis licite habere recursum. Si vero pro aliis fratrum necessitatibus aut commodis nominetur aliquis vel praesentetur ab eis, potest ille commissam sibi eleemosynam sicut dominus conservare vel apud spiritualem . . . amicum . . . deponere . . ." (*Epitome*, ed. Eubel, p. 238b).

[2] Clément, "L'administration des biens", chap I (a), section 3 (a).

[3] "in ius et proprietatem beati Petri" (*Epitome*, ed. Eubel, p. 239a).

properties.[1] Strictly speaking, could it be called property at all, when the Bull allowed the friars, the supposed users, a right of alienation at will at any rate over the movable goods of small value? It is an essential attribute of property that it should bring some temporal benefit to its owner. This the Franciscan goods never did.

It was not unprecedented for the Papacy to receive goods without intending to make a temporal gain from the transaction. Ugolino, for example, with the approval of Honorius III, received a number of houses of Poor Clares in Tuscany into the property of the Holy See from 1217 to 1219.[2] Clearly, there could be no possibility of any temporal gain accruing to the Papacy in this instance.

But the object of the transaction with the Clares was quite different from that made with the first order in *Ordinem vestrum*. It was not intended to safeguard the poverty of the Clares. Ugolino can never be shown to have taken pains to ensure that the Clares renounced property, like the members of the first order. Later on he did all he could to see that, on the contrary, they had a sufficiency of property outside their small enclosures.[3] The object which he and Honorius had, in receiving the property of the Clares' houses and enclosures, was to ensure that other, more powerful bodies did not encroach on their rights.[4] For that purpose it did not matter whether or not the Papacy could justly be called the owner of the goods received from the Clares. It was

---

[1] Balthasar, *Armutsstreit*, p. 75, n. 2.

[2] *BF* I, no. iii, pp. 3–5 (Monticelli, near Florence); no. xi, pp. 10–11 (Lucca); no. xii, pp. 11–13 (Siena); no. xiii, pp. 13–15 (Monteluce, near Perugia). These Bulls all quote letters of Ugolino dated in July 1219. He arrived as Legate in Tuscany in March 1217. *BF* I, no. i, pp. 1–2, dated August 1218, gives the Pope's approval for Ugolino's proceedings with regard to the Clares.

[3] See L. Oliger, "De origine regularum ordinis S. Clarae", *AFH* v (1912), 181–209, 413–47.

[4] The evidence is not wholly clear, and no modern writer appears to have investigated, *ex professo*, the significance of Papal ownership for the Clares. What has been said here must therefore be a tentative hypothesis. On the one hand, Clare herself does not seem to have made any such claim to total renunciation of dominion, in the literal sense, as was made by some members of the first order, largely on the strength of *Ordinem vestrum*. She seems to have accepted rights of property over the land used for the enclosure. See above, p. 87. On the other hand, the Bulls which received these houses "in ius et proprietatem Ecclesiae Romanae" (above, n. 2.) are concerned rather with the Clares' safety and freedom, than their poverty.

enough that the protection of the Holy See had been invoked. For the friars in 1245, on the other hand, it was of the first importance that the new rights which the Papacy assumed through *Ordinem vestrum* should fulfil the technical requirements of ownership, since their whole claim to have renounced property depended upon it. The starting point, Balthasar suggests, for the juristic interpretation which attributed the ownership of Franciscan goods to the Papacy was the arrangement made for the basilica at Assisi by Gregory IX in 1228.[1] Under this scheme the Papacy held the property of the church, while the friars served the church and paid a token rent annually of one pound of wax. *Ordinem vestrum*, one could say, was an extension of this scheme, omitting the rent, to cover the goods of the whole order.

Where one church alone was concerned, as in this instance at the basilica, the Papacy would make some gain from the property rights it held. At Assisi the Papacy always exercised a more direct control than over any other church of the order.[2]

But when the property of a whole order is received, clearly there can be no question of benefits accruing to the new owner; the scheme is a pure legal fiction. The acid test for a scheme of this kind is this: what happens when the property-owner exercises his rights?

Under the Gregorian system, if the benefactor wishes to exercise his rights, he may take back his property. The effect of his action will be that the friars have lost the property they enjoyed, without having any right to claim it back. When, however, in the course of time, the Papacy under John XXII decided to exercise its rights and cancelled the arrangements made by *Ordinem vestrum*, the decree had hardly any practical effect at all. There was as a result much heartburning in the order over their renunciation of property, which had apparently been rendered null by this decree; there was no question of there being any interruption caused to the friars' enjoyment of their goods.[3]

In one point the Franciscan renunciation of common property, under both the Gregorian and the Innocentian systems, brought

[1] *BF* I, no. xxix, p. 46; Balthasar, *Armutsstreit*, p. 35, and n. 2.
[2] See, esp., *BF* I, no. xlix, pp. 60–2; Balthasar, loc. cit.
[3] On John XXII's action, see below, pp. 230–1; for its effects, Clément, "L'administration des biens", chap. III.

genuine inconvenience to the friars. They had no free right of disposing of their goods. *Quo elongati* expressly laid down that they might not sell, exchange, or alienate their movable goods in any way outside the order without first obtaining the permission of the cardinal protector.[1] *Ordinem vestrum* followed on the same lines, forbidding alienation of movable goods, houses, or settlements without the permission of the cardinal protector or the Papacy.[2] This could only be dispensed with in the case of movable goods of small value, at the discretion of superiors.

Soon, however, even this minor inconvenience was to be taken from the brothers. Less than two years later, and a month after Crescenzio had been absolved from office,[3] Innocent followed up *Ordinem vestrum* with a supplementary decree, doing away with the cumbrous mechanism of making application to the cardinal protector for every major alienation of goods. By the new Bull, *Quanto studiosius*, the friars received the right of appointing procurators who, while acting on behalf of the Papacy as administrators of the goods which the Franciscans enjoyed, would be entirely at the disposal of superiors.[4]

The procurators might, as the Franciscans directed, make any use whatever of these goods. They could sell, exchange, or alienate any gifts made to the Franciscans, and, with money obtained from such transactions, buy necessities or commodities for them. As Clément has shown from the evidence of the acts of nomination as well as that of the Bull, the new Papal procurators were able to combine the functions of administrator of Papal goods with all the powers once enjoyed by the *nuntius* and *amicus spiritualis*.[5] In some respects their powers were greater, since the Innocentian procurators had the right to act against recalcitrant detainers of gifts or bequests to the friars; their position, in fact, was similar to that of the lay representatives appointed for the basilica since 1240, who were permitted to go to law to defend the rights of the church.

With the issue of *Quanto studiosius* in August 1247, the formal

---

[1] *Epitome*, ed. Eubel, p. 239a.

[2] Ed. cit., p. 230a.

[3] On the dating of the chapter of Lyons which absolved Crescenzio, see Gratien, *Évolution*, p. 238, n. 31.

[4] *BF* I, no. ccxxxv, pp. 487-8.

[5] Clément, "L'administration des biens", chap. I (b), section 2.

development of the observance of poverty by means of Papal privileges reached its term, for the time being. It was still hardly more than twenty years after the death of Francis. In that short time, which could easily be included in a single life-span, the friars through the use of intermediaries had gone a long way towards obliterating the distinctive features of their observance of poverty.

At first, in the primitive period, Francis had had no occasion to make a breach in his prohibition of money or to receive for his community any property of significance. Later, in 1221, he may have allowed an exception to the money prohibition—the MS. evidence is uncertain.[1] Certainly in 1223, for two special sets of circumstances only, the care of the sick and the clothing of the brothers, he permitted the friars to make their needs known to a money-agent, the *amicus spiritualis*.[2]

Quo elongati widened this concession to cover any "imminent necessity", and added a new agent, the *nuntius*, who, with certain restrictions, could be employed to pay for any necessity of the brothers. Any alienation of movable goods required the assent of the cardinal protector.

Fifteen years later *Ordinem vestrum* virtually dropped the distinction between the *nuntius* and the *amicus spiritualis*, and extended the field of action of the money-agents still further to cover "commodities" as well as "necessities". All rights of dominion over goods enjoyed by the friars were received into the hands of the Papacy. Finally, under *Quanto studiosius* almost all the rights of a property-owner in Franciscan goods were transferred to a single agent, who was appointed by the friars and acted at their direction.[3] Short of obtaining a privilege allowing them to act for themselves, accept property, and handle money, the friars could hardly have gone farther than they did in abandoning the actual observance of the renunciation of money and of property which they held, and maintained in controversy, to be the distinguishing marks of their poverty.

---

[1] *Regula prima*, 8; *Analekten*, ed. Boehmer, p. 8, line 22 and n. 17. Where St Francis says none of the brothers shall receive money, "immo nulla occasione", certain MSS. add "nisi propter manifestam necessitatem infirmorum".

[2] *Regula bullata*, 4; *Analekten*, ed. Boehmer, p. 32.

[3] It should be noted that, despite Clément's work, there is still some obscurity about the exact relation in practice between the money-agent of the friars and the Papal procurator.

There is thus a marked change in the actual practice of poverty in these years. There is, too, what has been somewhat overlooked, a shift in the theory of poverty. Two Bulls, *Quo elongati* and *Ordinem vestrum*, had dealt with the question of the common property of the order. The first of these had set it down that the friars were obliged by their Rule to make a total renunciation, as an order, of all forms of dominion or property rights. The second had put forward a theoretical system, a legal fiction indeed, which would enable the order to observe this total renunciation.

Questions of theory had not yet become of great significance in the order. The brothers were still preoccupied with the practical needs of their life. But when the theory of poverty did become of vital significance, when the way of life of the friars came under attack from the secular masters at the universities, then these Bulls would come into their own.

There had been, in these years, a quiet shift of emphasis away from the renunciation of actual goods, which we saw was the heart of Francis's interpretation, to the renunciation of rights and especially of property rights. All this was to have its effect when Bonaventura, as the representative of the order, set down the doctrine of the absolute poverty of Christ and the apostles in the sixth decade of the century. Our fifth chapter will describe how the new Franciscan theory of poverty, developed in these years, and St Francis's concept of poverty came together in the exposition of St Bonaventura.

But before we describe St Bonaventura's doctrine, it will be desirable to place him in his historical setting as minister-general of the order. The following chapter is not intended to pursue our central theme, the development of the doctrine of the absolute poverty of Christ: it has been included, primarily, to maintain the continuity of our account of the practice of poverty within the Franciscan order. Its subject matter will again be historical: it will describe the plateau period, from 1247 to 1274, in which the two greatest ministers-general the order has ever had, Blessed John of Parma and then St Bonaventura, struggled to check and bring to a halt the development of the observance of poverty.

4

JOHN OF PARMA AND BONAVENTURA

IT WOULD have been remarkable if the developments outlined in the previous chapter had not caused disquiet in some
quarters within the order. *II Celano*, which was published in
1246, reveals the anxiety felt by the companions about the state of
the order. The chapter-general of Lyons, which absolved Crescenzio from office, elected in his place, whether by accident or
design, a man opposed to the modification of poverty, whose
chief aim was to recall the order to the days of its primitive purity.

The new general, John Buralli of Parma, was the first to succeed
St Francis whom the companions could greet as one of their own
kind. Giles, recalling his less sympathetic predecessors, said to
him: "Well and opportunely have you come, but you have come
late."[1] First and foremost, no doubt, Giles was thinking of the
personal qualities of John, which earned him beatification in the
eighteenth century—the genius for personal relations, the quality
of *curialitas*, so much like Francis's own, the humility, the rigour
of his private life.

But on the question of Franciscan obligations John's views
also corresponded with those of the group of companions and of the
Spirituals who were attached to them. If we can trust the witness
of the late Spiritual historian Angelo da Clareno, John shared the
rigorists' view of the Testament as the vital key to the understanding of the Rule. Angelo quoted him as saying: "And it is not
possible for anyone who rejects the testament to have a spiritual
understanding of the Rule or to observe it faithfully."[2]

Moreover, he was on close terms with Hugues de Digne, a friar
of Provence, who in his views on the Rule, his Joachimism, and
his attraction of a circle of lay followers anticipated the later
rigorists, and has indeed been called "the father of the Spiri-

---

[1] Angelo da Clareno, *Historia*, ed. Ehrle, *ALKG* II, 263.
[2] Ed. cit., p. 275.

tuals".[1] Salimbene, his fellow-townsman and admirer, who gave a full account of John in his chronicle, said of this relationship: "Brother Hugues de Digne in all things and through all things had the same view as brother John."[2]

Without sharing fully, as far as one can see, in the rigidities and extremism of later Spirituals, like Angelo or Ubertino, which were in large part the product of the exceptional circumstances of the late thirteenth century, John of Parma was nevertheless in essentials one of the rigorist party. He was the only one of their number to hold supreme office in the undivided order. There is therefore a unique interest in seeing what his policy was and how well he fared in his self-appointed task of reforming the order.

One of the first things to strike one about his generalate, when compared with that of his predecessors, is the great stress he laid on personal methods. His predecessors had generally ruled the order from the centre, sending round deputies to fulfil their visitation duty. Elias had been immersed in the building of the basilica, Crescenzio had been too old, Haymo, though he made some visitations, had generally been preoccupied with putting into effect the new regulations of 1239. But John, soon after taking office, began the systematic visitation of the provinces. He was the first general ever to do this. Salimbene describes with admiration how, travelling on foot, he wore out his companions and had to be supplied with secretaries in relays.[3] Angelo, writing from the traditions of the Spirituals, also describes these astonishing journeys. This is what he says:

> So in the first three years of his administration, clad in one tunic and a habit of poor cloth, which he kept right to the end of his life, he visited the whole order; he never used an ass or a horse or any vehicle, was content with one companion or two at most, and was so humble and insignificant in appearance as he went, that the great men whom he happened to salute by the roadside thought him unworthy of acknowledgement.[4]

He goes on to describe how John would arrive unawares in different provinces as a simple brother, see for himself the state

---

[1] Hugues de Digne, *De Finibus Paupertatis*, ed. C. Florovsky, *AFH* v (1912), 279.
[2] *Cronica*, ed. Holder-Egger, p. 232.
[3] Ed. cit., pp. 298, 553. Parenti conducted personal visitations, according to the *Chronica XXIV Generalium*, *AF* III, 211.
[4] *Historia*, ed. Ehrle, *ALKG* II, 267-8.

of the observance, and correct abuses on the spot. He would always say his hours erect, and would eat with the meanest of the brothers in the refectory. It was all very much in the Spiritual tradition. Angelo da Clareno, when later on he became the leader of a small independent congregation of friars, governed his followers in much the same way, either by direct visitation or by sending personal letters dealing with the spiritual life of his subordinates.[1]

An analogous feature which also differentiates him from his predecessors is his aversion from the various additional regulations which the friars brought out in order to interpret the Rule. He was no law-maker. When the ministers and custodians at the chapter-general of Metz asked to issue some new constitutions, they received the chilling reply: "Let us not multiply constitutions, but keep well those we have."[2] Where Papal privileges were concerned, he was similarly conservative. On his 1248 visitation, coming to preside over the chapter of the province of France, he discovered that the provincial and diffinitors had already performed the duty reserved by the Rule to the minister-general, and had examined the province's candidates for the office of preaching. Space was short, and the officials had felt that they were within their rights in doing this, since two Bulls, *Prohibente regula* of 1240, and, subsequently, *Ordinem vestrum*, permitted the general to depute this duty to the provincial and the diffinitors in their chapters.[3] So the candidates were examined, and sent away. But John insisted that the candidates be recalled. He refused to recognize the action of the chapter: *Prohibente regula*, he explained, could only be used in the absence of the general. If the general was present the Rule must stand.[4]

Where Papal privileges went beyond convenience and con-

---

[1] F. Ehrle, "Die Briefsammlung des fr. Angelus de Clarino", *ALKG* I (1885), 533–69, *passim*; also L. von Auw, *Angelo Clareno et les Spirituels Franciscains*, Lausanne, 1952, commentary, pp. 36–8, further details of MSS., pp. 39–58.

[2] Salimbene, *Cronica*, ed. Holder-Egger, pp. 300–1.

[3] *Prohibente regula, Epitome*, ed. Eubel, no. 295, pp. 28–9; *Ordinem vestrum*, ed. cit., p. 239b. *Regula bullata*, 9; *Analekten*, ed. Boehmer, p. 33.

[4] Salimbene, *Cronica*, ed. Holder-Egger, p. 221. The witness of this chronicler has been used more than once in this work; but it is well to remember that he is not reliable. He said, for example, that John of Parma before his election was vicar for Crescenzio da Jesi at the Council of Lyons (ibid., p. 176); in fact Bonaventura of Iseo acted for Crescenzio. See E. d'Alençon, "Fr. Bonaventure d'Iseo Vicaire du Ministre Général des Mineurs au 1er Concile de Lyon, en 1245", *Études Franciscaines*, xxxiii (1921), 519–28.

flicted with essential principles of the Rule, he wished the order to exercise its right of refusal. *Ordinem vestrum* and *Quanto studiosius*, as we have seen, by giving such wide powers to the friars' agents to use money and hold dominion, did betray these principles. It was perhaps John's greatest triumph to have persuaded the chapter to suspend the operation of these Bulls in all clauses where they went beyond *Quo elongati*. The details are obscure. Eccleston places the episode at the chapter-general of Genoa, held either in 1249 or 1251, and gives the chief credit for persuading the chapter to his own provincial, William of Nottingham.[1] But it is at any rate clear from his account that a small, zealous minority at the chapter swayed the opinions of a less willing majority—and it would be unreasonable not to put the minister-general among the leaders of the zealots on such an occasion.

In effect, this action of the chapter was the first serious check to the process of modification of poverty.

Intellectually, John shared the Spirituals' weakness for prophesyings and apocalyptic, based on the genuine and spurious works of the twelfth-century Cistercian abbot, Joachim of Flora. This was indeed a weakness not confined to the Spirituals, or even to the Franciscans generally, although the contemplative strain among them, and perhaps their lighter intellectual training, made them particularly open to its temptations.[2] Salimbene, who was cer-

---

[1] ". . . ubi fere contra totum capitulum generale causam feliciter obtinuerunt, ut privilegium indultum a domino papa de recipienda pecunia per procuratores penitus destrueretur et expositio regulae secundum dominum Innocentium, quantum ad ea in quibus laxior est quam Gregoriana, suspenderetur." *Eccleston*, ed. Little (1951), p. 42. Gratien (*Évolution*, p. 243, n. 44) would put this event forward to the chapter of Metz in 1254, because of the injunction in the *definitiones* of the chapter of Narbonne in 1260: "Declaratio domini Innocentii maneat suspensa, sicut fuit in capitulo Methensi . . ." ("'Diffinitiones' Capituli Generalis Narbonensis (1260)", ed. F. M. Delorme, *AFH* iii (1910), no. 13, p. 503). Little, however, (loc. cit., note b) supports Eccleston's dating, and the evidence lies on his side. The chapter of Metz may well have repeated the decision first made at Genoa.

[2] "It is no accident that, among the mendicants, the Franciscans in particular adopted Joachimism. . . . They were not at the outset like the Preachers, a learned university order. . . . They were not armed against extravagances by as solid a theological training. Of the intellectual methods of the time, many of them only knew how to use the worst: they were accustomed to allegorical and symbolic interpretation, and had a mania for multiple, concealed meanings." E. Jordan, "Joachim de Flore", *DTC* VIII, ii (1925), 1425-58. Jordan's article may still be taken on the influence of Joachim, but on the seer himself, for a short account, see M. Reeves, "The *Liber Figurarum* of Joachim of Fiore", *Medieval and Renaissance Studies*, II (1950), 57-81.

tainly not a Spiritual, was for some time an ardent Joachimite.[1] Grosseteste and Adam Marsh corresponded, with some secrecy, about Joachim, and obtained a book of prophecies attributed to him.[2] The curia under Innocent IV went so far as to invite Hugues de Digne to entertain them with an exposition of Joachimite prophecy.[3]

The genuine works of Joachim, in which he applied traditional methods of exegesis to Scripture for the purpose of prophecy, had never been condemned; only the fourth Lateran Council had condemned the Trinitarian doctrine contained in a *libellus* of his directed against Peter Lombard, and that with an explicit recognition of Joachim's personal submission to the Papacy.[4] Nor had any ban been laid on the spurious works, in which other, clumsier hands brought Joachim's prophecies up to date, and gave them a more definite relevance to current political events.

In the first years of his generalate, therefore, John's *penchant* for Joachimite prophecy, which he shared with some eminent figures, was no source of danger to him.

But in 1254 the position suddenly changed. In that year, when both the mendicant orders were embroiled in a dispute with the secular masters at the University of Paris, a young Franciscan at the house of studies, Gerard of Borgo San Donnino, published a work of his own without the consent of his superiors, the *Introductorius in evangelium aeternum*.

It was an extreme and heretical adaptation of the Joachimite doctrine of the ages of the world.[5] About the year 1200, Gerard believed, the spirit of life had left the Old and New Testaments, and had passed to the three major works of Joachim, the *Concordia Novi et Veteris Testamenti*, the *Expositio in Apocalipsim*, and the *Psalterium decem chordarum*. Joachim was the angel of the Apocalypse

---

[1] Salimbene, *Cronica*, ed. Holder-Egger, pp. 174, 236–7, 302–3.

[2] Adam Marsh, *Epistolae*, ed. J. S. Brewer, *Monumenta Franciscana* II, London, 1858, pp. 146–7.

[3] Salimbene, *Cronica*, ed. Holder-Egger, pp. 226–31.

[4] J. D. Mansi, *Sacrorum Conciliorum . . . Collectio* XXII, Venetiis, 1778, pp. 982–6.

[5] The original is not extant; extracts, however, are to be found in a reliable source, the report of the commission of Anagni, set up by the Papacy to investigate the *Introductorius*. See H. Denifle, "Das Evangelium aeternum und die Commission zu Anagni", *ALKG* I (1885), 49–142. A summary of Gerard's views is given by Denifle, art. cit., pp. 57–62: on this the present account is based.

flying in the midst of heaven, and "having in his hand the everlasting gospel".[1] His three major works, the *evangelium aeternum* of
the title, would form the canonical scriptures of a new age.
Francis, appearing at the same period as Joachim, was the angel
of the sixth seal in the Apocalypse "who had the sign of the living
God".[2] His order was to be entrusted with the eternal gospel, and
would proclaim it to the men of the new age. This last, Gerard
said, was close at hand; the *Introductorius*, which was his own commentary on Joachim, was intended to prepare the faithful for its
coming.

The book gave the secular masters the chance they needed to
discredit the mendicants with the Papacy; in the ensuing scandal
Innocent IV deferred to their arguments, and in the last month of
his pontificate withdrew the mendicants' privileges of exemption.[3]
His successor, Alexander IV, although he restored the privileges,
found himself obliged to appoint a commission, which examined
the works both of Gerard and Joachim, and condemned Gerard.[4]
Meanwhile, William of St Amour, at the head of the secular
masters, used the *Introductorius* as the starting-point of an attack
on the whole *raison d'être* of the two mendicant orders.[5]

Even though Gerard's work was not typical of the pseudo-
Joachimite treatises popular at this time,[6] it served to discredit all
forms of Joachimism. At this juncture, with the order struggling
for life against the seculars, the office of general was occupied by a
man fatally compromised. He was a friend of the Joachimite
Hugues de Digne. He had used Salimbene as his agent to copy

---

[1] Rev. 14.6.
[2] Rev. 7.2.
[3] *Etsi animarum, Epitome,* ed. Eubel, no. xxviii, pp. 259–61.
[4] Denifle, art. cit.
[5] For the whole controversy, see D. Douie, *The Conflict between the Seculars
and the Mendicants at the University of Paris in the Thirteenth Century* (Aquinas
Society of London, Aquinas Paper no. 23), London, 1954. William of St
Amour, in his *De periculis novissimorum temporum,* turned Gerard's theory back
on to the Franciscans' heads by asking if they were not, in fact, the ministers
and heralds of Antichrist.
[6] On this point, H. Grundmann, *Studien über Joachim von Floris,* Leipzig,
Berlin, 1927, esp. section iv, "Das Fortleben der Joachimschen Ideen", pp. 157–
92. Both Grundmann and Denifle stress Gerard's comparative isolation from
the main stream of Joachimism at this time. Grundmann notices that Gerard
wished to popularize the genuine works of Joachim, while the majority of
Joachimites were interested in the apocryphal works (op. cit., p. 160, n. 3).

out a Joachimite MS.[1] Under the circumstances he could hardly stay in power.

Moreover, as a strong general, he had made enemies, and these were ready to use their influence against him. Peregrino of Bologna, a contemporary chronicler, who claimed to have acted as the intermediary between him and the ministers at John's last chapter, in 1257, has this to say about John's loss of the generalate:

Afterwards in the course of time he came to have many and great men envying him, who made accusations against him to the pope and so much influenced him that he ordered John in secret to renounce office and not to consent in any way if the ministers wanted to confirm him in office.[2]

So he resigned office at the next chapter-general. The truth of the matter seems impossible to determine. Angelo da Clareno simply says he went because he was weary of the abuses in the order.[3]

Franciscans who were not Spirituals were conscious of the loss to the order sustained by his going. Salimbene quoted a friend of his, Bartolomeo Calaroso, of Mantua, who lamented the waste of his talents brought about by his partiality for Joachimite prophecies. He said:

. . . brother John of Parma troubled himself and his order, because he was of such great learning and sanctity and most excellent life, that he could have put the Roman curia in order, and they would have trusted him to do so. But after he followed the prophecies of fantastic men, he disgraced himself and did his friends no small harm.[4]

The ministers at the chapter in 1257 begged him to stay in office, and when he refused, asked him instead to name his successor. He chose a friar who was not at the chapter, whom he had himself promoted at Paris—John of Fidenza, better known as Bonaventura, the most famous, and to all appearance the most successful, of the thirteenth-century generals.[5]

John's choice of Bonaventura as his successor has generally been

---

[1] Salimbene, *Cronica*, ed. Holder-Egger, p. 294.

[2] "Chronicon abbreviatum", *Eccleston*, ed. Little (1909), Appendice II, p. 144.

[3] *Historia*, ed. Ehrle, *ALKG* II, 270.

[4] *Cronica*, ed. Holder-Egger, p. 302.

[5] Salimbene, op. cit., pp. 309–10; Angelo da Clareno, *Historia*, ed. Ehrle, *ALKG* II, 271.

taken as an admission of failure on John's part. It has been assumed that John was, in effect, saying: "I, as a Spiritual, have failed with my policy of drastic reform; now I hand the order to the finest representative of the Conventuals I can find, who will see what success more moderate measures can have."

Undoubtedly, there is much truth in this view, provided at any rate that we restrict our gaze to the public aspects of Bonaventura's career. Where John of Parma had the characteristic Spiritual mistrust of Papal privileges, Bonaventura, like the rest of the Conventuals, used them freely. There is no sign in his generalate of any gesture, like that of John of Parma in his speech to the University of Paris,[1] moderating Franciscan legal claims in the face of outside opposition. On the contrary, a brief reference to the *Bullarium Franciscanum* in his time will show how he pressed for Papal confirmation of all pre-existing rights and used the customary legal defences against the enemies of the order. There is nothing here of the other-worldly intransigence of the Testament.

Again, on the question of poverty, the whole stress of John of Parma, like his fellow rigorists, was on the Rule without the Papal glosses, while the aim of Bonaventura's official policy was to restore the observance of the Rule with the original gloss of Gregory IX, the Bull *Quo elongati*. John of Parma wanted learning in the order but would not forgo the strict observance of poverty in order to have it; Bonaventura, on the other hand, was prepared to moderate the observance of poverty if it conflicted greatly with the pursuit of learning, as, of course, it did at the houses of studies at Universities.

Thus far we have a picture of John of Parma as the uncompromising reformer, contrasted with Bonaventura, his successor, the man of the golden mean, who attempted to provide for the order a middle-of-the-road poverty, which should satisfy both the rigorists, who looked back to the standards of St Francis's day, and the relaxed, who looked forward to an apostolate unhampered by the regulations of poverty.

Those who have discussed Bonaventura's generalate have usually made their judgements with some such assumptions as

---

[1] Salimbene, op. cit., pp. 299–300; *Eccleston*, ed. Little (1951), p. 74, note 2r, and refs. given.

these in mind. Some have treated his generalate as a blessing of providence which by its moderation saved the order from collapsing in confusion after a few more decades of enthusiasm. This school of thought has its best representative in Ehrle [1] and includes, probably, a majority of Franciscan historians.[2] Historically speaking, it was the view of the Conventuals separated from the main body by Leo X, and of some more moderate sections of the Observants.

Others have regarded the policy of the generalate as a betrayal of Francis's ideal which, by permitting relaxation under the guise of moderation, led the order on to its later degradation. This was the view of the Spirituals and their descendants in the order; it is also that of Sabatier and his school, and of a number of modern Franciscans.[3]

But all these critics have tended to discuss the generalate from a somewhat distant, *a priori* point of view.

The defence, for example, has tended to appeal chiefly to the long-term effects of Bonaventura's rule on the life of the order. His claim to the title of second founder has been justified by the use made of his constitutions by reforming legislators in later times, and by the effect of his example and writings in providing, down to our own times, a basis for unity among divided sections of the friars.

[1] See, esp. his "Der heilige Bonaventura, seine Eigenart und seine drei Lebensaufgaben", *FS* viii (1921), 109–24.

[2] For example, Isidorus a Buscomari, *S. Bonaventura ordinis Fratrum Minorum minister generalis*, Roma, 1874, an elegant panegyric written by an Observant on the sixth centenary of Bonaventura's death; Léonard de Carvalho e Castro, *St Bonaventure, le docteur franciscain*, Paris, 1923—"Bonaventura came providentially after St Francis to complete his work" (p. 255); L. Lemmens, *Der heilige Bonaventura Kardinal und Kirchenlehrer aus dem Franziskanerorden (1221–74)*, Kempten und München, 1909, the standard biography—for its weaknesses, see the review by L. Oliger, *AFH* iii (1910), 344–8; Gratien, *Évolution*—"He was the man destined by providence to defend the order of St Francis against its enemies, both within and without" (p. 249).

[3] For example the Capuchin, René de Nantes, in his *Histoire des Spirituels dans l'ordre de saint François*, Couvin and Paris, 1909: originally a series of articles in *Études Franciscaines*. René de Nantes in fact adds nothing to Ehrle, presents the Spirituals simply as unlucky reformers, and quite neglects their top-hamper of doctrine. See also the Observant, Holzapfel, *Handbuch*, pp. 34–5, a moderate criticism, which none the less accepts that there was a considerable division between the ideas of Bonaventura and Francis. It is interesting to notice that there was opposition in certain circles in the order to Bonaventura's canonization in 1482.

On both the hostile and the favourable side, much time has been devoted to investigating the relationship between Francis and Bonaventura. Hostile critics have tried to prove that there is an essential difference between them, that, in Sabatier's words, Bonaventura "has not understood him whose disciple he wanted and believed himself to be";[1] favourable critics have argued in defence that these differences are quite superficial, and that Bonaventura's policy was nothing more than a logical and organic development of the ideas of St Francis, as set out in the Rule of 1223.[2]

Both sides in this dispute have relied to a very large extent on *a priori* deductions. The defenders of Bonaventura have staked their case on making deductions about Francis's intentions from the Rule of 1223, while the hostile critics, as the Dutch Franciscan, Onings, points out,[3] have based theirs on the presupposition that the Rule of 1223 did not fully correspond to Francis's wishes.

Neither of these approaches will take us very far. A more secure method will be to approach through the contemporary evidence about Bonaventura. The amount of this is considerable, but it is one-sided. There is a notable lack of personal information. Bonaventura held office as general from 1257 to 1274, a period, that is, longer than any other thirteenth-century general. After his election he devoted himself almost exclusively to the care of the order. He wrote a series of treatises on Franciscan poverty, some for the defence of his order against its enemies among the secular masters at the University of Paris, some for the training of his fellow-friars. He reassembled the constitutions of the order in a more precise and coherent form. He wrote a new

---

[1] P. Sabatier, *Examen de quelques travaux récents sur les Opuscules de Saint François, Opuscules de Critique Historique*, fasc. x, Paris, 1904, p. 161, n. 1.

[2] This was the position of Lemmens in his biography, and of E. Gilson, following him, in his *La Philosophie de Saint Bonaventure*, Paris, 1924, section 2 of the first chapter, pp. 43–88. See the summary given by I. Onings, "De H. Bonaventura als 'Tweede Stichter' van de Orde der Minderbroeders", *Collectanea Franciscana Neerlandica*, I, 's-Hertogenbosch, 1927, pp. 138–9. This discussion has been based on Onings's article.

[3] "Their conclusions are not based directly on Bonaventura himself but on their interpretation of the intervention in the work of Francis by the Church, particularly by Pope Gregory IX, from the time when he was still Cardinal Hugolinus. If one condemns that one must also inevitably condemn the attitude of Bonaventura. . . ." Onings, art. cit., p. 137; see also his two questions, p. 139.

biography of Francis. All these writings of his own have survived. Yet no contemporary biography has come down to us; the earliest extant is a work written by Petrus Galesinius for his canonization in 1482.[1]

Although he held office for so long, and was so generally esteemed, no other contemporary historians have much in the way of personal accounts of him. Salimbene, who has so much to say about John of Parma, can provide little on his successor.[2] Eccleston comes to an end at the start of his generalate. Angelo da Clareno gives a few biased notes.[3] Bernard of Besse, once his secretary, has a little.[4] There is a description of him from an eye-witness, who was present at the Council of Lyons, where Bonaventura died.[5] Whether this paucity of biographical material is due to chance, or whether it can be put down to a certain elusiveness in the man himself, it has handicapped later historians.

The result has been to throw investigators back onto his own writings. Here again, the same difficulties reappear. The man is concealed behind the minister-general. It is believed that every one of his writings on the Franciscan order, and on the question of poverty, derives from the period after 1257, and must therefore have been written when he was minister-general.[6] They have an official tone. A number of them are controversial works, such as the *Quaestiones de evangelica perfectione*[7] and the *Apologia pauperum*,[8]

---

[1] See Oliger, *AFH* iii (1910), 344. He believes there would have been no paucity of material on Bonaventura if he had been canonized earlier.

[2] Ehrle suggests a reason: that Salimbene would have been out of *rapport* with Bonaventura. "Of course the profoundly religious general must have been somewhat alien and incomprehensible to the chronicler, who remained all his life a true child of this world" ("Der heilige Bonaventura", *FS* viii (1921) p. 110, n.c.). But, on the same grounds, one would expect Salimbene to be out of *rapport* with John of Parma.

[3] See, for example, *Historia*, ed. Ehrle, *ALKG* II, 277, 280-1, 285. His account of Bonaventura's investigation into John of Parma's Joachimite beliefs is markedly hostile. (See below, pp. 115, 123.)

[4] See "Catalogus ministrorum generalium", ed. O. Holder-Egger, *MGH Scriptores* XXXII, 653-74, and Ehrle, art. cit., p. 110, note b.

[5] Ehrle, art. cit., p. 110, note a, and refs. given.

[6] R. Silic, *Christus und die Kirche nach der Lehre des heiligen Bonaventura*, Breslau, 1938, pp. 6-8; cited by Esser in *FS* xxvii (1940), p. 150, n. 6. The *Quaestiones de evangelica perfectione* form an exception. See S. Clasen, *Der hl. Bonaventura und des Mendikantentum*, Werl.-i.-W., 1940, p. 5; and for the relation of Bonaventura's work to the secular-mendicant controversy generally, op. cit., pp. 1-30.

[7] Bonaventura, *Opera Omnia*, V, Ad Claras Aquas, 1891, pp. 117-98.

[8] See below, chap. 5.

9

which defend the Franciscan doctrine of poverty, or the *Quare fratres minores praedicent et confessiones audiant*, which defends their claim to the apostolate.[1] Since these are aimed at an audience outside the order, they are not likely to reveal much of Bonaventura's own views about the observance of poverty inside the order. Similarly with the works intended for the reading of the friars, such as the *Legenda maior*. For one reason or another they do not take us much below the surface of things. The *Legenda*, for example, a beautifully constructed work, has nothing of the judgements on the contemporary order which were written into *II Celano*. The Sermons, of which there is a collection of over three hundred, are not concerned with the detail of the observance of poverty.[2] The one exception to the official tone of Bonaventura's writings is the *Epistola de tribus quaestionibus ad innominatum magistrum*, a work addressed to a private individual and not intended for general publication, which touches the three crucial questions of the Franciscans' observance of poverty, their attitude to manual labour, and the development of academic work in the order.[3] Here alone we have a glimpse of personal views.

We have, therefore, very imperfect evidence on Bonaventura. Nevertheless, certain tentative conclusions may be suggested by the evidence which we have.

The first is that, while there is a real distinction between Bonaventura and John of Parma, this distinction should not be overdrawn or allowed to obscure the considerable body of ideas which they had in common. Each of these two generals supported the development of study in the order. Bonaventura, as we know, emerged from the exclusively academic environment of the University of Paris to hold office; but John of Parma also had been *lector* to the friars at Naples and Bologna.[4] For Bonaventura the development of learning out of the simplicity of the early days had been one of the attractions of the order for him—as he said, in a rare moment of self-revelation, in the *Epistola de tribus quaestionibus*: "I confess before God, that this is what has made me love the way of life of St Francis: that it is like both the beginning and the

---

[1] Bonaventura, *Opera Omnia*, VIII, Ad Claras Aquas, 1898, pp. 375–85.
[2] Ehrle, "Der heilige Bonaventura", *FS* viii (1921), 118–20.
[3] *Opera Omnia*, VIII, 331–6.
[4] Salimbene, *Cronica*, ed. Holder-Egger, p. 298.

perfection of the Church, which first started from fishermen and afterwards advanced to the most renowned and skilful doctors."[1] For John of Parma learning, if not of the same personal significance, was certainly an essential aspect of Franciscan life. According to Eccleston, he said that the structure of the order was raised on two foundations, good life and learning.[2]

John was a Joachimite and fell from office because of it. Bonaventura, most probably in 1262 at the provincial chapter at Città di Pieve,[3] initiated an inquiry into John's Joachimite beliefs. As a result of it John went into retirement at the hermitage of Greccio for virtually the rest of his life. In Angelo da Clareno's account of this affair only the intervention of a friendly Cardinal saved him from more severe penalties.[4]

But, despite this action, dictated no doubt by the attacks on the order by the secular masters, Bonaventura was himself not immune from Joachimite influences. In the prologue to the *Legenda maior* he included an identification of Francis with the angel of the sixth seal in the Apocalypse. He said:

> And so by a true prophecy of the other friend of the Bridegroom, the Apostle and Evangelist John, he is given a description not unworthy of him under the type of the Angel ascending from the rising of the sun and having the sign of the living God.[5]

Now this identification was used for the first time, so far as we can tell,[6] by Gerard of Borgo San Donnino in his *Introductorius*; it was included, although without being censured, in the excerpts made by the Papal commission at Anagni.[7]

---

[1] *Opera Omnia* VIII, 336.

[2] "Dixit autem idem pater, quod cum ex duobus parietibus construatur aedificium ordinis, scilicet moribus bonis et scientia, parietem scientiae fecerunt fratres ultra coelos et coelestia sublimem, in tantum ut quaererent, an Deus sit; parietem vero morum permiserunt ita bassum esse, ut pro laude magna dicatur de fratre: 'securus homo est' . . .", *Eccleston*, ed. Little (1951), coll. xiii, p. 74. The stress on the inadequacy of the friars' personal lives perhaps smacks of the Spirituals; but the point still holds.

[3] See M. Bihl in his review of the Italian translation of L. Lemmens, *Der hl. Bonaventura, AFH* xv (1922), 533–4.

[4] *Historia*, ed. Ehrle, *ALKG* II, 286.

[5] *Legenda Maior*, prologus, 1; *AF* X, 558.

[6] S. Bihel, "S. Franciscus fuitne angelus sexti sigilli? (Apoc. 7, 2)", *Antonianum* ii (1927), 62. I am indebted for the reference to this article to Dr M. Reeves.

[7] H. Denifle, "Das Evangelium aeternum", *ALKG* I, 101. The report of the commission, which Denifle edits, begins: "Hec notavimus et extraximus de

Elsewhere in Bonaventura's writings Joachimite symbols and phrases recur, especially in the *Collationes in Hexaemeron*, produced at the end of his life.[1] Tondelli, in the introduction to the recent edition of the *Liber figurarum* of Joachim, had this to say about Joachim's influence on Bonaventura:

> These contacts have normally escaped the notice of students, so that even a student of Joachim and his historical influence as profound as Bonaiuti can still maintain that St Bonaventura was completely impervious to his ideas and expectations. A study of them is necessary here because the similarities between the thought and sometimes even the phrases of the saint and the Calabrian abbot are so precise and frequent in the *Libro delle figure* that a dependence on this, rather than the other writings of Joachim, which were doubtless known to him, seems to me to be certainly demonstrable . . .[2]

It may well be that we have here, as Van Ortroy put it, "du joachimisme anodin";[3] on the other hand, one would be reluctant to dismiss all Bonaventura's Joachimism as a matter of tactics.

In the observance of poverty Bonaventura's generalate was in several ways a continuation of, rather than a contrast to, that of John of Parma. John's greatest achievement, as we saw, was to persuade the chapter-general to suspend the operation of the relaxing Bulls, *Ordinem vestrum* and *Quanto studiosius*. The suspension was not lifted by Bonaventura. The *definitiones* made at the chapter-general of Narbonne in 1260 included the clause:

> The declaration of the lord Innocent should remain in suspension, as was decided in the chapter of Metz; and we strictly forbid the use of it on those points in which it contradicts the declaration of the lord Gregory.[4]

Introductorio . . ." (art. cit., p. 99). The section which contains the identification of Francis with the angel of the sixth seal concludes: "Istos errores et fatuitates invenimus in isto libro . . ." (art. cit., p. 102). But the report is concerned primarily with Gerard's exposition of the doctrine of three ages, and one would imagine that it is the linking of Francis with the gospel of the third age, superseding the New Testament, which is condemned, and not this particular identification from the Apocalypse.

[1] S. Bihel, *Antonianum*, ii (1927), 67–9; L. Tondelli, *Il Libro delle Figure dell' Abate Gioachino da Fiore*, I, 2nd edn. Torino, 1953, pp. 249–50, and 250, n. 1.

[2] *Il Libro delle Figure*, I, 250.

[3] F. Van Ortroy, in *Analecta Bollandiana* xviii (1899), 205; he is referring to the Joachimite identification in the prologue to the *Legenda Maior*.

[4] "'Diffinitiones' Capituli Generalis Narbonensis (1260)", ed. Delorme, *AFH* iii (1910), no. 13, p. 503.

In other words, the observance was to be cut back to the standard of *Quo elongati*, in 1230.

Another feature of John's rule which was carried over into Bonaventura's was the attempt to regain the full control of the minister-general over the order. On it, in the last resort, depended the success of the reforming policy of both these generals. John of Parma had required that, for example, there should be no transferring of the sites of convents without his permission. Such transfers, often made necessary by the condition of the primitive sites of convents, strained the friars' resources and prepared the way for abuses of poverty. Bonaventura in the encyclical which he issued after his election renewed the decree, mentioning that he did so "iuxta praedecessoris mei mandatum".[1] Similarly, John of Parma, in this following some earlier precedents,[2] had forbidden friars to take office in the households of great men and withdraw themselves from the common life, or to receive ecclesiastical dignities without consent.[3] Bonaventura in turn, soon after his election, renewed the enactment against the reception of dignities, and, possibly recalling the complicity of the Papacy in some un-Franciscan transactions, added to it the more far-reaching prohibition of the use of any Papal privileges without the consent of the general.[4]

More surprising than any of these administrative similarities between the generals is the coincidence of ideas between them, or, to put it more exactly, between Bonaventura and the Spirituals. Bonaventura's most personal work, the *Epistola de tribus quaestionibus*, has been shown to be little more than a compilation from an earlier Exposition on the Rule written by no less a person than Hugues de Digne, the Spiritual, who was so close a friend of John of Parma. Esser, who made this discovery, demonstrates that nine out of the thirteen sections, plus an *additamentum*, in which it is comprised in the Quaracchi edition, are either based closely on Hugues, or taken word for word from him.[5] The substance of the

---

[1] *Epistolae Officiales*, I, 4; *Opera Omnia* VIII, 469b.
[2] *BF* I, no. c, p. 383; no. cxlv, p. 422.
[3] *BF* I, no. ccxxxi, p. 485; no. ccci, pp. 529–30; no. cdiv, pp. 605–6.
[4] *BF* II, no. ccclxxiv, pp. 253–4, and see Sbaralea's note b, p. 253; no. cdxiv, pp. 282–3.
[5] K. Esser, "Zu der 'Epistola de tribus quaestionibus' des hl. Bonaventura", *FS* xxvii (1940), 149–59.

work is a series of arguments designed to convince a critic that all
the current developments in Franciscan life, the reception of
money through intermediaries, the use of houses and land, the
adoption of academic work, and the dropping of manual labour,
do not represent a betrayal of Francis, his Rule, or his intentions.
They are the arguments which we should expect Bonaventura to
use to convince a Spiritual of the legitimacy of his own compromise
settlement in the order; yet in fact they come, for the most part,
out of the mouth of a Spiritual. It is clear, after a reading of
Esser's article, that some readjustment is needed in our views of the
relation between Bonaventura's thought about the practice of
poverty and that of the more responsible Spiritual leaders, like
John of Parma and Hugues de Digne.

A second tentative conclusion, not entirely unrelated to the
first, is that there is no ground for supposing, as a few pro-
Spiritual historians have done, that Bonaventura tacitly favoured
certain relaxations of poverty. To some critics, as the Spiritual
leader Olivi said in the 1280s,[1] God himself would seem an example
of relaxation. But if we distinguish between prudence and mere
relaxation, we shall discover little sign of the latter in Bonaventura.

Some critics have been impressed by the divergence between the
encyclicals, with their stern denunciation of breaches of poverty,
and the *Determinationes quaestionum circa regulam*, an apologetic
work, often over-eager in finding excuses for the mitigation of
poverty. The distinction has led them to doubt Bonaventura's
determination to uproot abuses, even, sometimes, his sincerity in
denouncing them. This is unnecessary. The *Determinationes* is, to
put it at the lowest, a doubtful work. All the MSS. of the first
part are derived solely from an area of German speech, a fact
which arouses suspicion about the attribution to Bonaventura.
The authenticity of the second part was questioned by the editors
in the original Quaracchi edition. We cannot therefore base any
criticism on the evidence of this work alone.[2]

The impression of an undue complacency towards abuses and
a certain prevaricating towards Francis's intentions in Bonaventura has been heightened by the critical examination of the
Legenda Maior. For centuries this Life was the only source of

[1] In his treatise on the *usus pauper*, extracts ed. Ehrle, *ALKG* III (1887), 516.
[2] On this point, see Clasen, *Der hl. Bonaventura*, p. 26.

information about Francis for the majority of the friars, and for the outside world; it was, perhaps, inevitable that the rediscovery of the older Lives which lay behind the *Legenda* and had been deliberately suppressed in its favour[1] should have led to a general lowering of esteem for Bonaventura's work. There are, however, signs that the reaction against the *Legenda* has been carried too far. It is essentially a compilation of the two older Lives by Celano. As such, it inevitably omits large sections of its sources. Critics have taken it that all such omissions must have a "political" significance deriving from the state of the order at the time Bonaventura made his compilation. Moorman, in this respect a typical representative of the critics of the last half-century, makes this comment on the omissions in the *Legenda*: "Bonaventura glosses over or suppresses many things for the sake of reconciling conflicting parties in the Order or to bring credit on the Order in the eyes of the world."[2] It should be pointed out on the other side that in many instances Bonaventura was probably guided by no more significant principle than lack of space. Where he does omit details, what Moorman calls "certain homely details in Celano which Bonaventura considers either undignified or unsuitable for a work of hagiography",[3] it may often be from a temperamental preference rather than out of policy. Newman, when giving casual descriptions of colleagues, always wrote in general, intellectual terms, omitting significant personal detail; and that was in private letters, where there was no thought of suppression. Nor can it be said that the omission of detail in the *Legenda* seriously obscures the picture of Francis's fierce love of poverty. In chapter seven, for example, we have the story of Peter Catanii's request to reserve goods for the friars from the property of postulants, and Francis's indignant refusal; Francis's simile of the learned man renouncing his learning to cast himself naked into the arms of the Crucified; the description of Francis, content to the day of his death with one tunic and a pair of breeches.[4]

---

[1] By the decree of the chapter-general of Paris, 1266: "Definitiones Capitulorum Generalium Ordinis Fratrum Minorum 1260–1282", ed. A. G. Little, *AFH* vii (1914), Paris, no. 8, p. 678.

[2] Moorman, *Sources*, p. 143.

[3] Op. cit., p. 147.

[4] *Leg. Maj.*, vii, 4; *AF* X, 588. *Leg. Maj.*, vii, 2; *AF* X, 587. *Leg. Maj.*, vii, 1; *AF* X, 587.

More effective is the criticism of Bonaventura which is based on the actions of his administration. Balthasar, while recognizing his claim to the title of second founder and applauding his work of defence against the enemies of the Franciscans, is noticeably cool in his judgements on Bonaventura as a reforming administrator. A doubtful arrangement made after his death whereby thirteen friars, who were careful to say they had no dominion, accepted the right to fixed incomes in a college for the study of Arabic at Majorca, he calls "wholly in the sense of Bonaventura".[1] On another case during his generalate, in Dalmatia, in 1264, where a bequest made in an illegitimate form to the friars was turned into cash, and then devoted to their needs, Balthasar comments:

> This example is significant for the interpretation which was gaining ground more and more, that the brothers could accept everything, but at the same time had to maintain the correct procedure.[2]

Further on, having agreed that in his writings intended for the reading of the order Bonaventura defended the standard of observance set by Gregory IX, he continues:

> Publicly he yet defended the prevailing modifications, and privately often yielded to the laxer party in the order.[3]

Balthasar's criticism rests on three selected examples of relaxation: the case at Dalmatia already mentioned, an instance from 1263, in which a friar was given permission from the Papacy to make a bequest of books,[4] and some appointments of procurators made by the Papacy in 1265 and 1268. In these last, so Balthasar claims, the forbidden Innocentian procurator made his re-appearance. In the 1265 case three burghers of Perugia were appointed by the Papacy to be procurators for the Franciscans in Umbria. They were given full powers over the goods used by the Franciscans, even down to the right to go to law on their behalf. It was specifically stated that they should act at the friars' will and under their control.[5] The one difference between this procurator and that envisaged in the formula of *Quanto studiosius*, which the friars

---

[1] *Armutsstreit*, p. 80; *BF* III, no. vii, pp. 253–4.
[2] *Armutsstreit*, p. 74; *BF* II, no. cxvii, pp. 532–3.
[3] *Armutsstreit*, p. 78.
[4] *BF* II, no. lxxiv, p. 476; *Armutsstreit*, p. 74.
[5] *BF* III, no. xxvi, pp. 24–5; *Armutsstreit*, pp. 74–5.

rejected under John of Parma's leadership, was that he was formally appointed by the Papacy and not by the friars. In 1268
procurators were appointed in the same terms in the province
of Milan and Upper Germany.[1]

Balthasar's criticisms of the administration of poverty have never
been refuted. Gratien, who relies to a great extent on Balthasar
for his knowledge of the *Bullarium Franciscanum*, contents himself
with citing his examples, and either arguing that they were not
in the true sense relaxations at all, or alternatively that they
occurred without Bonaventura's knowledge.[2]

In themselves Balthasar's examples do not stand against Bonaventura personally. The same difficulty about the use of procurators
arises under John of Parma. In his time the chapter-general sus-
pended the use of the procurator of the *Quanto studiosius* formula.
If we accept Eccleston's testimony, this took place at Genoa, therefore in 1249 or 1251. But the *Bullarium Franciscanum* shows us that
procurators of the Innocentian type were being appointed at
several places in Italy well after the decree of suspension, in 1252
and 1253.[3] These contraventions of the edict have not been held
against John of Parma personally; it has been assumed that they
occurred against his will, or without his knowledge. Bearing in
mind the evidence of strictness given by Bonaventura's authentic
writings, may we not also acquit him of laxity in like circumstances? The one case adduced by Balthasar where it is more
difficult to do this is the clause of the Bull *Virtute conspicuos*, obtained
under Bonaventura's generalate in 1265, which permitted the
friars to receive from their own postulants restitution money for
unlawful gains when the true owners could not be found.[4] This
privilege opened the door to the reservation of goods from the
possessions of postulants, and ran counter to a fundamental principle of Franciscan poverty; and it is difficult to see how Bonaventura as general could have passed it unwittingly. This aside, the
personal record of Bonaventura stands unblemished.

What these examples of Balthasar do suggest is that neither of
the two reforming generals was fully in command of the situation.

---

[1] *BF* III, no. clxi, p. 153, no. clxiv, pp. 154–5; *Armutsstreit*, p. 75.
[2] *Évolution*, pp. 295, and 298, n. 85.
[3] *BF* I, no. cccxcii, p. 595 (Offida); no. cdliv, pp. 643–4 (San Germano);
no. cdxcix, pp. 680–1 (Perugia); Balthasar, *Armutsstreit*, p. 44.
[4] *Armutsstreit*, p. 74; *Epitome*, ed. Eubel, no. xliii, p. 287b.

The fundamental problem was how to accept so much of the developments in the order which had taken place since Francis's time, and yet prevent mitigation of poverty being carried further.

The accepted standard was that of Gregory IX in *Quo elongati*. However just and lawful, this was not a standard to command general enthusiasm. For less academic minds, the distinction between, say, the Gregorian and the Innocentian form of intermediary, however valid the principle, might well seem a matter of words alone. Some use of intermediaries to hold dominion and accept money was absolutely essential if the friars were to maintain their form of life; the difficulty was to persuade the order to stop short at a moderate and legitimate use of them.

On the one hand there were the zealous but simple brothers, with scant experience of administration, who could not grasp the distinction between the legitimate and illegitimate use of intermediaries: these tended to reject them all outright. On the other there were the brothers eager for the exercise of the apostolate, who grasped the distinction, perhaps, but did not think it worth observing: these generally pressed for a virtually unrestricted use of them. Between them was a large undifferentiated mass, who at this stage cannot be placed in any definite party:[1] these, however, through inertia tended to gravitate to relaxation unless pressure was maintained upon them to safeguard poverty.

The task of both generals in mid-century was to rally a sufficiency of the friars to the support of their own solutions.

John of Parma, while retaining the support of the rigorist sections of the order, apparently lost that of others. The fact that he had failed to gain a general assent emerges from Peregrino of Bologna's account of the "aemuli", who disliked his rule and persuaded the Pope to get rid of him. It seems clear that he had failed when he left office.

It is not usual to say the same thing of Bonaventura. When he died, in 1274, while playing a leading part in the Council of Lyons, he had great prestige and a cardinal's hat. He had routed the opponents of the Franciscans in the outside world. As far as the internal administration was concerned, Balthasar admits:

---

[1] If the majority of the order had been divided into parties in this period, then surely it would have been impossible for John of Parma to have been elected in succession to Crescenzio da Jesi.

It is certain that in the eighteen years of his generalate he had given the order an improved organization in essentials and a more definite direction.[1]

Yet the suspicion remains that he, too, had not gained complete support within the order for his policy of stabilization.

The more primitive Spirituals did not wholly approve of him. It was not so much an active hostility as a grudging assent to his ideal: we can see that by comparing their utterances about Aquinas, whom they regarded as the enemy of Franciscan poverty. To some extent, their attitude was shaped by Bonaventura's investigation into the beliefs of their hero, John of Parma. But it was also influenced by their view of his observance of poverty.

These two elements can be seen at work in a symbolic dream related by John of La Massa, which became current in Spiritual circles and passed into Angelo da Clareno's *Historia septem tribulationum*.[2] He said that he saw a tree, which represented the Franciscan order: the brothers sat about in the branches. Francis was given a chalice from Christ, containing the spirit of life, which he offered to each of the brothers. Some refused it altogether and were put in darkness. Bonaventura received the chalice, drank half, and poured half on the ground. Only John of Parma and a few others drank all the contents, and they thereafter glowed with light. After a time Bonaventura replaced John of Parma, who moved farther down the tree. Then Bonaventura tried to attack John with his nails. John had to be protected by Francis from his attacks.

In many ways the story is typical of the Spirituals' view of the history of their order. Factually correct, it is yet unduly partisan. The complexities of the situation pass unnoticed. Events are interpreted solely in terms of personalities. One understands from this the difficulty of gaining the assent of such men for any compromise settlement.

The existence of other friars who, in practice, considered that Bonaventura's settlement did not go far enough, can be deduced from the incidence of relaxation under his rule. We have already seen Balthasar's evidence on this point. We might add to it the

---

[1] *Armutsstreit*, p. 52.

[2] Ed. Ehrle, *ALKG* II, 280–1. See also *Actus Beati Francisci et Sociorum eius*, ed. P. Sabatier, Paris, 1902, p. 216, n. 1, and refs. given.

evidence of the two encyclicals which Bonaventura directed at the order. The first, issued at his election, condemned a series of breaches of the observance of poverty;[1] the second, issued in 1266, complained as bitterly of excesses, and selected two breaches of poverty as especially worthy of notice, the pursuit of bequests and burial fees, and sumptuosity in building.[2]

In the long run, it may well be true that Bonaventura provided a middle way for the observance of the majority: his legislation is, after all, the basis of the observance of the majority of the friars at the present day. In the nineteenth century, the figure of Bonaventura acted as a rallying-point for the disparate bodies of the Observants who were reunited by Leo XIII. But under the circumstances of the thirteenth century the way of compromise foundered. It might even be suggested that, humanly speaking, it was bound to do so. If the learning and sanctity which Bonaventura brought to the support of the *status quo* could not maintain a permanently acceptable compromise, it might be that such a condition was, at that time, impossible. He was the type of a conciliator—"kind, affable, pious and merciful, full of virtues. Beloved of God and men . . ."[3]. As his master, Alexander of Hales, once said: "It seemed that in him Adam had not sinned."[4] When such a man as this is at the head of affairs, we should be inclined to seek for the causes of failure, not in his personality, but in the nature of his policy.

It is difficult to avoid the conclusion that the Bonaventuran settlement failed through inherent defects. In essentials, it was a legacy from the revolution of 1239. Bonaventura on his accession had very little freedom of action. The main pattern of observance had already been set for him by the existing Franciscan constitutions and the Papal legislation of the previous thirty years. These contained a basic contradiction—between the needs of the apostolate and the ideal of poverty. Given the circumstances of the time, with the pressures exerted against poverty on the one

---

[1] *Epistolae Officiales*, I, 2; *Opera Omnia* VIII, 468-9.
[2] *Epistolae Officiales*, II, 2; *Opera Omnia* VIII, 470.
[3] Quoted, Ehrle, "Der heilige Bonaventura", *FS* viii (1921), 113, n. 1.
[4] "Qui cum iuvenis intrasset ordinem, tanta bone indolis honestate pollebat, ut magnus ille magister frater Alexander diceret aliquando de ipso, quod in eo videbatur Adam non peccasse." "Catalogus ministrorum generalium", ed. Holder-Egger, *MGH Scriptores* XXXII, 664.

hand, the surviving enthusiasm of the early period and the still comparatively recent example of Francis on the other, it was most likely that these unresolved contradictions would destroy the settlement which Bonaventura had supported.

The process of destruction, however, still lay in the future: we shall describe it in three later chapters, dealing with the history of the observance in the last decades of the thirteenth century and the early fourteenth. What we must now discuss is the other great work of Bonaventura for his order: the exposition in scholastic form of the doctrine of the absolute poverty of Christ and the apostles.

5

THE BONAVENTURAN DOCTRINE OF
ABSOLUTE POVERTY

FOR FRANCIS, the nature of the poverty of Christ was an assumed fact. As we have seen, he never explained what it was, because he assumed that everybody already knew. Much the same was true of his immediate followers. The practical needs of their life in the early years of development pressed so hard upon them that they had neither wish nor opportunity to examine the intellectual basis of the doctrine of absolute poverty. Both for Francis and for the early Franciscans, the doctrine was expressed in terms which were devotional rather than academic.

With the opening of the secular–mendicant dispute at the University of Paris in 1253, the situation changed. The secular masters, who began by disputing with the friars about the exercise of their rights in the University and the outside world, finally came to launch a full-scale attack on the most fundamental issue: the legitimacy of the whole way of life of the new mendicant orders. What particularly came under fire was the claim of the mendicants to imitate the poverty of Christ and the apostles. Under this pressure, the Franciscans were compelled to think out the intellectual basis of their doctrine of absolute poverty and to defend it in scholastic form against the attacks of their enemies.[1]

In making this defence, the Franciscan controversialists drew on two principal sources: first, St Francis's idea of the poverty of Christ, and, secondly, the theory of poverty as it had been developed by his followers in the years after his death. With these as the twin poles of their argument, they pressed into service a large quantity of general texts relating to the practice of poverty which were to be found in Scripture and the Fathers.

The controversy developed in a series of attacks and counter-

---

[1] For details, ref. may again be made to Clasen, *Der hl. Bonaventura*, pp. 1–30, and Douie, *The Conflict between the Seculars and the Mendicants, passim.*

attacks. Both sides in the dispute in the course of time altered or developed their arguments. Among the Franciscan defences of absolute poverty, Bonaventura's *Apologia pauperum*[1] is, however, the classic exposition. It was his considered *apologia*, made in 1269, towards the end of his life. It became the accepted doctrine of the Franciscan order. It was even adopted as the official doctrine by the Papacy. Therefore, although other treatises may be found expounding the Franciscan view, the *Apologia pauperum* is the appropriate text for us to use here in explaining the development of the doctrine of the absolute poverty of Christ.

Gregory IX's decision in *Quo elongati* about the common property of the order is fundamental to the understanding of this development. Francis interpreted poverty, primarily, as a renunciation of material goods; but after Gregory IX gave his decision that the order should renounce all dominion, the tendency grew to interpret poverty as a renunciation of rights of ownership. By the time Bonaventura wrote, that trend was well established. The renunciation of all rights of ownership was seen as a primary mark of the poverty of the order, and careful arrangements were made to secure this renunciation in practice. Naturally Bonaventura took over the prevailing interpretation. When he defined Franciscan poverty, he did so in the terms suggested by *Quo elongati*. Equally naturally when he came to speak of the poverty of Christ and the apostles, he defined that, too, in terms of the renunciation of rights of ownership. Thus, as a result of the development in the theory and practice of poverty between 1226 and 1247, there appeared the full-fledged Franciscan doctrine of absolute poverty: the belief that Christ and the apostles, showing the life of perfection, had renounced all dominion.

Bonaventura's definition of poverty is given in the *Apologia* before the exegesis of the Scriptural texts relating to Christ's poverty. He says:

> Since there are two things to be considered with regard to the possession of temporal goods, *dominium* and *usus*, and *usus* is necessarily annexed to the present life; it is the nature of evangelical poverty to renounce earthly possessions in respect of *dominium* and *proprietas*, and, not to reject *usus* utterly, but to restrain it. . . .[2]

[1] *Opera Omnia*, VIII, Ad Claras Aquas, 1898, pp. 233–330.
[2] Ed. cit., cap. vii, para. 3, pp. 272–3. All refs. are to the Quaracchi edn. of 1898, cited as above.

Clearly, the definition is taken from the judgement given on Franciscan poverty by Gregory IX in *Quo elongati*:

> We say therefore that (the friars) ought not to have *proprietas*, either common or individual, but may have the *usus* alone of the utensils and books and movable goods which they are permitted to have. . . .[1]

This total renunciation of dominion, both individual and common, is taken by Bonaventura to be the highest form of poverty. He continues, in the same passage:

> And since the *dominium* of temporal goods can be renounced in two ways . . . so there is a twofold mode and a twofold perfection of evangelical poverty. For since there is a twofold dominion of things, individual and common, one pertaining to a determined person, the other to a determined college; and the first can be renounced while the second is retained, and the second can be renounced together with the first, there will be in accord with this twofold form a twofold perfect profession of poverty. . . . The form of the first poverty appeared in the crowd of believers, of which it is said in Acts: "And the multitude of them that believed were of one heart and of one soul: neither said any of them that ought of the things which he possessed was his own; but they had all things in common. . . ." Here also was given the form of monastic or cenobitic life. . . . The pattern and form of the second poverty appeared in the life of the Apostles, which Christ the master of perfection imposed on them, when he sent them out to preach, as one reads in Matthew: "Provide neither gold, nor silver, nor brass in your purses, nor scrip for your journey, neither two coats, neither shoes, nor yet staves: for the workman is worthy of his meat". . . . In these words, therefore, the Lord imposed on the Apostles and the preachers of truth a form of extreme and penurious poverty to be observed, not only as regards the lack of possessions, but also of money and other movable goods, whereby the common life of men is usually maintained or fortified . . . that thus they might bear the highest poverty both in action and in spirit, as a certain sign, so to speak, of perfection.[2]

Thus appears in the *Apologia pauperum* the proposition, that Christ and the apostles renounced all forms of dominion, both individual and common.

But while Bonaventura's exposition of the poverty of Christ owes much to the new Franciscan theory of poverty, developed

---

[1] *Epitome*, ed. Eubel, p. 230a. See above, pp. 85–8.
[2] Ed. cit., vii, 4–5, 273.

after Francis's death, the whole work is informed by the spirit of Francis. If an argument is required to clinch Bonaventura's case, it will be taken from the pattern of Christ's life. When, for example, Bonaventura is arguing for the superiority *per se* of the Franciscan observance of poverty over the way of life of those who hold Church goods, he makes his point by appealing to the example of Christ:

> It is true that church goods can be held without detriment to perfection; but to believe or to say that they are at the height of perfection, is as absurd as to say that the state and way of living of the present time is to be preferred to the life of Christ and the Apostles; which is most openly false.[1]

It is indeed the assumption of the whole work that the poverty of Christ and the apostles is in some way presented to Christians as a pattern for the imitation of those who wish to lead the life of perfection. Bonaventura, speaking of the observance of Christ and the apostles, says:

> This standard of poverty, perfect as by special prerogative, Christ observed in himself, and gave to the apostles to observe and gave as a counsel to those who desired to follow their steps.[2]

Again, Bonaventura, explaining how Christ on certain occasions condescended to the infirmity of men, adds that he did so in such a way "that yet the form and example of poverty should be secure, that he had especially come to show to men".[3] The words of Christ to the first missionaries, "Take nothing for your journey. . . . Provide neither gold nor silver nor brass in your purses. . . ." are, as we have seen, treated by Bonaventura as if they were a monastic Rule given by a founder to his novices. They represent to Bonaventura a fixed way of life, which is binding on all who wish to lead the life of perfection, and follow closely the way of life of Christ and the apostles. There can be no necessity to point out how closely this corresponds to the fundamental ideas of Francis. On points of detail, Bonaventura depended on the new Franciscan theory of poverty which stemmed from *Quo elongati*; for his most fundamental concept of the absolute poverty of Christ as the pattern for men's imitation, he was following Francis himself.

[1] Ed. cit., viii, 9, 289.
[2] Ed. cit., vii, 5, 273.
[3] Ed. cit.

We may now assemble Bonaventura's Scriptural exposition [1] in order to see exactly the nature of Christ's poverty as described in the *Apologia*. It may be grouped readily enough under the main headings of the renunciation of money, the practice of begging, and the renunciation of all forms of dominion.

The prohibition of money was contained in the words of Scripture. After that occasion none of the apostles used money under normal circumstances. Christ had none of his own when he was required to pay the tribute, and therefore in order to pay had to take the stater from a fish's mouth. [2]

The right to beg was given in the instruction to the missionaries: "Eat such things as are set before you." [3]

Christ and the apostles continued to observe this way of life after the return of the missionaries, for they depended for their daily sustenance on the offerings of the faithful. Christ himself begged. In a passage of the Psalms universally taken to refer to the Messiah, it was said: "Ego autem mendicus sum et pauper." [4] Moreover, Christ was, in effect, asking for alms when he said: "Zacchaeus, make haste, and come down; for to-day I must abide at thy house." [5]

The prohibition of dominion was implied in the instructions to the missionaries, for Christ told the apostles to take nothing for their journey. [6] It was repeated in his counsel to the young man: "If thou wilt be perfect, go and sell all thou hast . . .", [7] and the apostles' acceptance of it confirmed by the words of Peter which followed: "Behold we have forsaken all and followed thee. . . ." [8] If the apostles had made a total renunciation, as Peter said they had, then they must have given up both individual and common dominion. Dominion in all its forms can be given up, while use cannot. The apostles must then have given up common as well as individual dominion.

[1] All Scriptural refs. are to the A.V., unless otherwise stated. Bonaventura's Scriptural exposition will be found, particularly, in chap. vii, ed. cit., pp. 272–286; also, in chaps. viii–x, ed. cit., pp. 286–310.
[2] Matt. 17.27.
[3] Luke 10.8.
[4] Ps. 39.18 (Vulgate).
[5] Luke 19.5.
[6] Luke 9.3; Mark 6.8.
[7] Matt. 19.21.
[8] Matt. 19.27.

By the same logic Christ also must have given up common dominion. Scripture witnessed that neither he nor the college of apostles held any temporal dominion, for when the Passover was at hand they had no room of their own in which to eat it, and Christ said of himself: "The foxes have holes, and the birds of the air have nests; but the Son of Man hath not where to lay his head." [1] It was because of his renunciation of all temporal dominion that he was able to say to the apostles at the Last Supper: ". . . the prince of this world cometh, and hath nothing in me". [2]

Bonaventura, then, more or less precisely identifies the poverty of Christ and the apostles with the poverty observed by the thirteenth-century Franciscans.

But among the constituent elements of the poverty of Christ which he describes, the total renunciation of dominion has a special place. It acts as a distinguishing mark, separating the poverty of Christ from other, lesser forms described in Scripture. It is, in effect, a unique sign of that supreme poverty. Yet in the contemporary world it was a form of renunciation practised by no other order but the Franciscan. At the time when Bonaventura wrote the *Apologia pauperum*, no other order was making a comparable claim to the total renunciation of dominion. In Bonaventura's interpretation the order of St Francis, and no other religious body, was making a full imitation of the life of Christ and the apostles.

Naturally, such a claim was repugnant to other orders and groups in the Church. Tactful Bonaventura might be in pointing out that perfections differed in kind, and that no order could be said to be simply more perfect than another; [3] nevertheless, he was here claiming a definite superiority for the Franciscan order. The *Apologia pauperum*, although written as a work of controversy, amounted to more than a simple *riposte* to those secular masters who had made attacks on the Franciscan observance. It contained a doctrine of poverty and perfection which intimately concerned the lives of all the orders in the Church, and not solely of the friars minor.

Yet this doctrine of poverty, which had such far-reaching

---

[1] Matt. 8.20; cf. Matt. 26.17–19.
[2] John 14.30.
[3] Ed. cit., iii, 19, 249; also, xi, 3, 311.

implications, was by no means secure from criticism. At various times, both in the course of the thirteenth-century controversy and afterwards, two serious objections were levelled against it. Of these one originated in Biblical exegesis, and the other in the interpretation of the civil law.

The Biblical objection was perhaps the most obvious. Bonaventura's doctrine rested on a certain interpretation of Scripture. It was essential for the success of his argument for him to prove that Christ and the apostles renounced both individual and common dominion and the use of money, and that they maintained this renunciation as a rule of life, the *forma evangelicae perfectionis*. For this end he was able to deploy a series of authorities from Scripture and the Fathers, which purported to show that Christ and the apostles followed this way of life from the time of the first missionary journey and counselled it to those who wished to follow them.

But there was in existence an equally valid series of authorities which appeared to support an entirely contradictory view: that Christ and the apostles never consistently observed this way of life or recommended it as a way to perfection. Not a few texts in Scripture apparently revealed Christ and the apostles, after the missionary journey, holding dominion and using money. A significant number of Fathers denied that the instructions of Christ to the apostles on the first missionary journey represented anything more than precepts for the occasion, intended to last for the duration of the journey and no longer.

If the instructions on the missionary journey were a rule of life for the apostles, it might be asked, how was it that individual apostles were still apparently free to use money on various occasions? Christ assumed that Philip would have money to use when he said to him, before the feeding of the five thousand: "Whence shall we buy bread, that these may eat?"[1] The whole body of the apostles used money when in Samaria they went into the city to buy bread, leaving Christ alone at Jacob's well.[2] Some apostles still apparently held dominion, for the house which Christ entered to heal Peter's wife's mother was described as Peter's house,[3] and the boats which the apostles continued to use after the missionary journey were referred to in a manner which in no

---

[1] John 6.5.   [2] John 4.8.   [3] Mark 1.29.

way implied relinquished ownership.[1] How could this be, when the college of apostles had renounced all forms of dominion?

That these instances of the apostles holding dominion and using money were not passing episodes but part of a regular way of life, seemed amply demonstrated from the example of the bag which Judas carried. John's description of it might well suggest that Christ and the apostles were accustomed to holding a common dominion over the bag, and that they habitually used money for their own maintenance as well as for almsgiving.[2] Judas's bag was the classic example which, it was believed, exploded the Franciscan thesis of the absolute poverty of Christ and the apostles. All the secular masters used it as a decisive proof. The Franciscans on their side made it one of their principal tasks to prove that, as an example, it did not hold against their doctrine of poverty. If they could find a hypothesis to cover this, the most awkward piece of the Scriptural evidence, then it followed, *a fortiori*, that they should be able to deal with all the other Scriptural texts alleged against them.

Then, there was a second objection. The Franciscans laid claim to the full imitation of Christ and the apostles on the grounds that they had made a total renunciation of dominion. Bonaventura was following the tradition of the order when he claimed that the highest poverty consisted in this renunciation. But, in effect, by thus making the renunciation of dominion a criterion of poverty, he had adopted a legal definition and was bound to abide by a legal discussion.

Dominium and *usus* both carried legal implications. Gregory IX had declared that the Franciscans should retain *usus*, but renounce *dominium*[3] of every kind. At first, in pursuance of this decree, the friars retained dominion in the hands of their original benefactors; ultimately they found it more convenient to have a comprehensive arrangement and, by the terms of *Ordinem vestrum*, put the dominion over all their goods into the hands of the Papacy.[4] In each case, dominion and use were separated, more or less permanently in the *Quo elongati* system, in perpetuity in *Ordinem vestrum*.

---

[1] John 21.3; Matt. 14.13, 24–34; 15.39.   [2] John 13.28–9.

[3] The term he actually employed was *proprietas*, but no distinction is being made between it and *dominium*. See the full quotation, above, p. 86.

[4] See above, p. 97.

But was it possible in law thus to separate dominion and use? It is the nature of dominion that it should convey some temporal benefit to its holder. All the definitions of rights relating to material goods in the civil law assume this central axiom. The *Institutes* lay down, for example, that *ususfructus* shall not be separated in perpetuity from *proprietas*, lest the *proprietas* in this way cease to bring temporal benefit to its holder.[1] Similarly, in the case of *nudus usus*.[2]

Ordinem vestrum, in particular, assumed that the dominion and use of Franciscan goods would be separated in perpetuity. But, then, what is the value of such dominion to the Popes? If dominion and use are separated for ever, the Papacy will gain no temporal benefit, present or future, and cannot, in effect, be holding a true dominion.

Again, the *Ordinem vestrum* system of Papal ownership was held to cover all goods whatsoever used by the Franciscans. It must therefore comprehend goods consumable in use, such as food, clothing, and the like. But what temporal benefit does the Papacy gain from its dominion over such goods, when their substance disappears in use? Surely in such cases their dominion will be null. If these counter-principles can be shown to have a universal validity, what will be left of the Franciscan claim to total renunciation of dominion?

This was the question which the secular master, Gerard of Abbeville, asked when he cited these legal principles against Bonaventura's fellow-Franciscan, the author of the treatise *Manus quae*.[3] Gerard began by quoting the sentence in the Rule which permitted the Franciscans to receive "necessaria corporis" as the reward for their labour.[4] Did not Francis intend the brothers

---

[1] *Inst.*, II, iv, 1; *Corpus Iuris Civilis*, I, *Institutiones*, ed. P. Krueger, Berolini, 1928, p. 13.   [2] *Inst.*, II, v, 1; ed. Krueger, p. 14.

[3] The sequence of the controversy was as follows. William of St Amour attacked the friars. A Franciscan, probably Thomas of York, replied in 1256, or earlier, with the *Manus quae*. Gerard of Abbeville, taking up William of St Amour's theme, countered the *Manus quae* with his own *Contra adversarium*. After writing, he awaited a suitable moment, and published it in 1269, between July and October. Bonaventura then replied with the *Apologia pauperum*, attacking Gerard and defending the author of the *Manus quae*. See S. Clasen, "Tractatus Gerardi de Abbatisvilla 'Contra adversarium perfectionis Christianae'", *AFH* xxxi (1938), 277–83.

[4] Clasen, art. cit., *AFH* xxxii (1939), 133. *Regula bullata*, 5; *Analekten*, ed. Boehmer, p. 32.

to share the rewards of their labour? He quoted again—from the command to the ministers to take special care to look after the sick and to give clothing to the brothers.[1] Surely such food and clothing will be held in common? The brothers are in sin if they say they hold them as individuals. "Si sint propria", he said, addressing his opponent, "damnabiliter peccatis."[2]

But equally, he argued, it would be false to say that some other temporal agent could hold the dominion over such things which will be consumed by use:

> To say that the use of them is yours alone, and that the dominion pertains to those who have given them, until they are consumed by age, or until the food is taken into the stomach, will appear ridiculous to all, especially since among men use is not distinguished from dominion in things that are utterly consumed by use.[3]

If the dominion which the Franciscans have given up is null, then their claim to the highest poverty will also be made void. It was a telling criticism; and it had to be met by Bonaventura, for his whole treatise was intended to be an answer to Gerard of Abbeville and a vindication of the author of the *Manus quae*.

We may now examine Bonaventura's replies to the Biblical and the legal criticisms of the doctrine of absolute poverty.

His answer to the Biblical criticism is much the more important, and that to which he gave greatest space in the *Apologia*. The heart of this criticism was the example of Judas's bag. To meet it, Bonaventura propounded a doctrine of Christ's condescension to the imperfect.

We must distinguish, Bonaventura argued, among the actions of Christ. They may be considered from a subjective point of view, under the heading "opus interius", or objectively, under the heading "opus exterius". Taken as "opus interius" every action of Christ will be most perfect; but not if taken as "opus exterius".[4] Considered objectively, more than one action of Christ recorded in Scripture was imperfect. There was the case of Judas's bag, which appeared to show Christ departing from the highest perfection of life, and holding common dominion. There was Christ's

[1] Clasen, loc. cit. *Regula bullata*, 4; *Analekten*, ed. Boehmer, p. 32.
[2] Clasen, loc. cit.
[3] Ibid.
[4] Ed. cit., i, 10, 238-9.

neglect of the rules of fasting;[1] there was his flight from persecution;[2] there was his speech in the garden at Gethsemane, before the Passion: "Father, if thou be willing, remove this cup from me."[3] Imperfect as these actions were, they did not diminish Christ's own perfection: they were performed, not from weakness, but from charity, in order to give an example to the imperfect. They were a means adopted by Christ to show his weaker followers that he did not condemn their way of living. Bonaventura drew a parallel with the hypostatic union.[4] The bag did not hold as an example against the belief that Christ demanded renunciation of common dominion from entrants to the highest state of evangelical perfection, any more than his flight from persecution held against the belief that the perfect should suffer martyrdom gladly. Both were acts of condescension to the imperfect.

In support, Bonaventura appealed to the authority of Augustine. Augustine had asked how it was that Christ had had reserves of money carried in the bag, while Paul had had no reserves of wealth, and had lived by his own labour. "Sublimius Paulus", Augustine said, "nunquid et Christo?" But he gave his own reply: "Sublimius Christus, quia misericordius."[5]

The bag, Bonaventura admitted, acted as an example for later generations. For the imperfect, it was an act of condescension. Besides that, it was a pattern for Church administrators, who were thereby recommended to support the poor as well as themselves from church revenues.[6] It was a warning to the avaricious, for the apostle who carried the bag was the only one to be damned;[7] it was a declaration to confute heretics;[8] it was an example of the lesser, monastic form of poverty.[9] As for the apostles themselves, the example of the bag, like the rest of the "non-Franciscan" texts, represented one of the dispensations to which their Rule was subject.[10]

---

[1] Mark 2.18; discussed, ed. cit., cap. v, pp. 257–66.
[2] John, 8.59; discussed, ed. cit., cap. iv, pp. 252–7.
[3] Luke 22.42.
[4] See ed. cit., i, 10, 239.
[5] *Enarrationes in Psalmos*, ciii, 11, *PL* XXXVI, 1367–8; *Apologia*, ed. cit., i, 6, 237.
[6] Ed. cit., vii, 38, 284–5.
[7] Ed. cit., vii, 36, 284.
[8] Ibid.
[9] Ed. cit., vii, 37, 284.   [10] Ed. cit., vii, 39, 285.

One thing it was not, in Bonaventura's account. It was not an example of the most perfect way of living. Christ's call to the highest poverty remained intact. He concluded, in another para-doxical phrase:

> That so Christ held to poverty, that he did not condemn the state of the rich, so also he made himself conform to those who have money, that he kept perfectly the form of the highest poverty.[1]

After the bag, the rest of the "non-Franciscan" texts fell into place comparatively easily. In the case of the apostles, these texts represented only occasional, necessary, dispensations from their regular way of life. When, for example, the apostles in Samaria used money, they were in a hostile country; in effect, it was a time of persecution and they were enabled to relax their rule of renun-ciation of money. Christ himself, indeed, relaxed their rule when he said to the apostles in Luke:

> When I sent you without purse and scrip and shoes, lacked ye anything? and they said, Nothing. Then he said unto them, But now he that hath a purse, let him take it and likewise his scrip: and he that hath no sword, let him sell his garment and buy one.[2]

But after the death of Christ, when the persecution was over, the apostles returned to the rule of life they had been given. When Peter was asked for alms by the lame man at the gate of the temple, he had to reply to him: "Silver and gold have I none."[3] Again, when the members of the early Church sold their goods and brought them to the apostles' feet, the apostles acted only as administrators. The early Church had a common dominion over these goods; but the apostles still kept to their rule, and maintained their own total renunciation of dominion.[4]

Thus Bonaventura, while admitting the existence of contrary texts, reconciled them to his doctrine of absolute poverty. Here, then, we have the last essential development. Absolute poverty represented the regular way of life of Christ and the apostles. It was

[1] Ed. cit., vii, 40, 285.
[2] Luke 22.35-6.
[3] Acts 3.6.
[4] Acts 4.34-5. "Quamvis enim legatur in Actibus, quod multitudini creden-tium erant omnia communia, et quod rerum venditarum pretia ponebantur ad pedes Apostolorum: nequaquam est intelligendum, quod Apostoli proprium aliquid vel commune possederint, quia communitas illa non refertur ad Aposto-los, sed ad turbam. . . ." *Apologia*, ed. cit., vii, 32, 283.

dispensed from time to time. Christ himself relaxed the rule for himself, as an act of condescension to the imperfect; and for his apostles, as a concession in time of persecution. But the example to the perfect still stood. When Christ and the apostles showed to men the way of perfection, they still practised begging, the renunciation of money, and the total renunciation of dominion.

Bonaventura's reply to the Biblical objections, if somewhat tortuous, had the merit of resting on some traditional expositions. But the same can hardly be said of his replies to the legal objections, in some ways, perhaps, the weakest part of the *Apologia's* defence of his doctrine. A certain unease is reflected in the variety of arguments which he employs.

Two principal objections had been made to the Franciscan claim, that as an order they had made a total renunciation of dominion. One was the legal principle that use could not be separated from dominion in things consumable by use. Bonaventura denied that this had universal validity. The principle failed in the relation of a son to the *peculium*. A maxim of the Digest laid it down that: "A son under parental control is considered neither to retain, to recover, nor to acquire possession of his *peculium*."[1] In other words, the son had no rights of dominion over the *peculium*. Yet it was generally admitted that he had a use of the *peculium*. The *peculium* included things which were consumable by use. Therefore it was possible, in law, to hold use without dominion in things consumable by use, and the objection failed.

Alternatively, Bonaventura adopted a *reductio ad absurdum*. If use could not be separated from dominion in things consumable by use, then a monk would become an individual proprietor in such things—which was generally held to be false.[2]

The other principal objection was that since the Popes gained no temporal benefit from Franciscan goods, they had no true dominion over them. Bonaventura admitted they gained no temporal benefit, but argued that they did gain a spiritual benefit, by thus caring for their spiritual children, the Franciscans.[3] This answer involved a confusion of two disciplines—of theology and law.

---

[1] *Dig.*, L, 17, 93; *Corpus Iuris Civilis*, I, *Digesta*, ed. T. Mommsen, P. Krueger, p. 923. *Apologia*, ed. cit., xi, 7, 312.

[2] Ed. cit., xi, 8, 313.   [3] Ed. cit., xi, 7, 312.

Alternatively, he countered with another principle of the law: "A benefit is not conferred upon a person who is unwilling to accept it."[1] The Franciscans did not intend to receive, nor their benefactors to give dominion; therefore, they did not hold dominion, and again the objection failed.

Finally, he attempted to sweep all objections away by alleging, first, the Papal authority, which had sanctioned this system of ownership over Franciscan goods, and secondly, the example of Christ, who had made a total renunciation of dominion.[2]

It is not surprising that Bonaventura's reply to the legal criticism of absolute poverty should have been the weakest part of his treatise. He was not a lawyer at all, but a theologian. The legal part of his case, as that of the other Franciscan controversialists, rested on the decisions of the Papal Bulls, *Quo elongati* and *Ordinem vestrum*. Bonaventura inherited the concept of total renunciation of dominion; and, as we have seen, it sprang from the mind of Ugolino rather than from that of Francis. More than once, the *Apologia* gives the impression that Bonaventura does not have his heart in the legal discussions about the doctrine. He does not always get his Bulls right. He assumes that *Quo elongati*, and not *Ordinem vestrum*, received the dominion over Franciscan goods into the hands of the Papacy;[3] but this was untrue. The most that *Quo elongati* did in this direction, strictly, was to declare that any alienation of movable goods by the order would require the assent of the cardinal protector.[4] Through the whole body of the text, when he speaks of the rights of ownership renounced by the order, he uses undifferentiated terms; he does not define them; and only in one paragraph, apparently, does he split up these terms, and use more precise terminology from the civil law.[5] Later Franciscans developed the thought of this paragraph and erected on it a more precise doctrine of renunciation; but Bonaventura was prepared to cast off a few sentences and to leave the legal aspect of the Franciscan renunciation largely undiscussed.

The Franciscans at this time, and Bonaventura is the best

---

[1] *Dig.*, L, 17, 69; ed. T. Mommsen, P. Krueger, p. 922. *Apologia*, ed. cit., xl, 9, 313.

[2] Ed. cit., xi, 10–11, 313–4.

[3] Ed. cit., xi, 6, 312.

[4] *Epitome*, ed. Eubel, p. 230a. See above, p. 86.

[5] Ed. cit., xi, 5, 312.

example of them, showed themselves aware of the objections to their doctrine. They were prepared to argue effectively with the secular masters on their own ground. But they were not always deeply interested in the technical details of their renunciations. On the question of dominion, their feeling was very much that of Bonaventura, when answering the question: "So who will be assigned the *proprietas* over these things? I reply, that whoever it does belong to, it is not mine or the order's, and this is enough to satisfy the purity of my conscience." [1] Like Francis, the centre of their thoughts about poverty lay in the scenes of Scripture, which, as Douie so well says, became as real to them as the streets, churches, and lecture-rooms of medieval Paris. [2]

Gerard of Abbeville made no reply, and he and his kind were given a formal refutation by the Papacy, ten years after the appearance of the *Apologia*. The Papacy then gave official approval to Bonaventura's doctrine. We shall conclude our account of the development of the doctrine of absolute poverty by describing in the next chapter this official approbation.

---

[1] *Epistola de tribus quaestionibus ad innominatum magistrum*, 6; *Opera Omnia* VIII, 333. These are words corresponding very closely with the Exposition on the Rule of Hugues de Digne. For exact comparison see Esser in *FS* xxvii (1940), 152.

[2] "The conviction that the Franciscan ideal was to realize the Incarnation by following Christ in poverty, hunger, and nakedness made every incident in the gospel story as real to Bonaventura and Pecham as the streets, churches, and lecture-rooms of medieval Paris . . ." Douie, *The Conflict between the Seculars and the Mendicants*, p. 21.

6

EXIIT QUI SEMINAT

IN THE summer of 1273 Bonaventura received the red hat
from Gregory X. At Pentecost of the following year he presided over the chapter-general of Lyons, which elected his
successor, Jerome of Ascoli; shortly afterwards, exhausted by his
labours on behalf of the union between the Greek and Latin
churches, he died and was buried at Lyons.

Jerome was not a significant figure in the line of generals.
Much of his time in office was occupied with diplomatic missions
undertaken for the Papacy. After four years he was made a
cardinal. Finally, the chapter-general of Assisi elected in his place
his former deputy, Bonagratia of St John in Perseceto. As soon as
he was elected he received a request from the Pope, Nicholas III,
that he should confer with the chapter, in order to discover whether
they had any queries to raise with him about the life of the order.
Negotiations issued in a request for a Papal decision about the
Rule and the Franciscan observance. The initiative, it seems, came
primarily from the Pope, who until his election had been cardinal
protector to the order.[1] The result was the best-known of all the
Papal clarifications of the Rule, the Bull *Exiit qui seminat*, issued
in August 1279.[2]

In form, the new Bull resembled its predecessors, *Quo elongati*
and *Ordinem vestrum*. It consisted of a series of clauses, generally
introduced by quotations from the *Regula bullata*, in which the
Pope adjudicated upon difficult points in the Rule. Many of these
clauses touched on the same points as the previous Bulls. Sometimes, indeed, as in the case of the old problem of the obligation
of the Testament, the wording is the same.[3] One of the chief aims
of the Bull was the same as in the past: to quieten the anxieties of

[1] *Chronica XXIV Generalium, AF* III, 367.

[2] *Epitome,* ed. Eubel, pp. 290–300. It was received into the Sext by Boniface
VIII.

[3] *Exiit,* ed. cit., p. 299; *Quo elongati,* ed. cit., p. 229.

the friars about the extent of the obligations to which they were held by their vows. The Papacy here assumed its traditional rôle of the Franciscans' friend. Nicholas, in words reminiscent of Gregory IX, recalled his long-standing affection for the order, his work on their behalf as cardinal protector, and the personal contacts he had had with the surviving companions of Francis.[1] The prevailing tone is that of *Quo elongati*: we see here the same concern for tender consciences in the order, the same trend towards moderate canonist's solutions of difficulties.

Nevertheless, there are important differences. The two earlier Bulls were intended more or less exclusively for the friars themselves; this one was directed as much to the outside world as to the friars. Added to the traditional aim of quietening consciences within the order was a new one, that of putting an end to the attacks from outside upon the Franciscan way of life.[2] The previous Bulls dealt with the administration of Franciscan life; this one dealt also with its doctrinal basis.

The distinction will emerge from a comparison of the preambles to these Bulls: where in *Quo elongati* and *Ordinem vestrum* we have general expressions of esteem alone, in *Exiit* we have a sequence of dogmatic statements.[3] The Bull began with an adaptation of the parable of the sower. Christ went forth to sow the seed of his doctrine in the world. Some fell by the way, some on stony ground, some was choked by the cares of the world. Some, however, fell on good ground, that is, on the order founded by Francis. Through his Rule he carried the seed of the evangelical doctrine to his followers. Of these the Bull says:

> These are those who have professed that holy rule, which is founded on the words of the gospel, supported by the example of the life of Christ, secured by the words and actions of his Apostles, the founders of the church militant.[4]

Then, of the order:

> This is the way of religious life pure and immaculate with God and the Father, which came down from the father of all illumination,

---

[1] Ed. cit., p. 291b.

[2] ". . . visum est Nobis mordacibus huiusmodi vias mordendi praecludere, aliqua, quae in ipsa regula videri poterant dubia, declarare, nonnulla etiam per praedecessores nostros declarata pleniore claritate disserere, in aliquibus etiam regulam ipsam contingentibus puritati eorundem conscientiae providere" (*sic*), ed. cit., p. 291b.

[3] Ed. cit., pp. 290b–1a.   [4] Ed. cit., p. 291a.

was given by his Son to the apostles by example and word and finally given at the inspiration of the holy Spirit to St Francis and those who follow him, and so contains, as it were, in itself, the testimony of the whole Trinity.[1]

The Bull thus accepted the evangelical basis of the Rule, in the life and teaching of Christ and the apostles, and the inspiration of the Holy Spirit on Francis writing it.

In the body of the Bull Nicholas dealt directly with the evangelical basis of Franciscan poverty. Speaking of their renunciation of common dominion, he said:

> . . . we say that such renunciation of *proprietas* of all things, both individually and in common, for God, is meritorious and holy, and taught in word and confirmed in example by Christ showing the way of perfection and channelled on by the first founders of the church militant, as they had drawn it from that fount, through the streams of their doctrine and life.[2]

Here are several propositions, that Christ, when showing to men the way of perfection, renounced common dominion, that his apostles did likewise, and that their example was to be imitated by those who wished to follow the way of perfection. It will be noticed that these are exactly the propositions defended by Bonaventura against Gerard of Abbeville in his *Apologia pauperum*. It is clear that *Exiit* is giving an official sanction to the Franciscan doctrine of absolute poverty.

Immediately below, the objections to the Franciscan position are stated, and then resolved, just as they are in the *Apologia*.

First, we have the Biblical objection—the bag, which Judas carried.[3] It is met, as in the *Apologia*, by distinguishing between the works of Christ performed as an example to the perfect and those performed out of condescension to the imperfect. In origin, as we have seen,[4] this distinction derived from Augustine. But it

---

[1] Ibid.

[2] Ed. cit., p. 293a. In Eubel "vitam perfectionis" is a misprint in this passage for "viam perfectionis": see *Bullarium Franciscanum*, ed. J. H. Sbaralea, III, 407b, also *Seraphicae Legislationis Textus Originales*, Ad Claras Aquas, 1897, p. 191.

[3] John 13.29. For further details of the connection between *Exiit* and the *Apologia* and other writings of Bonaventura, see V. Maggiani, "De relatione scriptorum quorumdam S. Bonaventurae ad Bullam 'Exiit' Nicolai III (1279)", *AFH* v (1912), 3–21.

[4] See above, p. 136.

would appear that the Bull did not draw the distinction direct
from Augustine. It uses the same language as Bonaventura.
Exiit, speaking of other examples of Christ's condescension, has
this phrase: "non tantum carne, sed et mente condescendit
infirmis".[1] Bonaventura uses, in effect, the same words; but they
do not appear in Augustine.[2]

Exiit summarizes the doctrine of condescension to the imperfect
in words which correspond to those of the *Apologia*.[3]

It is clear that *Exiit's* treatment of the problem of Judas's bag
is nothing more than a compressed version of the *Apologia pauperum*.

Secondly, we have the legal objection to the Franciscan doctrine.

Here again there is a close correspondence between the Bull
and the *Apologia*. *Exiit* states the objection based on the maxim
of the civil law, that use cannot be separated from dominion in
perpetuity, lest dominion become fruitless to its holder. It is an
objection given in the *Apologia*. It is met by the same argument as
Bonaventura employed, that the retention of dominion by the
Papacy on behalf of the friars was not fruitless, since it brought
a spiritual benefit to the Pope. Again, there is identical wording,[4]
and a direct borrowing from the *Apologia*.

But the legal exposition of Bonaventura has not been transferred
to the Bull *in toto* and unaltered, as was his theological exposition.
There are omissions and alterations. The terms Bonaventura used
have been changed. In one paragraph of the *Apologia*, where he
dealt rather more precisely with the terms of the civil law, he had
adduced a list of four relevant legal terms. They were *proprietas,
possessio, ususfructus, simplex usus*.[5] *Exiit*, while taking over the
substance of Bonaventura's argument, changed the terms, presumably to give a greater precision. Five were now to be considered:
proprietas, possessio, ususfructus, ius utendi, and *simplex usus facti*. The
order, it was explained, held only *simplex usus facti* in certain
temporal goods: this was a license to use certain goods, revocable
at the will of the conceder.[6]

The other principal legal objection, that use cannot be separated

---

[1] Ed. cit., p. 293a.
[2] *Apologia*, ed. cit., i, 6, 237a.
[3] *Epitome*, ed. Eubel, p. 293a. Compare *Apologia*, ed. cit., i, 10, 239.
[4] *Exiit*, ed. cit., p. 293b; *Apologia pauperum*, ed. cit., xi, 7, 312.
[5] Ed. cit., xi, 5, 312. See above p. 139.
[6] Ed. cit., p. 293b.

from dominion in things consumable by use, was not so much as mentioned. Nor was Bonaventura's defence on this point. It can hardly have been left out by carelessness. The commission who drafted the Bull may be assumed to have read this passage of the *Apologia*, because they employed in another context the two legal examples brought forward by Bonaventura to counter this objection.[1] Also, we know that the commission had expert legal advice: Benedetto Gaetani, the future Boniface VIII, had a hand in the drafting.[2] Might it have been that they considered this legal objection too penetrating to be included in a defence of the Franciscan Rule? Whatever the motive, this omission was to be of some importance later on, when *Exiit qui seminat* came to be re-examined, in less favourable circumstances.

We may now reach our conclusion. The whole substance of the doctrinal exposition of poverty given in *Exiit* has been taken from Bonaventura's *Apologia pauperum*. Official sanction has been given to the Franciscan doctrine of the absolute poverty of Christ and the apostles. Bonaventura's reply to the Biblical objection has been taken over unchanged; his reply to the legal objection has been modified and given greater precision.

What was the significance of this decision in favour of the Bonaventuran doctrine? Later, in the fourteenth century, under John XXII, it became a matter of the utmost importance to decide whether it should be regarded as, in the full sense, a dogmatic decision from the Pope, or only an administrative arrangement. Discussion about it continued long after: Bellarmine wrote about it,[3] and the anti-infallibilist party at the time of the Vatican Council of 1870 included the case of *Exiit* among their arguments.[4]

Clearly, there can be no easy answer. This much may be said. On the one hand, *Exiit* was not a formal dogmatic decision comparable with those issued by a General Council. The decisions about the poverty of Christ were embedded in a series of clauses

---

[1] I.e., the example of the monk and of the *filiusfamilias*. *Exiit*, ed. cit., p. 294a; *Apologia*, ed. cit., xi, 7, 312, and xi, 8, 313.

[2] *Chronica XXIV Generalium, AF* III, 369.

[3] *De summo Pontifice*, IV, xiv; *Disputationes*, I, Ingolstadii, 1601, coll. 1019–21.

[4] They believed that there was a contradiction on the question of Christ's poverty between *Exiit* and the Bulls of John XXII. For refutations, see B. Jungmann, *Dissertationes selectae in Historiam Ecclesiasticam* VI, Ratisbonae, Neo Eboraci, Cincinnatii, 1886, "De Minoritarum turbis", pp. 174–88; I. Jeiler, "Armut", Wetzer and Welte *Kirchenlexicon*, I, 1393–1401.

dealing with the administrative arrangements of the friars. As far as can be seen, there was no preliminary discussion with any other interested parties apart from the Franciscans. The fact that Nicholas asked for doubts on matters discussed in *Exiit* to be referred to the Papacy suggests that he did not regard these decisions as irreversible.[1]

On the other hand, it is plain from Nicholas's language that he intended this Bull to be a final settlement of disputes about poverty. In his conclusion he referred to the failure of his predecessors' efforts to end attacks on the Rule, or to settle all doubts about the friars' observance. He demanded, from the friars, a strict adherence to his settlement of the internal questions of their observance, and, from the outside world, full acceptance of his decisions about the legitimacy of the observance.[2] He forbade the use of glosses, under pain of excommunication, and insisted on the literal interpretation of his words.[3] This last provision was curiously reminiscent of Francis's prohibition of glosses in the Testament;[4] and in the long run was hardly more effective than the words of the founder had been.

The Bull marks the end of the process of the development of the doctrine of the absolute poverty of Christ. We have now traced the elaboration of the doctrine, step by step, from its beginnings in the mind of St Francis, 1210–26, to its official approbation by the Papacy in 1279. We have attempted to re-create St Francis's view of absolute poverty. We have seen how the changes in the life of the order between 1226 and 1247 came to affect the definition of the doctrine of absolute poverty. We have examined St Bonaventura's exposition of the poverty of Christ, and, especially, his use of the concept of Christ's condescension to the imperfect. Finally, in this chapter, we have shown how the Papacy came to

---

[1] ". . . sed si quid penes aliquem in his ambiguitatis emerserit, hoc ad culmen praedictae sedis Apostolicae deducatur, ut ex auctoritate Apostolica sua in hoc manifestetur intentio, cui soli concessum est in his statuta condere et condita declarare", ed. cit., p. 300a.

[2] Ed. cit., p. 299b.

[3] "Itaque . . . districte praecipimus, ut praesens constitutio, cum ipsam legi contigerit, sicut prolata est, sic fideliter exponatur ad litteram . . . super ipsa constitutione glossae non fiant, nisi forsan per quas verbum vel verbi sensus . . . quasi grammaticaliter ad litteram vel intelligibilius exponatur . . .", ed. cit., pp. 299b–300a.

[4] *Testamentum*, 12.

accept the Bonaventuran doctrine of absolute poverty, and to give it official approbation. *Exiit* is the last step in the process: it marks the apogee of absolute poverty.

But our task is not yet done. We must now introduce the Spiritual–Conventual controversy within the order, which developed in the last decades of the thirteenth century and the early years of the fourteenth. The relevance of this conflict must be understood. It is not a detachable episode of Franciscan history, but an integral part of the history of the doctrine of absolute poverty. We have now a reverse process to describe: not the elaboration, and the formal acceptance, of the doctrine of the absolute poverty of Christ, but, instead, the discrediting of this doctrine, its misuse by rival factions, and its final condemnation. The Spiritual–Conventual controversy has a vital part to play in this process. It acts as a catalyst, exposing to the outside world all the weaknesses of the doctrine of absolute poverty as it had developed in the thirteenth century, finally drawing down the official condemnation of the Papacy. The Spirituals and the Conventuals each believed in the poverty of Christ, although the emphasis of their interpretations was different: between them they succeeded in bringing about its destruction.

The Spiritual–Conventual controversies, it should be stated, are not solely concerned with the practice of poverty. If their starting-point lies in the reaction of the most conscientious members to the developments in the observance, from the last quarter of the thirteenth century, the means of expressing that reaction are doctrinal as well as practical. There is a strong doctrinal element in the dispute. The Spirituals, in search of reform, put forward a theory of poverty which, despite traditional attachments, amounted to a new development. The Conventuals, in reply, gave a new emphasis to the traditional orthodox view of the poverty of Christ. The ultimate outcome of this doctrinal conflict was the condemnation of absolute poverty by the Pope.

But if the doctrinal issue is of central importance, it can only be understood in the context of the whole story of the internecine strife in the order during these years. Discords arose in the order, centring on poverty, but penetrating into many other aspects of the order's life, and being echoed back. Superiors inside the order, and authorities outside, by attempting to intervene succeeded only in exacerbating disputes and further disseminating the trouble-making doctrines. It will be necessary for us to mention each area of distribution and each intervention in order to provide a true picture and to show how many aspects of life were touched on here—philosophy, popular heresy, Joachimism, politics, both of States and Popes. For each of these factors affected the course of the dispute, and so the eventual outcome in the condemnation of the doctrine of absolute poverty.

The story of the Spiritual–Conventual disputes needs to be retold. Much has been discovered and numbers of new texts edited since Ehrle, and later Douie, wrote their accounts. Yet there has been no attempt to relate this new work to a wider theme. Knowles, speaking of this time in his *Religious Orders*, says: "The extreme complexity of the subject, the fragmentary nature of the sources and the controversial topics involved have combined to deter scholars from dealing with this period of Franciscan history."[1] Undoubtedly this is true, provided that it is applied to general surveys; and so a fresh narrative is worth attempting.

We shall then take up the thread of the history of the observance of poverty in the order where we left it, towards the end of the generalate of St Bonaventura. The object is to explain the background of the controversy on the poverty of Christ under John XXII: to show how the logic of events and the rigour of the Pope's intellect drove him to see behind all the troubles and disturbances of the Franciscan order that vital doctrine of the absolute poverty of Christ.

[1] D. Knowles, *The Religious Orders in England*, I, Cambridge, 1948, p. 246, n. 1.

7

RELAXATION AND THE GROWTH OF
PARTIES

AT THE start of the period which we shall now cover the
Franciscans had recently emerged from a twenty-seven
year period of stabilization, dominated by the generalates
of two of Francis's greatest sons, John of Parma and Bonaventura.
They had routed their opponents among the secular clergy and
the masters in the universities. In *Exiit qui seminat* their doctrine
of poverty had been accepted by the Church, and their practice
of poverty officially sanctioned. To judge from the benefactions
they received, their prestige remained high in the outside world;
within the order also, despite some sporadic disturbances and
despite a certain undertow of anxiety about the practice of
poverty, there was still unity and, for the most part, a comparatively strict observance.

At the end of this time, in the last years of Clement V and the
vacancy between his death and the accession of John XXII,
matters stood otherwise. Then, divisions among the Franciscans
had grown so serious that it had been necessary for the Papacy
to appoint a commission to inquire into their affairs. Evidence of
relaxation had been uncovered and published to the world in a
new Papal Bull, *Exivi de paradiso*. Rigorists in Provence had been
withdrawn into separate convents; in one convent friars had come
to blows; elsewhere rigorist groups had broken into revolt, and
left the order to form congregations of their own.

The disputes which had brought the Franciscan order to this
pass, though complicated by other issues, still centred on the
observance of poverty. They were a recrudescence of earlier
conflicts—but with a difference. The rigorists were now a much
stronger force. They were stronger numerically. They acquired
some powerful patrons outside the order. Through the hands of
their leader, Olivi, they assumed a new weapon, that of the

doctrine of the *usus pauper*, which claimed that restriction in use was as integral a part of Franciscan poverty as the renunciation of dominion.[1]

The Conventuals, similarly, closed their ranks. To counter the *usus pauper*, they put forward their own view, that the vow of poverty was comprehended in the renunciation of dominion alone, and did not itself demand a restriction in the use of earthly goods. A characteristic type of superior began to emerge among them, lax where the suppression of abuses of poverty was concerned, rigid to a fault when it came to breaches of obedience by the Spirituals. Moderates like Bonaventura, who cared for the detail of the observance of poverty, diminished in numbers or lost influence. Gradually it became apparent that the Community was either unable or unwilling to check relaxations; the protests of the Spirituals, far from assisting to this end, tended rather to stiffen opposition to reform.

Under the stress of persecution, the Spirituals tended to become more fanatical and extravagant. As they saw their policy rejected by the main body of the friars, the revolutionary demand for separation from the Community began to gain ground among them. For a time, while the Papal commission made its investigation, they hoped that they might gain the ear of the Papacy, and thus impose their policy on the order. When, however, this failed, the demand for separation became too strong. Individual groups broke away, and in doing so discredited their more moderate fellows who remained under obedience.

Indeed, the whole history of the Spiritual movement among the Franciscans can be written in terms of the betrayal of more moderate reformers by the fanatics in their entourage. In the fourteenth century, it was more than all the presence of extremist groups in Provence, both Franciscans and their lay supporters among the Beguins, which prevented the Spirituals from gaining the recognition for which they hoped. These extremists, with their Joachimite dreams and their plans for the redemption of the whole Church through poverty, brought discredit on the movement for the reform of the order. Ultimately, as we shall see, they brought

---

[1] *Usus pauper* is a technical term employed throughout the subsequent controversy to indicate the obligation imposed on the friars by their vow of poverty to restrict their use of things to rigid necessities.

discredit also on the doctrine of the absolute poverty of Christ, which lay at the heart of the Franciscan observance, of both Spiritual and Conventual alike.

The ministers-general in the last quarter of the thirteenth century did not make their mark upon the order in the way that their predecessors had done. Less will be heard of them in this chapter. Throughout the decades which followed *Exiit*, the dominating figure seems not to be the general, but an individual friar, who never, as far as we know, held office other than that of *lector*, the Provençal, Petrus Johannis Olivi.[1]

It was a disturbed and confusing time in the history of medieval thought. The reception of Aristotelianism led to great controversy and a series of condemnations. In 1277 we have the condemnations of the Aristotelians by Kilwardby and Étienne Tempier; again, similar action by Pecham at Oxford in 1284. There is the literature of the *correctoria*, the measures taken, after some hesitation, by the Dominicans to inculcate Thomism, and by the Franciscans to maintain their unity and doctrinal tradition against Thomism. There are other sources of controversy, particularly between Franciscans and Dominicans, on such issues as the observance of poverty and the degree of obedience owed to a superior. Generally, it was a time of unsettlement, in which superiors were unusually conscious of their duty to suppress doctrinal deviations.[2]

It is against this background that one should set the genesis of the long disputes about Olivi's writings, which split the order and did so much to bring about the decline of the Franciscans in the fourteenth century.

The first difficulties about Olivi arose some time before the issue of *Exiit qui seminat*, when Jerome of Ascoli examined certain theses put forward by him.[3] Olivi later claimed he was exculpated on this occasion;[4] certainly he lost scant prestige by the examination, for when negotiations were begun in preparation for the

---

[1] In strict form, Olieu rather than Olivi. A. Thomas, "Le vrai nom du Frère Mineur Petrus Johannis Olivi", *Annales du Midi*, Toulouse, 1913, p. 68f. But the less correct form, Olivi, is now too well established to be supplanted.

[2] On this background, D. Laberge, "Fr. Petri Ioannis Olivi O.F.M., tria scripta sui ipsius apologetica annorum 1283 et 1285", *AFH* xxviii (1935), 118–19, and refs. given.

[3] F. Ehrle, "Petrus Johannis Olivi, sein Leben und seine Schriften", *ALKG* III (1887), 413–14.

[4] Art. cit., p. 414, n. 2 and 3.

issue of the Bull, at Rome in 1279, he was asked by his provincial to submit a memorandum on Franciscan poverty for the guidance of the Papal commission.[1]

This was apparently concerned only with the renunciation of dominion by the Franciscans; but before *Exiit* Olivi had also written a *quaestio* expounding his doctrine of the *usus pauper*.[2] In this he began by supporting the traditional and Bonaventuran thesis, that the Franciscan Rule excludes individual and common dominion. Having proved this, he turned his attention to another aspect of Franciscan poverty, not discussed in any detail by Bonaventura in his writings in defence of the order. This was the *usus pauper*. He put the question: Is the *usus pauper* included in the counsel or vow of evangelical perfection, so that it is of its substance and integrity? He gave a strong affirmative in reply. The reasons, he said, which have been adduced to prove that the highest poverty is one of the principal counsels of evangelical perfection better prove this proposition than the necessity of renunciation of common dominion. He supports this view by authorities from the order, Pecham, and Bonaventura in his encyclicals, urging the necessity of a moderate use of the goods which the Franciscans are permitted to enjoy by their owners. The relation, he said, of the *usus pauper* to the renunciation of dominion is as that of form to matter; this he justifies by an appeal to common sense: "Omnis homo deridet. . . ."[3] Finally, he discusses the relation of the obligation of the *usus pauper* to the vow of poverty taken at profession. Will breach of the *usus pauper* involve breach of the vow, and thus mortal sin? The evident dangers of imposing too strict an obligation lead him to the conclusion that not every deviation from the *usus pauper* is a mortal sin, but only a deviation so great that the use could be called rich rather than poor. To go on horseback without due reason once would not be a mortal sin; to do so habitually would be.[4]

What rigorist attitudes were involved in practice in this doctrine of *usus pauper* may be seen from Olivi's subsequent discussion of the position of Franciscans who had been made bishops, and of the legitimacy of the use of procurators. In the first case he insists

---

[1] Ehrle, art. cit., p. 415.
[2] Extracts ed. Ehrle, *ALKG* III, 507–14.
[3] Ibid., p. 508.   [4] Ibid., pp. 509–10.

that such Franciscan bishops, once elected, have no cause to be dispensed from the obligation of the *usus pauper*; indeed at one moment he comes close to saying that the observance of the *usus pauper* was essential to the office of any bishop. Of the Franciscan bishops he said they were obliged to the *usus pauper* when they were elected "aliquo modo amplius quam antea", and he followed this up with the more perilous statement that the office of bishop was not held in full perfection unless it was held with the observance of evangelical perfection.[1] This in turn involved the obligation of the *usus pauper*: it was in fact imposed on the apostles by Christ at the time of the first missionary journey. In the second case he gave only a most grudging assent to the appointment of procurators: they were allowed "per indulgentiam" and then only provided that they were not appointed direct by the friars.[2]

For the time being, Olivi's doctrine of the *usus pauper* appears to have been uncontested. *Exiit qui seminat*, without using Olivi's term, did, for the first time in the series of Franciscan Bulls, include a general warning about the Franciscan use of material goods.[3] In this there was implied Olivi's view, that renunciation of dominion necessarily involves restriction in use; on the other hand, a full discretion over the use of goods was given to ministers and custodians, and there was no mention of his most characteristic thesis, of the relation of the obligation of the *usus pauper* to the vow of poverty. It cannot be said that *Exiit* specifically supports Olivi's *usus pauper*. Bonagratia of St John in Persiceto, however, did give it some official backing in two encyclicals to the order. Both, unfortunately, have been lost; but we have the witness of Olivi's disciple, Ubertino da Casale, that they did put forward his

---

[1] ". . . cum status episcopalis et eius sublimitas et eius principalia officia quantum est de se summe exigant perfectionem evangelicam in hiis, qui ad ipsum assumuntur et in tantum, quod nunquam status ille habetur in plena decentia et perfectione sua, nisi simul cum perfectionis evangelice observantia teneatur . . .", ibid., p. 511. [2] Ibid., p. 513.

[3] "Insuper nec utensilia nec alia, quorum usum ad necessitatem et officiorum sui status executionem licet habere (non enim omnium rerum habere debent usum, ut dictum est), ad ullam superfluitatem, divitias seu copiam, quae deroget paupertati, vel thesaurisationem, vel eo animo, ut ea distrahant seu vendant, nec sub colore providentiae in futurum, nec alia occasione, quinimmo in omnibus appareat in eis quoad dominium omnimoda abdicatio et in usu necessitas. Haec autem secundum exigentiam personarum et locorum ministri et custodes simul et separatim in suis administrationibus et custodiis disponant. . . ." *Epitome*, ed. Eubel, p. 294b.

doctrine. He adduced this fact in controversy with the Community before the Council of Vienne, and it was never denied by his opponents.[1]

In other quarters Olivi's doctrine was not so well received. Opposition among his fellow-friars led him to write a second treatise, this time solely concerned with the *usus pauper*.[2] It was sharply polemical; in it Olivi compared his opponents with the enemies of the order among the secular masters and the Dominicans, who were bent on destroying the Franciscan doctrine of evangelical poverty. No names were given, and the work can only be given a *terminus a quo*, in 8 October 1279, the date of a document of Bonagratia's cited in the text.

Two more writings, both undated, reveal the existence of a conflict between Olivi and other Franciscans. One is a controversial work, concerned especially with the question of poverty, and directed against another Franciscan, a certain "fr. A.",[3] the other a personal *apologia*, addressed to a group of Olivi's supporters, and defending his position on nineteen articles, all of them dealing with philosophical matters.[4] The last document makes it clear that Olivi was faced with a general inquiry by the minister-general into all his works and not merely those relating to poverty.

Joseph Koch, who has written a series of articles on Olivi as part of his studies of the theological condemnations of 1270 to 1329, has produced a hypothesis linking all three documents. The genesis of the trouble about Olivi, he says, was the controversy with "fr. A." It was based on the *usus pauper*. The Franciscans unnamed in the treatise on the *usus pauper* were "fr. A." and his friends. In the conflict on poverty "fr. A." was unsuccessful, because Olivi had the support of the minister-general, Bonagratia. Failing here, he turned his attention to Olivi's philosophical work. Certain articles were excerpted; an inquiry was put in hand by

---

[1] See *ALKG* III, p. 82, lines 14–20.

[2] Extracts, ed. Ehrle, *ALKG* III, 514–17.

[3] *Petrus Johannis Olivi Provencalis Ord. Min., Quodlibeta et impugnationes quorundam articulorum; item defensiones aliorum articulorum*, Venetiis, 1509, foll. 42ra–53ra. This has proved unobtainable: ref. has been taken from the article of Joseph Koch cited below, p. 155, n. 1.

[4] Extracts in Gratien, "Une lettre inédite de Pierre de Jean Olivi", *Études Franciscaines*, xxix (1913), 414–22. See also Ehrle, "Petrus Johannis Olivi, sein Leben und seine Schriften", *ALKG* III, 426–7, 469, 477–8.

the minister-general; Olivi wrote the *apologia* to his supporters; and thus the long controversy began.[1]

If the views of Olivi on poverty were the starting-point of the conflict, as Koch suggests, general issues of philosophy and theology soon displaced them at the centre of the stage. In 1283 a commission of seven Franciscan masters and bachelors of the University of Paris, appointed by Bonagratia to examine Olivi's doctrine, made their report to the minister-general. They censured a series of excerpts from Olivi, and issued a list, the *Littera septem sigillorum*, containing twenty-two articles, supposedly reversing Olivi's theses, on which they were all agreed. Of these twenty-two, four only could be said to be in any way concerned with the question of poverty.[2] Among the excerpts there was a similar disproportion between the items treating poverty and those touching other topics current in the Schools. Of some thirty-four items, dealing with such matters as the Divine Essence, the union of soul and body in man, matrimony as a sacrament, and the bestowal of grace and habitual virtues by baptism, five at most were related to poverty.[3]

It could, of course, be assumed that the miscellaneous philosophical and theological points raised against Olivi were intended to act as a cover for the items concerned with poverty, the one true ground for dispute. One of the thirty-four excerpts dealt with the *usus pauper*, the centre of the controversy with "fr. A."; Olivi's teaching on this point was censured by the commission as "commonly false and perilous to our state".[4] Another dealt with the closely allied question of the obligation of the *usus pauper* for

---

[1] J. Koch, "Die Verurteilung Olivis auf dem Konzil von Vienne und ihre Vorgeschichte", *Scholastik* v (1930), 489–522. For his list of documents and editions of Olivi, see pp. 490–1.

[2] No. 12 (on the *usus pauper*); no. 13 (on Franciscan bishops); no. 14 (on the burial of the dead); no. 15 (on the right of burial). See *Littera septem sigillorum*, ed. G. Fussenegger, *AFH* xlvii (1954), 45–53.

[3] The document which contained the excerpts from Olivi together with the marginal comments of the commission is generally known as the *Rotulus*. No primary text of it is extant, but it has been quoted fully by Olivi in the *apologia* he made to his censors in 1285. This is the second of the three works of Olivi edited by Laberge in 1935–6. See *AFH* xxviii (1935), 130–55, 374–407. The issues relating to poverty are as follows: burial rights, discussed by Olivi, ed. cit., pp. 378–81, the *usus pauper*, pp. 381–6, Franciscan bishops, pp. 386–90, procurators, pp. 390–4, the Rule and the gospel, pp. 394–5.

[4] Laberge, "Tria scripta apologetica", *AFH* xxviii (1935), p. 382, lines 7–8.

Franciscan bishops.[1] Later, we know, in the 1290s and before the Council of Vienne, the doctrine of the *usus pauper* was potentially the most dangerous of Olivi's teachings, and therefore one to be most rigorously suppressed by the Community.

But we are not thereby justified in assuming that the *usus pauper* was the vital issue confronting the commission of bachelors and masters at Paris in 1283. Since Ehrle produced his fundamental article on Olivi in the *Archiv für Litteratur und Kirchengeschichte* in 1887, much more work has been done on Olivi as a thinker, particularly by the Jesuit, Jansen. Perhaps the most important result of these investigations has been to reveal the common ground between Olivi and the later nominalists.

There are significant points of similarity, for example, between Olivi's work and that of Durandus of St Pourçain, a Dominican censured in 1314 by his colleagues for nominalist views.[2] Ockham, it has been proved recently, borrowed from Olivi one of his most fundamental tenets, a thesis on the predicaments which had been censured in article fifteen of the *Rotulus*.[3] It is becoming increasingly clear that the basic charges brought against Olivi in 1283 were the same as those alleged against the nominalists in the fourteenth century. The censuring of Olivi, we conclude, was based on real issues, and not trumped up to conceal an attack on his doctrine of poverty.

The difficulties encountered by judges in the fourteenth century who examined the work of nominalists are well known. No doubt the commission of seven masters and bachelors in 1283 found the task of examination no easier than did their successors. We may reasonably assume that it was the complexities in the material before them which led the commission to adopt new methods. They made actual excerpts from Olivi's works. Before this, it had been the custom to summarize a theologian's doctrine in a series of concise theses. In their conclusions, they employed a graduated sequence of censures, ranging from "haereticum" to "temerarium", whereas judges had hitherto been content with the one undifferentiated term, "error". The *Rotulus*, in which the

---

[1] Ibid., pp. 386–90.
[2] Koch, "Die Verurteilung", *Scholastik* v (1930), 513–514.
[3] Laberge, "Tria scripta apologetica", *AFH* xxviii (1935), 129; A. Maier, "Zu einigen Problemen der Ockhamforschung", *AFH* xlvi (1953), 174–81.

commission assembled the excerpts from Olivi and their own judgements on them, was an event in theology. It was, as Koch puts it,
"the first list of errors with strictly graduated censures . . . ."[1]

There were unusual features, not only in the actions of the
commission, but also in the proceedings of the minister-general
which followed. In itself, the report of the commission was
couched in purely intellectual terms. No condemnation of Olivi
personally was envisaged. "Bonagratia wanted an expert judgement on Olivi's doctrine, and that he obtained."[2] Yet, once having obtained this judgement from the commission Bonagratia
acted as if it were a personal condemnation of Olivi. Through his
deputy, he forced Olivi to give a public assent, in an assembly of
friars at Avignon, to the propositions of the commission contained
in the *Littera septem sigillorum*. He ordered the *Rotulus* and the
Littera septem sigillorum to be read out in all the convents of Provence, Olivi's own province. He had all Olivi's writings collected,
and put under guard at Avignon.[3] The stiffness of these measures,
following after the academic judgement of the commission, it may
be suggested, was due to a desire to destroy Olivi's influence over
his humbler followers in Provence. What Bonagratia and his
agents had to fear was not that Olivi would make nominalists of
his supporters, but that he would turn them into poverty-fanatics.
Here in Provence, we may suspect, the poverty issue bulked much
larger than the philosophical and theological.

To Olivi the proceedings of Bonagratia and the commission
seemed a great injustice. For two years he was deprived of his
writings. He had no copy of the *Rotulus*, and so could not make any
reply to the charges made against him. In 1285 copies of these fell
into his hands, and he was able to compose a defence for his judges
of 1283. In it he complained that he had not been allowed to speak
in his own defence. The commission, he said, by forcing him to
assent to their own propositions in the *Littera septem sigillorum*, were

[1] "Die Verurteilung", *Scholastik* v (1930), 507. See also his article, "Philoso-
phische und Theologische Irrtumslisten von 1270–1329. Ein Beitrag zur
Entwicklung der Theologischen Zensuren", *Mélanges Mandonnet* II, *Bibliothèque
Thomiste* XIV, Paris, 1930, pp. 305–29.

[2] Koch, "Die Verurteilung", *Scholastik* v (1930), 507.

[3] F. Ehrle, "Des Ordensprocurators Raymund von Fronsac Actensammlung
zur Geschichte der Spiritualen", *ALKG* III, p. 14, cap. xxx–xxxi. *Chronica
XXIV Generalium*, AF III, 374–6. Laberge, "Tria scripta apologetica", *AFH*
xxviii (1935), 120–1, 132–3.

setting themselves up as a dogmatic authority, and usurping the place of the Papacy.[1] His anger against the commission was all the greater because he could have hoped to have become a master at Paris himself, and, as he hinted in a letter to his supporters, had been prevented from attaining it through suspicions about his orthodoxy.[2]

His feelings at this juncture could not have been concealed from his followers. We know that he was in the habit of corresponding with a group of them from time to time. Later, when his writings were again the centre of dispute, before and during the Council of Vienne, the *Apologia* to his judges was the principal source on his doctrine used by both sides; through it others of his party, who had had no direct contact with him, would learn of the prejudice of his accusers. In this way the proceedings of 1283 helped to inflame feeling and to make the Olivi case a more potent source of division in the order.

The action against Olivi, having been taken so far, now halted, for Bonagratia died in October 1283. While the generalate was vacant, the case hung fire. In 1285 the chapter-general of Milan elected a new general, Arlotto of Prato. At the time he was absent, lecturing on the Sentences at Paris. The chapter merely enjoined provincials to collect Olivi's works and forbid their use "until other ordinance should have been made by the minister-general".[3] Arlotto had sat as a member of the commission of seven masters and bachelors in 1283; the evidence, however, suggests that as general he was not ill-disposed to Olivi.[4] Nothing is heard of proceedings in his short rule. He died within a year of election, and again there was a vacancy. In 1287 the chapter-general of Montpellier elected Matthew of Aquasparta to succeed him. He vindicated Olivi's orthodoxy. Under his rule, the chapter-general heard Olivi expound his doctrine of the *usus pauper*. If we can trust Ubertino's reporting, the exposition was given in restrained terms. Olivi kept close to the phrases of *Exiit qui seminat*,

---

[1] Ibid., pp. 131-2.

[2] Koch, "Die Verurteilung", *Scholastik* v (1930), p. 496, n. 27.

[3] *Acta Capituli Generalis Mediolani celebrati an.* 1285, ed. A. Callebaut, *AFH* xxii (1929), 289; *Responsiones*, no. 3.

[4] Laberge, "Tria scripta apologetica", *AFH* xxviii (1936), 122-3, and refs. given.

and took care to delimit the operation of the doctrine.[1] The chapter accepted this version, and Matthew appointed Olivi *lector* at the *studium* of Santa Croce, in Florence. No suspect teacher could be appointed to such a post. Matthew's action, coupled with the chapter's acceptance of the *usus pauper*, amounted to an acquittal of Olivi on all the charges yet made against him, on poverty, general philosophy, and theology alike.

It was, however, unlikely that an agreement on points of theory alone would make an end of controversy. There remained Olivi's simpler followers in Provence. Already these had become suspect to the authorities. In 1285 the provincial, Arnald of Rochafolio, and thirty-five other friars of Provence had drawn up a memorandum, in which they accused Olivi of being the head of a superstitious sect in the province.[2] Transferring Olivi to Florence might remove Olivi's direct influence from these men; it could not heal the dissensions aroused by them.

In Tuscany the ground was prepared for the sowing of rigorist doctrines. A friar from the province of Genoa, Ubertino da Casale, had been a *lector* at Santa Croce since 1285. After leaving the University of Paris, where his views had been those of the majority of his fellows, he had learnt the Spirituals' view of Francis's intentions for the order. He had met Angela of Foligno and Margaret of Cortona. At Greccio he had visited John of Parma. Olivi, on his arrival at Santa Croce, found him a ready listener.[3]

To judge from later events, there were others in the province who were already inclined towards Spiritual views.[4] Elsewhere

[1] "In hiis vero, que ad victum atque vestitum, divinum cultum et sapientiale studium spectant, sub rationali circumstantiarum moderantia usum artat et restringit. . . . Hanc autem moderantiam, que nichil aliud est quam virtutis paupertatis medium, non secundum rem sed secundum adequationem sumptum, non intelligo sic precise includi in voto paupertatis evangelice, quod omnis excessus aut immoderantia sit mortale peccatum . . . sed solum quando est talis et tanta, quod merito debet censeri enormiter ledere statum evangelice paupertatis. Alie autem immoderantie tanquam peccata venialia censebuntur. . . ." *ALKG* II, 401.

[2] F. Ehrle, "Des Ordensprocurators Raymund von Fronsac Actensammlung", *ALKG* III, p. 14, cap. xxxii.

[3] On Ubertino's biography, see F. Callaey, *L'idéalisme franciscain spirituel au XIVe siècle. Étude sur Ubertin de Casale*, Louvain, Paris, Bruxelles, 1911, and, for a correction of Callaey's attempt to alter the traditional chronology of his life, Godefroy, "Ubertin de Casale", *DTC* XV, ii (1950), 2020–34. The prime source for these details is the prologue to Ubertino da Casale's *Arbor vitae*.

[4] "On the first beginnings of the Tuscan Spirituals, the sources hitherto

in Italy, rigorists had been active. Conrad of Offida and other, less well-known, friars had been spreading the Spiritual tradition of St Francis, handed down from the early companions.

In at least one case, in the March of Ancona, the proclaiming of zealot views had led to violent action. There, a group of rigorists had protested against a proposal to impose the ownership of common property on the Franciscans. The proposal was a false rumour, the echo of the discussions taking place about the mendicant orders at the Council of Lyons in 1274; but it served to act as a focus for the latent discontent in the province. Ultimately, the dominant Conventuals decided for a policy of draconian severity, and condemned the ringleaders of Spiritual agitation to perpetual imprisonment.[1] At this time the story of the events in Ancona was not generally known in the order; later, after the ringleaders had emerged from prison, and there had been a recrudescence of the disturbances, the Spirituals of Ancona defended the doctrine of the *usus pauper* and hailed Olivi as their master.

In several provinces of the order in the 1280s there was thus a rising agitation from the Spirituals. Olivi was not responsible for the growth of the Spirituals' complaints; these had a much longer history, as we have seen, and owed much more to contemporary conditions. Nevertheless, in every region so affected he was in some way connected with these dissensions among the friars. His name was taken with reverence, and his doctrine of the *usus pauper* adopted for radical schemes of reform. Inevitably, therefore, the settlement at Montpellier came to be abandoned, and the Olivi controversy continued.

After 1287, however, the dispute ceased to be one primarily concerned with Olivi's academic opinions. It acted, rather, as one outlet, perhaps the chief one, for the general, diffused agitation about the observance of poverty, which troubled the order at this period.

[The grounds for this agitation are not far to seek. They lay in current abuses of poverty. The common standard of observance,

known leave us in obscurity. It is, nevertheless, probable that the rigorist tendency had its representatives there, as in the rest of Italy, from the time of brother Elias." L. Oliger, "Spirituels", *DTC* XIV, ii (1941), 2538.

[1] Angelo da Clareno, *Historia*, ed. Ehrle, *ALKG* II, 301–4. But see also Ehrle's note, p. 302.

it is generally agreed, declined in the decades following the issue of *Exiit qui seminat.*

The means by which the modifications of poverty were effected, and the causes of that modification, were very much the same as those which obtained in the first twenty years after the death of Francis.[1]

But in the last decades of the thirteenth century the extremist group, who made free with the poverty regulations, seem stronger and the moderate majority less able to check their relaxations than ever before. The question of the appointment of procurators, for example, will illustrate the extent of the division between the friars of the past and the new men. Under the system of Papal ownership for Franciscan goods, the position of the intermediary between Pope and friars was crucial. An improper use of the intermediary could make null the Franciscan claim to total renunciation of dominion. The chapter-general in John of Parma's time, who refused the Bull *Quanto studiosius*, well realized this, and rejected an arrangement which put the appointment of procurators into the hands of the friars and gave them full control over their activities. Under Bonagratia, the question of the Papal procurator arose once more. *Exiit*, by an oversight, permitted the use of a procurator in certain circumstances but omitted to lay down a procedure for his use.[2] Martin IV, attempting to fill the gap, in 1283 issued a new Bull, *Exultantes in Domino*, which decided how the friars might appoint and use their intermediaries. They were allowed to appoint them direct without recourse to the bishops or to the Papacy;[3] they were given full powers of direction over them; they were enabled to remove them from office at pleasure. The intermediaries, although technically the syndics of the Papacy, administering the goods which the Holy See permitted the friars to use, buying, selling, and going to law in the name of the Papacy and not of the friars, were thus to all intents and purposes Franciscan agents. This was *Quanto studiosius* over again. But what did the chapter-general do on this occasion? At Milan in 1285 they gave permission for this Bull to be used; the most they

[1] See above, chap. 3.

[2] *Epitome*, ed. Eubel, p. 297. See F. M. Delorme, "Praevia nonnulla Decretali 'Exultantes in Domino' (18 jan. 1283) de Procuratorum institutione", *AFH* vii (1914), 55–65.

[3] *Epitome*, ed. Eubel, p. 301.

provided by way of safeguard was an exhortation to the brothers not to multiply litigation.[1]

There was always a certain artificiality about the Franciscan claim to total renunciation of dominion. The Martinian solution to the problem of intermediaries, it might be said, put aside unnecessary complications. If the Franciscans were not to return to the extreme simplicity of early days, then *Exultantes* was the easiest way of recognizing the fact that the Franciscans must, in practice, enjoy the fruits of dominion.

There is something to be said for this view; but on the other side it must be recalled that ever since the time of Gregory IX the Franciscans had adopted the total renunciation of dominion as a distinctive badge of their order. They could not abandon it now. If on this one matter, the detail of the renunciation of dominion, they allowed too wide a gap to open between practice and precept, the consequent demoralization would affect all other aspects of their observance of poverty.

Among the Franciscans, neglect of forms at the highest level has very generally led to real relaxations at the lowest. In fact the Martinian syndic opened the way to a whole series of easily recognizable abuses. Ehrle, in a passage of his classic essay on the origins of the Spirituals in the *Archiv für Litteratur und Kirchengeschichte*, revealed how in certain circles in the late thirteenth century the syndic was being used to smooth away many of the realities of Franciscan poverty. He said:

> It was the task of the "syndacus", as plenipotentiary of the Holy See, the true owner of almost all Minorite property, to dispose of or exchange movable and immovable goods, according to the desires of those in authority. The clear meaning of the Papal letters and constitutions of the order was that immovable property should be limited to the convent, the fairly small garden surrounding it, and the church. The collected alms held by the "nuntius" were not to make daily begging unnecessary, but were to be sought and accepted only in proportion to such extraordinary needs in the way of clothing, building alterations, books, etc. as had to be satisfied in the immediate future. Instead of this, however, the "nuntius" of those

---

[1] "Item placet capitulo generali, quod privilegio domini pape Martini de nominandis procuratoribus provincie possint uti. Caveant tamen a multiplicandis litibus et quod nichil fiat contra ordinis honestatem." *Acta Capituli Generalis Mediolani*, ed. Callebaut, *AFH* xxii (1929), 283; *Constitutiones*, no. 23.

convents in which that extreme faction was in control accepted the administration of benefactions, wills, and annual incomes in such measure that the brothers were as good as completely relieved of all need to care for their own maintenance and household. From legacies and other benefactions, vineyards, estates, gardens, and houses were turned over to the "syndacus", not in order that he should dispose of them for the benefit of the brothers, as Nicholas III had ordained, but that he should administer them and turn the rent and income from them to the use of the convent, at times, indeed, of individual brothers. Such convents, therefore, lived from their incomes and estates no less than did the Benedictine abbeys, even if the appearance of having no possessions was preserved.[1]

One should not imagine that convents as lax as these were in a majority in the order; on the other hand the available evidence suggests that they were to be found in more than one province, and that the tradition of relaxation might be handed on from one generation to the next. At Venice, for example, the brothers had been receiving a fixed rent annually under a will for ten years, apparently undisturbed, before they asked the Pope to alter the terms of the bequest for them.[2] At the basilica we find the brothers again asking for, and receiving from the Papacy, this time in 1288, permission to take exceptional measures for the collection of money.[3] In other cases specific abuses were denounced in provincial constitutions, in definitions at chapters-general, and in encyclicals issued by ministers-general; but the very repetition of these denunciations suggests that attempts at reform were having no very great success.

The Spirituals claimed that the denunciations were always ineffective because they were not followed by stern enough measures against offenders. The Community, they said, too often turned a blind eye. There is much to support this notion. Certainly these Conventual documents themselves reveal that in individual cases relaxation had been taken to great lengths. Gratien cites clauses from three sets of provincial statutes, of the March of Treviso, of Aquitaine, and of Provence, to show that in these provinces friars had been in some way taking private ownership

---

[1] "Die Spaltung des Franciscanerordens in die Communität und die Spiritualen", *ALKG* III, 594–5.

[2] *Epitome*, ed. Eubel, no. 1818, p. 185; Balthasar, *Armutsstreit*, pp. 92–3.

[3] *Epitome*, ed. Eubel, no. 1630, p. 167; Balthasar, *Armutsstreit*, p. 93.

of money.¹ If individual friars could sink as low as this, what might be said of the general standard of observance? In one example, the provincial statutes of the March of Treviso, there is a clause urging the brothers to take great care to preserve title deeds or equivalents for the property they used.² The fact that such an injunction could have been included in provincial statutes of Franciscans is, in its way, more damning than any amount of isolated and more extreme examples of relaxation.

Probably what one should expect to find at this time is, beside the areas of great relaxation, a general decline over the body of the order from the standards associated with the name of Bona-ventura. England, a province not apparently touched by the gross abuses which can be found in certain parts of Italy and France, may well be a good example to cite in this connection. Of this period in the history of the English province, Little said there was a steady and general rise in the standard of living. Between roughly 1270 and 1320, he decided, there was a great expansion of building, an expansion not made necessary by any corresponding growth in numbers.³ Building, over and above the limits of necessity laid down by Bonaventura in the constitutions of Narbonne, was a grievance frequently brought against the Community by the Spirituals. Ubertino da Casale gave details of names and places in order to convince the Papal commission in 1311 that excesses in building were palliated by Franciscan superiors.⁴ His views were supported by less biased authorities. Much earlier Pecham, who shared the standards of his master Bonaventura, had called these over-large buildings "monstra professionis".⁵ Excess in building, as we have seen earlier, by overstraining the legitimate resources of the friars led directly to a relaxation of the standard of poverty. The motive for these excesses was often no more than the understandable wish to do credit to the order, in a worldly sense; in other circumstances it might have been regarded as praiseworthy, but Francis had set the standards of his order so

¹ *Évolution*, p. 367, n. 17.
² Quoted, Gratien, op. cit., p. 370, n. 26.
³ *Studies in English Franciscan History*, p. 72.
⁴ F. Ehrle, "Vorarbeiten zur Constitution Exivi de Paradiso vom 6 May 1312", *ALKG* III, 164.
⁵ ". . . unde fateor multa edificia ordinis esse monstra professionis." *Tractatus Tres, Tractatus Pauperis*, ed. A. G. Little, p. 37.

high that even the least falling-off was magnified and became a betrayal.

Naturally enough, decisive evidence to support such large generalizations about the state of the observance is hard to find. The impression, however, that there was a decline at this time over almost all sections is borne out by evidence provided by the Community. From time to time, as *definitiones* were issued by chapters-general, it was found necessary to make new redactions of the constitutions of the order. If we compare Bonaventura's redaction, made at Narbonne in 1260, with that made by the chapter-general of Paris in 1292, we shall discover that in the great majority of cases, where there has been a change of regulations concerning poverty, the change has been in one direction only—towards mitigation of earlier austerities.

Some changes fell on small details. Narbonne laid it down that no brother should have two tunics; Paris altered this to read: no brother should have two new tunics.[1]

Others dealt with wider issues. Paris, while denouncing the use of begging-boys to gather money for friars, permitted the use on long journeys of an "honestus nuntius", who appeared to be, in principle, not much different from a begging-boy.[2] Again, Narbonne had ordered the brothers not to influence anyone to make a will in favour of themselves or their relatives; Paris, while including some salutary new regulations about wills, nevertheless allowed an exception to this prohibition. Friars might influence testators to whom they were related, and in doing so, and in all gathering of alms, they were to remember the needs of the Paris convent.[3]

Finally, there was at Paris a change in the theory of renunciation. Narbonne, defining the *pecunia*, which was forbidden to the brothers, had decided that the term included not only *denarii*, or coinage, but any object which was received in order to be sold. At Paris the definition was dropped.[4] In practice the change might

---

[1] *Statuta Generalia*, ed. M. Bihl, *AFH* xxxiv (1941), 43, 44, Narbonne, Paris, II, 7.

[2] Paris, V, 7; art. cit., p. 66. Compare Narbonne, V, 7; art. cit., p. 63. It should be noted, however, that the clause about the "honestus nuntius" first appears in the redaction of Assisi, in 1279.

[3] Narbonne III, 7, art. cit., p. 46; Paris III, 7 and 7a, art. cit., pp. 49–50.

[4] Narbonne III, 2, art. cit., p. 45; Paris III, 2, art. cit., p. 49.

not be very significant; it did, nevertheless, mark in words the general shift in attitudes, away from the stricter prohibitions of Bonaventura's day and on to a more formal and legalized interpretation of poverty.

Olivi's stay at Florence lasted roughly two years. Ubertino, his fellow *lector* at Santa Croce, had been there since 1285. He was already inclined towards the Spirituals when Olivi arrived; Olivi now completed his conversion. In addition to thus crystallizing his views on poverty, Olivi also introduced Ubertino to the apocalyptic speculations of Joachimism.[1] These Ubertino absorbed with enthusiasm. In Olivi Joachimism remained very largely speculative. However dear to his heart, however closely linked to his views on Franciscan poverty, Joachimism in his works was subject to many restraints and caveats. In Ubertino, on the other hand, who was a man of no academic subtlety, these reserves were cast aside. In him Joachimism was far more literal, and correspondingly more dangerous. Unfortunately for the peace of the order, it was Ubertino's type of exposition and not Olivi's which came to be the vogue among the Spirituals and their lay supporters in the next decades.

In 1289 master and pupil were separated. The chapter of Assisi in that year elected a new minister-general to succeed Matthew of Aquasparta. He was Raymond Gaufredi, by origin of a noble house in Provence. His election was a breach with precedent. Gaufredi was a non-Italian, the first in the generalate since Haymo of Faversham, and a non-academic.[2] The change soon benefited the Spirituals. Gaufredi appointed Olivi *lector* at Montpellier,[3] thus completing the exculpation begun by Matthew of Aquasparta, and incidentally restoring Olivi to his Provençal followers. Ubertino did not stay in Santa Croce without Olivi, but began a prolonged preaching mission lasting for some ten years in Tuscany, the Valley of Spoleto, and the March of

---

[1] Ubertino had gained some knowledge of Joachimism earlier, from John of Parma; but his full initiation came from Olivi. See Godefroy, "Ubertin de Casale", *DTC* XV, ii, 1950, coll. 2021, 2027, and ref. given to book v of the *Arbor vitae*.

[2] On the background of the new general, and the possible motive for his election, Balthasar, *Armutsstreit*, pp. 174–7.

[3] F. Ehrle, "Petrus Johannis Olivi, sein Leben und seine Schriften", *ALKG* III, 431.

Ancona.[1] There he developed the extravagance of his thought, and, together with his orthodox preaching, mixed Spiritual ideas on poverty and Joachimite prophecies. Meanwhile, Gaufredi's election benefited other rigorists in Italy. The new general went on visitation to the provinces, and discovered in the March of Ancona the victims of the former disturbances still lying in prison. He asked what their crime had been, and, on hearing that they had been condemned for an excess of zeal in their observance, is reported to have said: "Would that all of us and the whole order could be convicted of such a crime."[2] He promptly released them and, to get them out of the way of the Conventuals, sent them as missionaries to the crusading kingdom of Armenia.

The respite brought by Gaufredi to the Spirituals was nevertheless very short. A fresh sequence of persecution began in Provence in 1290, where Nicholas IV intervened to command Gaufredi to take action against certain brothers "condemning the state of other brothers and giving themselves out to be more spiritual than others. . ."[3] Investigation was entrusted to a Franciscan Inquisitor,[4] and the results were brought before the chapter of Paris in 1292. Again Olivi was required to give an explanation of his doctrine of the *usus pauper*; again he escaped with a tactical evasion, although this time, if we can believe the pro-Conventual sources, it was something not far from a recantation.[5]

The Spirituals from the March of Ancona were hardly more fortunate. In Armenia they found no peace from Conventuals. They were denounced to the King of Armenia. Their leader was treated by other friars as an excommunicate. At length they determined to abandon the mission and make for home in order

---

[1] Godefroy, "Ubertin de Casale", *DTC* XV, ii, 1950, col. 1022.

[2] Angelo da Clareno, *Historia*, ed. Ehrle, *ALKG* II, 305.

[3] *Chronica XXIV Generalium*, *AF* III, 420. There has been some doubt whether Nicholas IV's intervention was directed against Olivi and his followers. See Ehrle, "Olivis Leben und Schriften", *ALKG* III, 434–5, Douie, *Fraticelli*, p. 11. The doubt was based on Ubertino's statement in his *Apologia* for Olivi (*ALKG* III, 389); but see, on the other side, L. Amorós, "Series condemnationum et processuum contra doctrinam et sequaces Petri Ioannis Olivi (e cod. Vat. Ottob. Lat. 1816)", *AFH* xxiv (1931), 405.

[4] F. Ehrle, "Raymund von Fronsac Actensammlung", *ALKG* III, pp. 14–15, cap. xxxv–xxxvi.

[5] *Chronica XXIV Generalium*, *AF* III, 421–2; F. Ehrle, "Raymund von Fronsac Actensammlung", *ALKG* III, p. 15, cap. xxxvii.

to seek better guarantees for their freedom. Two of them, the leader
and his companion, Angelo da Clareno, made their way direct to
the minister-general. He in turn referred them to the Pope. As it
happened, they had arrived at a propitious moment. The unsym-
pathetic Franciscan, Nicholas IV, had died, and in his place the
cardinals had chosen Celestine V. This eccentric figure, a hermit
brought from his cave in the Abruzzi, was cast for the role of the
papa angelicus who, in the Joachimite prophecies beloved of the
Spirituals, was to come to cleanse the Church. In him the rigorists
found a kindred spirit. He listened to their request, gave them
freedom to observe the Rule to the letter, as Francis had willed
in the Testament, and enrolled them in his own foundation, the
order of the Holy Spirit of Maiella. The leader, Brother Liberato,
was given power to act as a religious superior. A cardinal, Napoleon Orsini, was made the protector of the future community.
Liberato and those who should follow him were absolved from
obedience to the Community.[1] The first rent was made in the
seamless robe of St Francis.

Yet again hopes were dashed. Before six months were up, Celestine made the great refusal. Unable to bear his responsibilities, he
resigned, and was succeeded by Boniface VIII. The new Pope
cancelled the exemption of the Celestinian Spirituals. What could
the little group do? If they returned to their superiors now, they
could expect little but persecution. Their freedom had been
granted to them so recently that they could not believe that they
had lost it again. Moreover, their authority, Celestine, had left
office by the doubtful means of resignation. A Pope, some argued,
was so wedded to the Church that he could not resign. If Celestine
was still rightful Pope, their exemption was still valid. By such
arguments they were drawn into schism. They decided, in Angelo's
words, to give place to wrath, avoided the Conventuals, and took
ship for Greece.[2]

The event brought out differences, hitherto unrecognized,
between Olivi and the simpler rigorists. In September 1295 he
wrote a letter in formal terms to Conrad of Offida, the *doyen* of the
Italian Spirituals, condemning errors similar to those which had

[1] Angelo da Clareno, *Historia*, ed. Ehrle, *ALKG* II, 308–9.
[2] Ibid., 309–10, 312.

led to the flight of the Celestinians.[1] His language made it plain that he spoke from the heart.[2] The first error was the belief, so relevant to the case of the Celestinians, that a Pope could not resign office. It was supported, among the simpler Italians, by a series of mystical and Joachimite analogies, assimilating the position of the Pope to that of Christ. These Olivi soon dissipated by an appeal to logic and canon law.[3] The second was the belief that the Papal constitutions, *Quo elongati* and *Exiit*, by abrogating the Testament, permitting the use of money through inter-mediaries, and allowing the friars to have more than two tunics, had betrayed the Rule. This point he dealt with somewhat less easily. He denied that there was conflict between the Testament and the Papal constitutions. *Quo elongati* had praised Francis's intention. In the Testament Francis had meant only to ensure that the Rule should be observed without fraud and deceitful comment. As for the use of money, did not the Apostle Paul make collections for the poor in Jerusalem? To allow more than two tunics, he said, was justified by the discretion given to the ministers in the Rule.[4] Finally, a third error justified secession from the Community out of the text of the Apocalypse: "Come ye out of her, my people, that ye be not partakers of her sins and that ye receive not of her plagues." In reply to this he gave the examples of the early companions, Giles, Leo, and Masseo, who did not desert the order.[5]

Olivi's letter, if occasionally disingenuous, was generally an excellent refutation of the wilder notions of the Italian Spirituals. And yet it had no discernible effect at all. The Celestinians were not restrained from their course of action. Spirituals in Italy continued to believe in the illegitimacy of Celestine's renunciation: in 1297 several of them, including Jacopone da Todi, counter-signed the manifesto issued by the Colonna who revolted against

[1] See his *De renuntiatione Papae Coelestini V Quaestio et Epistola*, ed. L. Oliger, *AFH* xi (1918), 309–73.
[2] "Attendant igitur isti temerarii presumptores quam turpiter et quam brutaliter errant", art. cit., p. 367. In his conclusion he refers to these errors as "dementia", and shows his fear of their effects on the cause of the Spirituals. Ibid., p. 372.
[3] Art. cit., pp. 366–70.
[4] 1 Cor. 16.1–4. Art. cit., pp. 370–2.
[5] Art. cit., pp. 372–3. Rev. 18.4.

Boniface VIII.[1] Ubertino continued to believe that the Papal
constitutions were a betrayal of the Rule, and that the successors
of Celestine were usurpers; these ideas all reappeared subsequently in his writings.[2] From this time it was apparent that
Olivi was no longer master of the spirits he had conjured up.[3]

The Celestine episode formed the prelude to further persecutions. Angelo, in his History, called it the beginning of the sixth
great tribulation of the order.[4] First, Gaufredi was lost to the
cause. Boniface summoned him, late in 1295, offered him a bishop-
ric, and, when he declared himself unworthy of such a position,
deposed him from the generalate.[5] Then, the chapter in the following year elected to the generalate John Minio de Murrovalle. He
was a friend of Boniface VIII. He was by origin of the March of
Ancona, an area with a tradition of strong action against rigorists.
He had taken part in previous proceedings against Olivi: as a
bachelor at Paris, in 1283, he had put his seal to the *Littera septem
sigillorum*. He was of strict life. Even Angelo was unable to accuse
him of relaxation, and the best that the Spiritual spokesman,
Arnald of Villanova, could do in the way of attack was to compare
him to the ostrich, the hypocritical bird.[6] He was a persecutor on
principle—and therefore the more effective.

His talents were soon displayed. The Celestinian Spirituals were
ferreted out in their refuge on an island in the Gulf of Corinth.
Their persecutors attempted to discredit them with the accusation
of Manichaeism. When this failed, they turned to the Papacy,
and, with Murrovalle's aid, brought the case before Boniface.
At first he was disinclined to take action. He gave them a rough
answer: "Leave them to serve God: they do better than you."[7]
Now, however, the Spirituals' adherence to Celestine began to
bring in its harvest. The friars tried again, and this time mentioned
that the group were supporters of Celestine, and had denied the

---

[1] H. Denifle, "Die Denkschriften der Colonna gegen Bonifaz VIII und der
Cardinäle gegen die Colonna", *ALKG* V (1889), 514.

[2] In book v of the *Arbor vitae*. See Balthasar's summary, *Armutsstreit*, pp.
248–54; also Godefroy, "Ubertin de Casale", *DTC* XV, ii, 1950, coll. 2027–8.

[3] Ehrle's phrase: "Olivis Leben und Schriften", *ALKG* III, 438.

[4] *ALKG* II, 125–6.

[5] Wadding, *Annales Minorum*, ad. ann. 1295, xiv, vol. V, Romae, 1733,
p. 338.

[6] Balthasar, *Armutsstreit*, p. 246, and ref. given.

[7] Angelo da Clareno, *Historia*, ed. Ehrle, *ALKG* II, 316.

legitimacy of Boniface's succession. Boniface acted, and gave orders for their arrest and excommunication. The group avoided capture; but they were expelled from their hiding-place, and forced to set out on their wanderings once more.[1]

In Italy Conrad of Offida, who had advised recourse to Celestine, and had apparently considered joining the group in Greece, was accused of favouring schism, and of teaching that the Community did not observe the Rule. He was summoned before Minio de Murrovalle, and narrowly escaped punishment.[2]

In Provence the followers of Olivi were subjected to an attack more thorough than anything which had gone before. At the chapter-general of Lyons in 1299 Olivi's teachings were condemned outright, and all who kept or used his writings were excommunicated.[3] Armed with this decision, Murrovalle sent out visitors to investigate Olivi's followers and to punish the culpable.[4] At the same time the provincial made his own inquiries. Olivi was now out of the way: he had died at the convent of Narbonne, in 1298.[5] The attack appears to have followed stages. Murrovalle directed a series of letters against the Olivi supporters. In the first he gave orders for the sect of Olivi to be extinguished and its members, where necessary, to be expelled from the province.[6] In the second, because the sect was still strong, he gave orders for Olivi's writings to be collected under pain of excommunication.[7] In the third, Murrovalle was constrained to justify his action. He recalled the past history of Olivi's writings: how his writings had been burnt by one minister-general, and forbidden by another. He concluded by ordering imprisonment for the obstinate.[8] In the fifth he went further: he ordered Olivi's writings to be burnt.[9]

---

[1] Ibid., pp. 316–17.   [2] Ibid., pp. 311–12.

[3] Amorós, "Series condemnationum", *AFH* xxiv (1931), p. 504, no. 4. The source places the chapter at Paris; Amorós believes it was in fact Lyons. Art. cit., p. 504, n. 7.

[4] See the statement of Gaufredi in the Papal investigation at Avignon: F. Ehrle, "Die Erwiderung Raymunds und Bonagrazias auf die von Gaufredi eingereichte Beantwortung der vier Fragepunkte (c. Juni 1311)", *ALKG* III, p. 144, lines 23–6.

[5] See the *libellus* of Olivi's Beguin supporters, the *Transitus Sancti Patris*: Bernard Gui, *Manuel de l'Inquisiteur*, ed. and tr. G. Mollat, I, Paris, 1926, pp. 190–3.

[6] Ehrle, "Raymund von Fronsac Actensammlung", *ALKG* III, p. 15, cap. xl.

[7] Ibid., pp. 15–16, cap. xli.

[8] Ibid., p. 16, cap. xlii.   [9] Ibid., p. 16, cap. xliii.

The provincial chapter asked Murrovalle what were the articles of the doctrine for which Olivi's followers were dubbed superstitious. He gave them a short reply, which put the guilt on the defenders of Olivi's doctrine of the *usus pauper*.[1] The Spirituals themselves appealed to Boniface VIII. It was an unwise move. Boniface merely chose the provincial of Genoa, William de Cherio, to act as his representative, and he, after investigation, imposed further penalties on his own account.[2]

Customary weapons had already been used against the followers of Olivi in Provence. The Murrovalle persecution, however, added something new. A form of abjuration was drawn up, and a commissary, the provincial of Aragon, appointed to receive submissions.[3] The points of doctrine on which abjuration was required are significant. They were purely theological and popular. There were three points in all. The first, as expected, was Olivi's doctrine of *usus pauper*. The remaining two broke new ground. They were concerned with the darker side of Olivi's influence over his humbler followers.

One dealt with Olivi's teaching on the spear-wound, which, in St John's Gospel, was inflicted on Christ after his death. In his Postill on John, Olivi included a passage in which he speculated on the timing of this spear-wound. The text of John, as it stood, was clear enough: the soldiers coming round to break the legs of the victims at the Crucifixion desisted when they came to Christ, for they saw that he was dead already. But, John added, one of the soldiers then pierced his side with a spear; whereupon there came out blood and water.[4] Nevertheless Olivi saw fit to expound certain mystical reasons which would have made it more fitting for the spear-wound to have been inflicted while Christ was still alive. He knew that a saintly man, worthy of credence, had learnt in a vision that in fact the spear-wound had been inflicted not after but before the death of Christ. So, with due submission to the

---

[1] ". . . sic duxi breviter respondendum: omnes superstitiosos et pernitiose doctrine iudicari debere, qui usum pauperem rerum esse de substantia voti paupertatis asserere audent." Quoted by Ubertino in his *apologia* for Olivi: F. Ehrle, "Ubertinos von Casale Vertheidigungsschrift des Petrus Johannis Olivi und der Spiritualen", *ALKG* III, 385–6.

[2] Amorós, "Series condemnationum", *AFH* xxiv (1931), pp. 504–5, no. 5.

[3] Ehrle, "Raymund von Fronsac Actensammlung", *ALKG* III, p. 17, cap. xlv, xlvi.

[4] John 19.32–4.

Church, purely as a hypothesis, "absque aliqua assertione . . . inquirendo solum", as Ubertino put it later, he put forward the view that the spear-thrust had been inflicted before, and not, as the text of John had it, after the death of Christ.[1]

In many ways this passage was typical of the more doubtful side of Olivi. It was a dangerous piece of speculation. The matter in itself was insignificant; but the text of Scripture had been put in doubt, and a private revelation adduced as if it was in some way an argument against the plain words of John. Doucet, the editor of this section of the Postill on John, observes that, although Olivi put forward his views as a hypothesis only, he did so in terms which were so exaggerated as to induce error in the minds of simpler followers.[2] From this spear-wound exposition, with its mystical arguments, and its mention of the vision "of a saintly man", one catches a glimpse of the cloudy, visionary atmosphere in which Olivi exerted his influence over his Provençal followers. One sees, too, that the Community had grounds, quite outside the poverty issue, for making an attack on Olivi and his followers.

The third item for abjuration was on similar lines. The Provençal zealots were required to abjure the practice of giving honours of canonization to those unrecognized by the Church.[3] This, of course, meant Olivi. We know, from other sources, what exaggerated respect the rigorists felt for Olivi. Angelo, in the *Historia septem tribulationum*, speaks of him as, like Dominic and Francis, the fulfilment of old prophecies. He says, for example:

> For that prophecy, which was given to St Cyril by an angel, calls brother Petrus Johannis the sun on account of the clear and everlasting incorruptibility of his virtues and on account of the splendid diversity of his wisdom and knowledge which were divinely given him. . . .[4]

This is the exaggerated language of Joachimism. It is also the reflection of the sufferings of the zealots, sufferings indeed in which Angelo himself shared most fully. To bear their persecutions, the

---

[1] See V. Doucet, "De operibus manuscriptis Fr. Petri Ioannis Olivi in Bibliotheca Universitatis Patavinae asservatis", Appendix, *Documenta*, I, *AFH* xxviii (1935), 436–41.

[2] Art. cit., *AFH* xxviii (1935), 170.

[3] Ehrle, "Raymond von Fronsac Actensammlung", *ALKG* III, p. 17, cap. xlv.

[4] *ALKG* II, 290.

zealots required a mythology. They needed to have a saint and martyr for their leader; and so they made Olivi into one. Veneration for his real virtues; the heightening of the emotions which always accompanied Joachimism; the need for a centre of devotion—all combined to produce the *cultus* at Narbonne which the Community was now endeavouring to suppress. The policy of "thorough" had its limitations, however. Unless the new persecution destroyed the Spirituals, it would fail. The effect of the draconian measures in that case would only be to make the obstinate irreconcilable, and to increase their unhealthy devotion for Olivi.

Ubertino da Casale, alone of the Spiritual leaders, escaped the persecution of the time. While his fellows were suffering in Provence, he continued his preaching tour in central Italy unscathed. Trouble for him came comparatively late, after the death of Boniface VIII, in 1303, and then not through Spiritual views on poverty but through Joachimism. He was preaching in Perugia when it was noticed that his use in his sermons of the Joachimite concept of the *ecclesia carnalis* appeared to be a veiled attack on the contemporary Papacy. Enemies delated him to Rome, and he found himself summoned before the new Pope, Benedict XI. He escaped. The Pope apparently took his Joachimism lightly. Envoys arrived to plead for him from the municipality of Perugia, and he used his own dialectical skill to clear himself. His superiors in the order nevertheless refused to allow him to continue his preaching, disciplined him, and sent him to the hermitage of Alverna.[1]

The punishment gave him the opportunity for reflection. At Alverna, living on the mount where Francis received the stigmata, with an indulgent guardian and sympathetic friars, he felt himself free to express his view. At the request of the brothers, he began to write the *Arbor vitae crucifixae Jesus*.[2] In form it was a devotional treatise based on a lesser work of Bonaventura, his *Lignum vitae*; in fact, it served as a compendium of Spiritual views. Ubertino's plan was to describe a tree, its root in the history of the world from

---

[1] Ibid., 132–3.

[2] The original has not been used here: Godefroy gives a summary, "Ubertin de Casale", *DTC* XV, ii, 1950, coll. 2024–5, and, generally, 2025–9. See also Douie, *Fraticelli*, pp. 132–42; Callaey, *Étude sur Ubertin de Casale*, pp. 58–64, 83–134.

the creation to the redemption, its branches the works of Christ, its fruits the deeds of the elect; in practice, his own preoccupations led him to give chief place to Joachimism and the struggle over poverty.

It was an unbalanced work. One part of it contained mystical reflections of great merit. In this section Ubertino can stand comparison with the masters of mystical exposition; indeed, the *Arbor* played a significant part in the development of devotions to the person of Christ. St Bernardino of Siena, the fifteenth century Observant, borrowed extensively from the *Arbor* for his sermons: devotion to the Holy Name, the theme of the universal mediation of Mary, the patronage of Joseph, devotion to the Sacred Heart were all practices popularized by St Bernardino, but derived from Ubertino in the *Arbor*.[1] In all this Ubertino is in the main stream of the Franciscan tradition of meditation on the sufferings of Christ. He enlarges it, directs it further on to the internal rather than the external sufferings, and adds to it something of his own intensity.

Other parts, however, stand in glaring contrast. These are the sections where Ubertino surveys the contemporary scene. Joachimism, always expecting the imminent approach of the end of the world, causes him to exaggerate the woes of the present. He speaks savagely of the Community, and draws a clear distinction between the Franciscan life intended by the founder and that permitted by the Papal constitutions. He calls *Exiit qui seminat* "a millstone tied to the belly of the order".[2] He casts some doubt on the right of the Papacy to dispense from the Rule. He allows that the Papacy may interpret the Rule, and will admit that those who follow its interpretations will not endanger their salvation; but he stresses that the Pope may not interpret the Rule and declare it to be the life intended by Francis for his order. To illustrate, he takes an example from monastic life: "And although the Pope can make a monk cease to be one, he can never make a monk observe his rule and have property of his own."[3] Callaey, the biographer of Ubertino, is thinking particularly of these sections of the *Arbor*

---

[1] E. Blondeel d'Isegem, "L'influence d'Ubertin de Casale sur les écrits de S. Bernardin de Sienne", *Collectanea Franciscana* v (1935), 5–44.

[2] ". . . ac si lapis molaris fuisset appensus ad ventrem ordinis." Quoted, Balthasar, *Armutsstreit*, p. 252, n. 4, from bk. v of the *Arbor vitae*.

[3] Quoted, Balthasar, *Armutsstreit*, p. 252, n. 3.

when he makes this contrast between his subject and Francis: "He only half knew the humble beggar of Assisi: the ardent enthusiast for poverty fascinates him, while the friar who has charity for all failings, physical as well as moral, leaves him cold."[1]

The rigorism which we see in Spirituals like Ubertino is not only displayed in their attitude to poverty; it is, one may suspect, a temperamental strain, which emerges elsewhere, in quite distinct topics. In Ubertino, for example, it is interesting to find him taking up the most harsh position about the damnation of unbaptized infants—an attitude for which he was later taken to task by Denis the Carthusian.[2] On current Popes, his *penchant* for condemnation combined with his Joachimism to produce extravagant descriptions. He denied the legitimacy of Celestine's renunciation, called Boniface VIII the mystical Antichrist, and made Benedict XI one of the beasts of the Apocalypse. It was apparent that the accusations at Perugia were more than justified.[3]

This two-sidedness was characteristic of the Spirituals. We find it, to a greater or less degree, in all the Spiritual leaders about whom we have any information: John of Parma, with his sanctity, and at the same time his interest in doubtful Joachimite works, Olivi, similarly tainted, now Ubertino. Angelo da Clareno presents the most straightforward front; but even he supported a schism, and was on occasion guilty of prevarications about obedience. In the case of Ubertino, the *Arbor*, the chief evidence against him, circulated at this time only in circles sympathetic to the Spirituals; it remained unknown to the Community. In a direct sense, therefore, its darker passages did not harm his credit in the order. On the other hand, they were there to influence his own followers. Also the ideas revealed in them remained in the mind of the author, as the background to his own conduct.

Meanwhile, in Provence, the persecution had not abated with the death of Boniface. Before the end of his pontificate, Boniface gave Murrovalle the red hat. He did not give up office immediately, but continued to govern the order until the next chapter-general, held at Assisi in 1304. Three years later, he became

---

[1] *Étude sur Ubertin de Casale*, p. 189.
[2] Ibid., pp. 91–3, and refs. given.
[3] Godefroy, "Ubertin de Casale", *DTC* XV, ii, 1950, coll. 2027–8, and refs. given.

cardinal protector and so continued to influence policy. In his place the chapter elected Gonsalvo of Valboà, the first Spaniard to hold the generalate. He followed the same policy as his predecessor.

Olivi's writings continued to be the focus of persecution. Gonsalvo's rigour was no less than that of his predecessor. Ubertino cited the case of a friar who was condemned under his rule to imprisonment, not for refusing to give up Olivi's works but for saying that if he had any, he would not give them up to the order, only to the Papacy.[1] The same penalties were applied: banishment, imprisonment, deprivation of office and books. Ubertino believed that in the whole course of the Provençal disturbances some three hundred friars were punished in this way.[2] He was not always strictly truthful, and he wrote in a controversy; nevertheless the figure, however approximate, does suggest a persecution of formidable proportions. The Spirituals were thus, numerically, a strong force; and the continuity of repressive measures does also suggest that they were obstinate in clinging to their opinions.

We know, too, from other sources, that they had succeeded in spreading their views among Provençals outside the order. The Inquisition records of John XXII's time reveal the presence of numbers of Beguins in Provence who had imbibed a compound of Joachimism and a crude version of the Spiritual doctrines of poverty; the circumstances make it clear that they had derived this from a somewhat earlier period.[3]

How was it, we may ask, that Provence should have been the province above all others where Spiritual doctrines took hold, both in the order and among laymen outside?

We may attribute much to the influence of Olivi. It is plain that, as Douie says, there was some drawing power in his personality which has not been reflected in his writings.[4] Nevertheless, the influence of one man seems hardly adequate to account for the strength of the movement. Provence was not an area visited by Francis or the early companions. The rise of the Spirituals in Italy

---

[1] In the *apologia* for Olivi: Ehrle, "Ubertinos von Casale Vertheidigungsschrift", *ALKG* II, 386.
[2] Ubertino da Casale in the *Declaratio* of 1311: F. Ehrle, "Die Replik Ubertinos von Casale (c. August 1311)", *ALKG* III, 192.
[3] See below pp. 217–8.
[4] *Fraticelli*, p. 95.

13

is less surprising, for here their influence remained until comparatively late. Because Francis died young and often had youthful
companions, some of them long outlived him. Leo, for example,
did not die until 1271. These could convey the germ of Spiritual
ideas—but not, at any rate directly, in Provence.

Two points may be made in answer to this question. In the first
place, the tradition of rigorism and Joachimism in Provence goes
back before Olivi. We should regard Olivi rather as a passive
recipient of this tradition than its initiator. In mid-century, in the
time of Crescenzio and John of Parma, Hugues de Digne was active
in the province. We know from his writings, particularly the *De
finibus paupertatis*, which was used extensively as a source by the
later Spirituals, that he belonged to the rigorist section of the
order. He was a close friend of John of Parma. He was a notable
Joachimite. We know from Salimbene's famous description of the
doctors and lawyers assembled in his cell to hear him expound
Joachimite prophecies at Hyères that he had a lay clientele for his
views. We can trust Salimbene on this point: he had acted as a
carrier between Hugues de Digne and John of Parma.[1] Hugues de
Digne's work would have made it possible for Spiritual views to
take hold in the province well before the persecutions began in the
late thirteenth century.

There remains a further point: how was it that Provence should
have been fertile soil for Spiritual doctrines? Here we may venture
on a less certain hypothesis. Provence in the previous century had
become a hotbed of Catharism; and heresy was eliminated, at least
in its outward manifestations, by armed force rather than by per-
suasion. The influence of Cathar doctrines lingered on after open
resistance had ended. The Spirituals themselves were not Cathars:
they were as hostile as other religious to these doctrines. Yet in
their outward practice of poverty they did resemble Cathar *perfecti*.
The same qualities which had drawn the devotion of the Provençal
populace to the *perfecti* would appear also in the Spirituals. Might
it not be that the success of the Spirituals in Provence was, in part,
due to the existence, hardly recognized, of Cathar sympathies in
the province? It would be very difficult to prove the connection
between Spiritual success and Catharism. But until any investigation is made, the theory of Cathar influence may be put forward

[1] For refs. see above, p. 109.

to account for at least part of the strength of the Spiritual move-ment in Provence, and for its long persistence under persecution.

By the time of Gonsalvo the position of the Spirituals in Pro-vence was becoming desperate. They would not simply submit; the Community was not assured of success; and so the persecutions continued. Their one hope was to escape from the closed circle of protest and punishment. But how? The constitutions gave ministers almost unlimited rights of coercion. The last two gene-rals, Murrovalle and Gonsalvo, were committed to the Conventual side. At the curia, Murrovalle as protector after 1307 was able to block their appeals. The most that the zealots could hope for was that some patron of theirs would intervene, on a personal level, with the Pope.

They did have friends in high places, although not always of the highest repute. One such was Arnald of Villanova, the papal physician.[1] A Catalan of humble birth, he had risen to power through his medical skill. He became physician to Peter III of Aragon, and then, through him, became known to the Popes. He treated both Boniface VIII and Clement V, who tolerated his foibles for the sake of his skill. Like other great men, like, for instance Michelangelo with his sonnets, he had a fondness for another field, in which he had no special aptitude. In the case of Arnald, this was theology. He believed he had a divine mission to announce the coming of the end of the world and to reform the Church. He wrote Joachimite treatises, was linked with the Beguins, and occupied himself in translating devotional treatises into the vernacular.

He is apparently one example of a Spiritual supporter who was led to hold the rigorists' views about poverty from his interest in Joachimism.[2] In him, unlike the Spirituals in the order, Joachimism

---

[1] M. van Heuckelum, *Spiritualistische Strömungen an den Höfen von Aragon und Anjou während der Höhe des Armutsstreites*, Berlin, Leipzig, 1912, chap. i; J. M. Pou y Marti, "Arnaldo de Vilanova y Fadrique, rey de Sicilia", *Archivo Ibero-Americano* xi (1919), 142–231, in the series of articles, "Visionarios, beguinos y fraticelos catalanes (siglos XIII–XV)"; F. Ehrle, "Arnaldo de Villanova ed i Thomatiste, contributo alla storia della scuola Tomistica", *Gregorianum* i (1920), 475–501.

[2] His Joachimite work, the *Allocutio super significationem nominis Tetragrammaton*, was completed in 1292, at a date, that is, before he seems to have taken any special interest in poverty. But this is not certain. Pou y Marti, art. cit., pp. 146–8.

seems to have come first, poverty second. His first training in theology came from the Dominican school at the convent of Montpellier. Later, however, he broke with the Dominicans, partly because of their adherence to Thomism, and in 1303-4, probably for the first time, made contact with the Spirituals of Provence. He had already used his position at the Papal court to press his theological hobby; in 1304, in a *Rahonament* delivered to Benedict XI, he included in his discourse an appeal for the Spirituals. Thereafter he used every opportunity to put their case.

Arnald also acted as a carrier for Spiritual ideas outside the Papal court. Being in office to Peter III, he acquired influence over his sons, James II of Aragon and Frederick II of Sicily.[1] They allowed him to act as a theological adviser. He interpreted a dream of Frederick II, and for James II's children wrote an "Alphabetum catholicum". In all his surviving works, he constantly urges the cause of "evangelical truth", often with success. James II was never deeply interested, and was happy to use Arnald as a weapon for his own projects. When, for example, Arnald denounced the Templars for their neglect of poverty, James found it useful to encourage him, in hopes of getting a share of the Templars' wealth if they were suppressed.[2] But as soon as Arnald drew him in too deeply and in 1310 began to undermine his reputation for orthodoxy with Clement V, he abandoned Arnald, and, with him, the cause of the Spirituals.[3] Frederick II, on the other hand, had a sincere religious interest.[4] At one time he seems to have considered becoming a Beguin himself. He protected the Spirituals and under John XXII gave a refuge to some of their runaways.

Aragon and Sicily were not the only royal houses to be influenced by Spiritual ideas. The closely related house of Majorca was deeply involved. Here perhaps the source of influence was not Arnald, but the queen of James I of Majorca, Esclarmonde de

---

[1] On the southern kings, see, esp., Heuckelum, op. cit., chap. i. Heuckelum was a pupil of Finke, and leans heavily on the *Acta Aragonensia*.

[2] The case of the Templars illustrates Arnald's narrow fanaticism over poverty: because of their laxness in this, he approved of their overthrow. See Balthasar, *Armutsstreit*, p. 233, n. 3.

[3] Heuckelum, *Spiritualistische Strömungen*, pp. 18-20. See James II's repudiation of Arnald: H. Finke, *Acta Aragonensia*, II, no. 570, pp. 892-4.

[4] On the contrast between the brothers, Heuckelum, *Spiritualistische Strömungen*, pp. 12-15.

Foix, who was devoted to the Franciscans.[1] Of her four children, James renounced the kingdom and took the habit in 1299; Sancia, who became the queen of Robert the Wise of Naples, was a life-long supporter of Spirituals; Philip became a Beguin, and corresponded with Angelo da Clareno.

Support for the Spirituals was able to override political barriers: the house of Anjou was no less in their favour than its rivals of Aragon. At the end of the thirteenth century, despite their internal dissensions, the Franciscan order still had great prestige in the outside world. Often they were the favourite choice as chaplains in royal houses. With Franciscan influence, that of the Spirituals often came also. The house of Anjou is a case in point. Charles II was a patron of the order: he supported several of their houses, and in the summer made it a habit to stay by the convent of Sisteron, in Provence.[2] He was at the same time a supporter of the Community, and, at Gonsalvo of Valboà's request, assisted the persecution of a group of the Celestinian Spirituals.[3] His children, on the other hand, became Spiritual supporters. The three sons, Louis, Robert, and Raymond Berengar, when they were kept as hostages in Aragon, took Franciscans as tutors and chaplains. These were inclined to the rigorists, and influenced their protégés similarly, so much so indeed that the three sons wrote to Olivi in 1295, asking him to come and give them advice.[4] He refused, partly because he was aware of Charles II's hostility;[5] but the influence persisted. Louis renounced the throne in order to take the habit, surrounded himself with Spiritual friars, and as Archbishop of Toulouse brought on his death with excessive austerities. Robert, who succeeded his father in 1309, remained a Spiritual patron. There was therefore at the turn of the century a considerable body of support in the southern kingdoms for the Spiritual party in the order.

[1] On the family links, J. M. Vidal, "Un ascète de sang royal, Philippe de Majorque", *Revue des Questions Historiques* lxxxviii (1910), 361–4.

[2] Balthasar, *Armutsstreit*, p. 177.

[3] Angelo da Clareno, *Historia*, ed. Ehrle, *ALKG* II, 319.

[4] See Olivi's reply: F. Ehrle, "Olivis Leben und Schriften", Anhang, "Olivis Schreiben an die Söhne Karls II von Neapel aus dem J. 1295", *ALKG* III, 534–40.

[5] "Nam et michi a fide digno aliquo dictum fuit, quod eciam dominus pater vester timuerat vos inbeguiniri seu ut proprius loquar in divinis infatuari per eloquia oris mei." Ibid., p. 539.

In addition, the Spirituals had friends in the college of cardinals.[1] The Colonna, Peter and James, had used the Spirituals as makeweights in their propaganda against Boniface VIII. Peter's interest in them was always more political than otherwise. James, however, was sincere. Earlier on, he had been a personal friend of John of Parma. While the discussion about the Franciscans took place in the Council of Vienne, he received Angelo da Clareno as his guest.[2] Napoleon Orsini was another patron. He had old family links with the order. Celestine had made him the protector of the independent Spirituals in 1294. He continued to follow the fortunes of the group.[3] Early in the century, most probably when on his mid-Italian legation of 1306–8, he received Ubertino da Casale into his service. He made him his chaplain and employed him on various duties, including an investigation into a nest of heretics of the sect of the *Spiritus libertatis* in Umbria and the lifting of an interdict on the city of Siena.[4] The cardinals, perhaps more than the monarchs, could expect to gain the ear of the Pope.

Deliverance, when it finally came, was due to the efforts of a number of these outside supporters. In Angelo's version, given in the *Historia septem tribulationum*,[5] the impetus came from Arnald of Villanova. In 1309, Angelo says, he approached Charles II of Naples, who as Count of Provence ruled the area of greatest persecution, and persuaded him to write to the minister-general. The letter to Gonsalvo contained a threat: that if the Provence persecutions did not cease, the Pope would be informed. In addition, Arnald spoke privately about the persecutions to Clement V.

Angelo's account will probably stand: although he played no direct part in the discussions at the curia, he was present in the neighbourhood of Avignon from 1310 and had access to good sources of information. Arnald's *Rahonament* of 1309, delivered in

---

[1] On these, Balthasar, *Armutsstreit*, pp. 243–5, and refs. given.

[2] On Angelo's link with James see, esp., two of his letters: Ehrle, "Die Briefsammlung des fr. Angelus de Clarino", *ALKG* I, 543, and 555–6 (Ehrle's summary).

[3] Angelo, for example, c. 1305, consulted him; Napoleon offered to take him with him on his journey to Bordeaux. F. Ehrle, "Die Epistola excusatoria des fr. Angelo da Clarino", *ALKG* I, 531.

[4] Callaey, *Étude sur Ubertin de Casale*, pp. 44–6. Angelo's account of his unmasking of the heretics, *Historia*, ed. Ehrle, *ALKG* II, 131–2, can now be supplemented by L. Oliger, *De secta Spiritus libertatis in Umbria saec. XIV, disquisitio et documenta*, Roma, 1943. I am grateful for some help with references to Callaey to my friend Mr F. Dreyer, of the University of St Andrews.

[5] *ALKG* II, 129.

secret consistory, has survived, and is published by Pou y Marti.[1] The only detail which appears doubtful is the name of Charles II, who had not hitherto given favour to the Spirituals. He died on 5 May 1309. We shall probably be correct if we substitute the name of his successor, Robert the Wise, a known Spiritual supporter.[2]

A further step was taken by lay supporters in Provence. On 17 August procurators from the municipality of Narbonne presented a petition to the Pope. It contained all the grievances of the Spirituals—first, that the books of Olivi were unjustly condemned; second, that the Rule was not observed by the Community; third, that the Spirituals were unjustly punished. Lastly, a point perhaps of significance for the motives of the municipality, it was requested that special reverence be permitted for the body of Olivi, which was now preserved in Narbonne.[3]

Finally, it seems that a cardinal, perhaps Napoleon Orsini, about this time pleaded the Spiritual case to the Pope.[4]

At last, impelled by this sequence of appeals, the Pope turned his attention to the Franciscan order. From his summer residence at Groseau, outside Avignon, in late August or early September, by *littera secreta*, he summoned the leaders of both Spirituals and Conventuals to the curia.[5] After conducting some preliminary hearings in person, he decided to depute the task of investigation to subordinates. A commission of cardinals was set up. A formal list of questions, concerned with Olivi's writings and the state of the order, was put to the Franciscan representatives, and auditors were appointed to receive their replies.[6]

The Spirituals now had attained one primary objective: the cessation of persecution and a full investigation of the order. It remained for them to present their case to the Papal commission.

---

[1] *Archivo Ibero-Americano* xi (1919), 183–200.

[2] But for a contrary view, see Oliger, "Spirituels", *DTC* XV, ii, 1941, col. 2534.

[3] Ehrle, "Raymund von Fronsac Actensammlung", *ALKG* III, p. 18, cap. i.

[4] This is suggested by the opening sentence of the Bull of exemption, *Dudum ad apostolatus*, which Clement V issued in favour of the Spiritual leaders in 1310: "Dudum ad apostolatus nostri notitiam frequenter et secreto, et tandem in consistoriis tam secretis quam publicis, nostris et fratrum nostrorum auribus extitit frequentius intimatum, quod nonnulla erant corrigenda in ordine vestro . . .", *BF* V, no. 158, pp. 65–6.

[5] Oliger, "Spirituels", *DTC* XV, ii, 1941, col. 2534.

[6] There were four questions: on the penetration of the sect of the *Spiritus libertatis* among the Franciscans, on the observance, on the doctrines of Olivi, and on the persecutions in Provence.

8

THE PAPAL INVESTIGATION 1309–12

WE HAVE now reached a dividing-line in our account of the Spiritual-Conventual disputes. Hitherto, despite a common attachment to Olivi and a fundamental unity of aim, the Spirituals have generally acted in isolation from each other. Their ideas have been bounded by their provinces. The Spirituals from the March of Ancona, for example, when they went to Celestine V to ask for freedom, were making their request for their own group alone. The Spirituals from Provence, similarly, were complaining chiefly of the injustices in their own province. With the summons to the curia the situation changed. Here the Spiritual leaders were able to act in unity. They were able to put forward claims which did not concern their province alone, but the whole order. For the first time they had the opportunity of imposing their ideas on the whole body of Franciscans.

Our concern in the previous chapter was to describe how the first disputes arose and gradually became so bitter as to necessitate the intervention of the Papacy. In this chapter, while maintaining a chronological sequence,[1] we shall concentrate attention on the claims which the Spirituals put to the Papal commission.[2] The best source material for the ideas of the Spirituals are the pamphlets which they exchanged ceaselessly with the Conventuals for some three years, until the conclusion of the controversy in 1312.

[1] This seems important. There is no up-to-date, chronological account of the struggle in the curia between the parties; and I hope here to fill a gap, at any rate for English readers.

[2] In fact, there were two commissions, one from 1309 to the opening of the Council of Vienne, another thereafter until the settlement of the dispute by Clement's Bulls. The personnel of the first commission were changed: for details see E. Müller, *Das Konzil von Vienne 1311–1312. Seine Quellen und sein Geschichte*, Münster-i-W., 1934, who gives a complete narrative of the Franciscan dispute from its beginnings in the investigation of Olivi's doctrine up to *Exivi de paradiso*, pp. 236–386.

They were written by various of the Provençal Spirituals, who were those first summoned by Clement V. But the best of all, and those which most impressed the commission, were those written by Ubertino da Casale, who came to reinforce the Provençals some little time after the opening of the inquiry. Moreover, a full selection of Ubertino's has been edited by Ehrle in the *Archiv für Litferatur und Kirchengeschichte*.[1] We shall therefore use Ubertino as our prime source for the views of the Spirituals.

The most general statement of his position was given by Ubertino in his first reply to the commission, the *Sanctitas vestra*, written in or shortly before January 1310.[2] In form, the pamphlet faintly recalled the *Arbor vitae*. It had the same type of arrangement, with subject-matter placed under a long series of headings, the state of the Franciscans consisting in poverty, simplicity, purity, prayer, etc., and their failings grouped accordingly. As in the *Arbor*, the sequence of headings and the true logical order bore no relation to each other. There, however, the resemblance ended. *Sanctitas vestra* had none of the extravagant condemnations or the Joachimism which had distinguished the *Arbor*. It was, for Ubertino, a sober presentation of the Spiritual case.

Ubertino's starting-point was the same as that of his Conventual

---

[1] The *apologia* for Olivi: "Ubertinos von Casale Vertheidigungsschrift des Petrus Johannis Olivi und der Spiritualen", *ALKG* II, 374–416. The *Sanctitas vestra*: "Ubertinos von Casale Beantwortung der vier Fragepunkte (Anf. 1310)", *ALKG* III, 48–9. The *Rotulus*: "Die von Ubertino von Casale gegen die Communität aufgestellten Anklageartikel und Raymunds von Fronsac Widerlegung derselben", *ALKG* III, 89–137. The *Declaratio*: "Die Replik Ubertinos von Casale (c. August 1311)", ibid., pp. 160–95. The only omission of importance is the *Super tribus sceleribus*, ed. A. Heysse, *AFH* x (1917), 123–74. (The complete article of Heysse includes an edition of the Community's *Circa materiam*, which Ubertino was attacking.) For a bibliography of all the works known to have been produced for the Franciscan controversy, 1309–12, see A. Heysse, "Anonymi Spiritualis responsio 'Beatus Vir' contra 'Abbreviaturam Communitatis'", *AFH* xlii (1950), 213–16.

[2] It would seem that Ubertino arrived at Avignon after the other Spiritual representatives. He came from Umbria. Gaufredi apparently gave this heading to his reply to the four questions put to the representatives: "Responsiones fratrum . . . ad articulos per sanctissimum patrem dominum Clementem . . . fratribus ad se vocatis de provincia Provincie traditos." *ALKG* III, 142. This would suggest that only friars from Provence were then acting in the investigation. Further, in the same work Gaufredi and his companions said they knew nothing of the sect of the *Spiritus libertatis* in Umbria (*ALKG* III, p. 142, lines 10–12); Ubertino, who had played an active part in its suppression, would have informed them if he had been present. For the date of the *Sanctitas vestra*, Ehrle, *ALKG* III, 49; the text, ibid., pp. 51–89.

opponents. He began with the accepted identification of Franciscan poverty with the poverty of Christ, much as it had been set out by Bonaventura and by *Exiit qui seminat*.[1] He went on, just as a Conventual might have done, to insist that evangelical poverty, in its highest form, required the renunciation of all dominion, individual and common. From that he deduced that the friars could not go to law, and could have no legal rights. So far, the positions of the two sides were identical, for the Community insisted as ardently as the Spirituals that the friars had no legitimate rights in law.

But after this, the two begin to diverge. Ubertino next appealed to the intention of St Francis. He recalled the words of the Testament, forbidding the friars to take Papal privileges, and characteristically reinforced this precedent with a quotation from one of the Leo-sources on the biography of Francis. He was not concerned with *Quo elongati's* abrogation of the Testament. Technically, he admitted, nothing Francis said in the Testament could have the force of law, since Francis when he wrote it had resigned office. Morally, however, he said, it still bound the friars, because it revealed Francis's intention in the Rule—an intention which was based on the inspiration of the Holy Spirit. The Testament therefore to all intents and purposes still stood, and it forbade the use of privileges. How, then, do the friars come to have privileges from the Papacy? He answered: "And our popes have been swayed by what we have said: with good intentions they have given us privileges, not knowing that they would be repugnant to our state and that we should abuse them."[2] This, of course, was a diplomatic reply: in the *Arbor* Ubertino was a good deal less accommodating about the position of the Popes who had imposed their interpretations of the Rule on the Franciscans.

Ubertino throughout the controversy had great difficulty in discussing Papal privileges. At bottom, like all the Spirituals of the later period, he wished to follow Francis in the Testament and reject them.[3] He argued that the Rule was clear and observable to the letter.[4] *Exiit qui seminat*, he said, was not, and could easily

---

[1] "Status iste, qui est evangelice perfectionis, fundatus est a Deo homine Yesu Christo et fuit a beato Francisco repetitus." Ibid., p. 51, lines 32–3.
[2] Ibid., p. 54, lines 18–20.
[3] Ibid., pp. 52–3.   [4] Ibid., p. 73, line 6.

be twisted against the intentions of Nicholas III.[1] In conclusion,[2] he explained that he did not wish to say anything against *Exiit*—but by implication his whole treatise is an attack on all the Papal Bulls interpreting the Rule.

The counter-authority to which he appeals is that of the founder, under the guidance of the Holy Spirit.[3] The Rule and the Testament had been sealed by Christ with the bestowal of the stigmata on the writer.[4] Both Gregory IX and Nicholas III appealed to the intentions of the founder. Ubertino claimed that it was legitimate for him to do the same, employing the evidence of Leo and the companions.[5]

Concessions, he said, did not bind those who do not wish to observe them, and the privileges were not imposed by the Popes but extorted from them.[6] The Popes had good intentions in thus conceding privileges: they wished to accede to the desires of the friars, and by legitimizing the existing state of the observance, by bending the Rule to the life, to prevent further relaxations. In fact this policy was mistaken, because privileges were merely used as a cover for further relaxations.[7]

We see that Ubertino is clearly distinguishing two ways of life, that permitted by the Papal privileges, from *Quo elongati* onwards, and the literal observance, which is that envisaged by St Francis and practised, when the Community permitted, by the Spirituals. To the first form of life Ubertino, as we have seen, is very grudging. He admits that it is not a sinful state. He agrees that the Pope might well order "that . . . no brother should say that the rule is not being kept, as far as is necessary to salvation, when the standard is that of the papal declaration . . ." (i.e. *Exiit qui seminat*).[8] But it is inferior to the second form of life, the literal observance. Ubertino will not admit any reason for departing from the literal standard. He assumes that any deviation is dictated by human weakness, and brushes aside all the reasons for

[1] Ibid., p. 86, lines 31–5.
[2] Ibid., p. 89, lines 14–16.
[3] Ibid., p. 54, lines 4–11.
[4] Ibid., p. 87, lines 8–13.
[5] *Quo elongati: Epitome*, ed. Eubel, p. 229a. *Exiit qui seminat: Epitome*, p. 291b. *Sanctitas vestra*, *ALKG* III, p. 85, lines 17–26.
[6] Ibid., p. 86, lines 23–5.
[7] Ibid., p. 69, lines 2–13.
[8] Ibid., p. 86, lines 26–8.

development as "falsa prudentia".[1] It is exactly the attitude of the
Speculum perfectionis, attributing to Francis denunciations of the
ministers of his time.[2]

Ubertino did not, however, simply equate the actual state of the
Community with the state of those who use the Papal privileges.
The Community in his view did not use the privileges in the way
which the Popes intended. Their state was a sinful state, *tout court*.
He gave a series of examples of abuses to prove this. He cited the
illicit reception of money, which had been made necessary by
superfluities in building and ornaments, especially in Umbria
and Tuscany;[3] the use of the *bursarius* by friars going on journeys;[4]
excess in church ornaments[5]—all the abuses which were at the
time being banned, officially, by the Conventuals in constitutions
and decrees of chapters-general. There can, indeed, be little dispute about their existence.

But Ubertino by the scheme of his treatise had to do more than
demonstrate the existence of abuses. He had to show that the state
of the order, to use his own words, was "collapsus"; that, in fact,
the general standard had fallen so low that only drastic remedies
could restore it.

His claim was that the cause of this decline was the adoption by
the order of the way of privileges. These opened the way to relaxation. They were not a secure standard, as the letter of the Rule was.
The only adequate solution to Franciscan problems, therefore,
would be to declare the literal observance to be the proper form
of life for the friars. This way should be presented to the body of the
friars by the Papacy. Then, if they refused it, they might be
allowed to follow the lesser standard, the way of privileges. But it
should be plain to all that this was a lesser standard, and not the
full observance, as the Spirituals practised it.[6]

Ubertino ended his discussion on poverty with a warning. It
would not be enough, he said, simply to restore the way of privileges, and force the Community to observe it, while allowing the
Spirituals their own observance, within the order, under favourable

---

[1] Ibid., p. 72, lines 33–5, p. 73, lines 1–3.
[2] Compare *Speculum*, ed. Sabatier (1928), cap. xi, para. 9, p. 36.
[3] Ibid., pp. 67–8.
[4] Ibid., p. 71.
[5] Ibid., pp. 70–1.
[6] Ibid., p. 87.

superiors. If this solution was adopted, it would not work. The way of privileges would not be kept, because it was too imprecise; the Spirituals would complain; persecution would follow, as before.[1] It was a penetrating, and, as it turned out, a prophetic observation.

What was the effect of this first blast from Ubertino? It is almost impossible to say, directly; but, in the following April Clement issued a Bull, *Dudum ad apostolatus*, in favour of the Spirituals.[2] It began with a sketch of the situation. Clement had heard that there was a need for reformation in the Franciscan order. Franciscan superiors have not corrected abuses, although often required to do so. He has therefore instituted an inquiry, summoning to the curia the minister-general and other leaders, and with them certain other friars "whom we believe to be fervent with the zeal of God in the regular observance of the order . . ."[3] This was already a blow for the Community. He had assumed the existence of abuses, and Conventuals' failure to correct them. He had publicly praised the Spirituals.

Worse followed. In the dispositive section, Clement exempted the Spiritual leaders from their superiors, and put them under the jurisdiction of the cardinals on the commission. He assumed that there would be danger to the Spirituals from the members of the Community, and warned the order against punishing other Spirituals in the provinces. Finally, he ordered the minister-general or his procurator to promulgate the Bull, so that they would be unable to make the excuse of ignorance.

First blood had gone to the Spirituals. In the same year, it seems, Ubertino began work on a second pamphlet, the *Rotulus*, which was to complete the damage.[4] Here his aim was to show, in greater detail, how the observance of the Community was in decay. A new list of transgressions was set down, this time under the heading of quotations from the Rule and *Exiit*. Little escaped that mordant pen. All the infractions of a religious society, some-times large, often trivial, but cumulatively effective, were set down by an eye-witness. Ubertino ranged from the over-indulgence

---

[1] Ibid., p. 87, lines 35-9, p. 88, lines 1-2.
[2] *BF* V, 65b-8a.
[3] Ibid., p. 66a.
[4] Text, together with the Conventual reply, ed. Ehrle, *ALKG* III, 93-137. For the date, ibid., pp. 90-1; Müller, *Das Konzil*, p. 270.

of the friars at chapters-general[1] and the excessive wearing of shoes by masters of theology[2] to serious criticisms of the use of money and the treatment of dominion. Most of these complaints were not new: the Conventuals indeed generally cited the decrees and constitutions which condemned these abuses as evidence of their own innocence as a body. But in the pamphlet the complaint was that much more effective because it was couched in the style of an anecdote, and not in the decorous language of a constitution.

As an example we may quote part of Ubertino's description of the abuses of money:

> Again in just the same way those who can, take with them *bursarii*, who are their servants, who so spend money at the order of the brothers, that in every respect the brothers appear to have dominion not only over the money, but also over the servants spending it. And sometimes the brothers carry a box with the money inside; and on the occasions when this is carried by the boys, they often know nothing of the contents, and it is the brothers who carry the keys. And although the servants may sometimes be called *nuntii* of those persons who gave the money for the brothers; yet neither the servants nor those who deposit with them, know that the money is in the dominion of anyone other than the brothers. . . .[3]

And another example:

> Again in some places the sacrists themselves have candles brought from the sacristy and have them put on a dish in the church, so that men and women come in, receive them, and offer them and put money in their place on the dish or box; and the servant looks after the brothers' dish and receives the money, so that the same candle is sold ten times over.[4]

The relevance of these abuses to the "way of privileges", which permitted the use of the *nuntius*, was obvious; while Ubertino's employment of detail carried its own conviction. Repeatedly precise facts were given about abuses—about, for example, the practice of cultivation for profit,[5] the use of granaries and cellars for wine,[6] the reception of bequests of horses and arms.[7] Repeatedly

---

[1] *ALKG* III, 102.
[2] Ibid., pp. 100–1.
[3] Ibid., p. 104, lines 30–8.
[4] Ibid., p. 105, lines 15–20.
[5] Ibid., p. 114, lines 23–6.
[6] Ibid., p. 115.
[7] Ibid., p. 114, lines 3–10.

the obvious contrast was made with the conditions of Francis's day—on building, for instance, the point that the buildings which Francis pulled down were still very humble, "nothing in comparison with the present ones".[1]

The conclusion which Ubertino drew from his indictment of the Community was that the only secure way of reform was to return to the literal observance of the Rule, which Francis had intended for his order. He said:

> . . . so we ask the Holy See humbly and earnestly for the perfect observance of our rule and the gospel of Christ, as it is contained in the rule, and according to the intention of our father St Francis, which he expressed in word and deed and plain exclusion of all the laxities mentioned.[2]

Against these criticisms the Community had little defence. They admitted some relaxations, but said that they were the work of isolated individuals. Because the Community forbade them in its constitutions, they were not responsible for them. Other abuses alleged by Ubertino were not real abuses at all, but usages legitimized by privileges from the Papacy. The use of *bursarii*, for example, was not a breach of poverty: it was as legitimate as the use of the *nuntius*, which Papal privileges had long allowed to the friars.[3] To carry the key of a purse was reprehensible in a friar; but only because the appearance was unseemly.[4] Dominion over the money remained in the hand of another; and so there was no offence. Privileges were not wrong. They had been granted by the Papacy, and to attack them would be to attack the wisdom of the Papacy in granting them.[5] The Community could thus produce nothing better than these narrowly legalistic arguments to defend its position. If the actual practice of poverty had been the only issue confronting the commission, then surely the Community would have gone down in defeat.

But in fact it was not. The two parties differed, not only on the

---

[1] Ibid., p. 116, line 24.
[2] Ibid., p. 137, lines 34–8.
[3] Ibid., pp. 107–8.
[4] "Tamen quia species non esset decens, idcirco hoc reprehensibile iudicatur. . . ." Ibid., p. 107, lines 33–4.
[5] Ibid., p. 99, lines 21–35.

practical question of the observance, but also on the doctrine of poverty which underlay it, and here, on this last point, the Spirituals were less effective. The central question was the doctrine of the *usus pauper*. Ubertino had taken over, more or less *verbatim*, Olivi's doctrine of the *usus pauper* and with it its weaknesses.[1] He argued, as Olivi had done before him, that the *usus pauper* was an integral part of the vow of poverty. He assumed that it would be incumbent on the friars all the time. Certainly some allowance was made for special circumstances, and Ubertino, here borrowing Olivi's caution,[2] conceded that only a serious and prolonged transgression of the *usus pauper* would amount to a breach of the vow, and thus be a mortal sin. Nevertheless the constant obligation, if it did not take away the discretion of superiors over the Rule, would at any rate much diminish it.

To the Spirituals this by-product of their doctrine was not a drawback—it was, rather, an advantage, since the majority of superiors in the order were unfavourable to them. To ecclesiastical authorities, on the other hand, it was a demerit of their doctrine that it took away so much of the superior's powers of discretion. As far as the commission was concerned, for example, acceptance of the Spiritual view of the *usus pauper* would mean breaching the long tradition in the West, which preferred widening the powers of superiors to tightening written regulations.

Furthermore, the precedents which Ubertino alleged for his doctrine from older Franciscan authorities, although they favoured some form of *usus pauper*, did not specifically put it in relation to the vow of poverty. The fact was that before Olivi's time this particular issue had seldom been discussed in the order. The *usus pauper* was a difficult issue. The disputes which had taken place over Olivi's doctrine while he was still alive suggested that even the learned found it hard to agree on the matter. Could it then be

---

[1] Ubertino's principal work on the *usus pauper* is the *Super tribus sceleribus*, ed. Heysse, *AFH* x (1917), 123–74. It shows him less effective on doctrine than on the discussion of the state of the observance. For his dependence on Olivi, compare the quotations he gives from Hugues de Digne, ed. cit., pp. 141–2, with those given by Olivi in his *apologia* to his censors of 1285, ed. Laberge, *AFH* xxviii (1935), 383–4. With one exception, they are identical. See also the borrowing of a long passage on the *usus pauper* in the *Sanctitas vestra* from Olivi, *ALKG* III, 134–5; note also the abrupt change of tone when Ubertino ends the quotation and adds two sentences of his own, ibid., p. 135, lines 34–9.

[2] And, as we have seen, his words. *ALKG* III, p. 134, n. 3.

legitimate to impose this doctrine of *usus pauper* on unlearned novices, whose consciences might be oppressed by this uncertain obligation? Tradition required that the vow should fall on some precisely delimited obligation; neither the *usus pauper*, nor the *usus lautus*, by their nature, could be given precise limits.[1]

Now the Spirituals were not reformers pure and simple. As we have seen, they did not wish merely to restore the official standards of the observance; they wished to impose their own standards. They insisted on the *usus pauper*. Ubertino said more than once that the acceptance of the *usus pauper* was essential. Indeed, he accused the Conventuals of heresy for denying that the *usus pauper* fell under the vow.[2] All Franciscans were agreed that their poverty corresponded to that of Christ and the apostles. Christ imposed the *usus pauper* on the apostles when he sent them on the preaching tour; and therefore to attack the *usus pauper* among the Franciscans was to undermine the authority of Scripture.[3]

What was the Conventual answer? They also appealed to the poverty of Christ and the apostles; but with a very different result. In their view, the substance of poverty consisted not in the restriction of use but in the renunciation of dominion. All the traditional proofs given by Bonaventura in the *Apologia pauperum* were pressed into service in order to show that it was only dominion and not use that was in question. Pierre Auriol, for example, used this argument. Christ was most perfectly poor. Therefore he was more poor than John the Baptist. But he was not more austere. Christ had a seamless robe, John camel's hair. Christ came eating and drinking, John fasted. In use John was thus poorer than Christ. It must have been the renunciation of dominion which made Christ the poorer—and this was shown by Christ's words. He said, "The Son of Man hath not where to lay his head", and yet he lived with Martha and Mary. When he said he had nowhere to

---

[1] This was the most effective argument of the *Circa materiam*, which Müller (*Das Konzil*, p. 336) calls "the most mature work on the side of the Community". See Heysse's edn., *AFH* x (1917), 118–19. Similarly, in the treatise of Richard of Conington, ed. Heysse, *AFH* xxiii (1930), 359.

[2] For example, *Sanctitas vestra*, ed. Ehrle, *ALKG* III, p. 82, lines 26–34, p. 83, lines 1–7.

[3] See the *Super tribus sceleribus*, ed. Heysse, *AFH* x (1917), 125–31, where a major argument is based on the identification of the poverty of the Franciscans with that of Christ and the apostles.

lay his head, he can only have been referring to his renunciation of jurisdiction, not to his restricting of use.[1]

Arguments of this type, used on both sides, were almost a caricature of the Bonaventuran exposition.

Generally, however, the Conventual case rested on technical arguments, drawn from law. The vow must fall on some determined obligation. The *usus pauper* has no determined limits. Therefore the vow of poverty cannot include the *usus pauper*.[2] Or again, in the observance the *usus pauper* is dispensable. The renunciation of dominion is not. Therefore the *usus pauper* is not of the substance of the vow of poverty, while the renunciation of dominion is.[3]

If the Spirituals unduly diminished the discretion of the ministers, the Conventuals on the other hand exaggerated it to an arbitrary degree. If the vow is to relate only to the renunciation of dominion, the superior has *carte blanche* to proceed as he wills in the use of material goods. There was not perhaps a total freedom. The Community admitted there should be some restriction in use, "ex condecentia status", and they allowed that restrictions in use, when put as precepts in the Rule, should be universally observed.[4] Nevertheless the tendency remained, and in the future issued in such extreme proposals as Gerald Odonis's request to John XXII, that he give permission for provincials to dispense at will from the Rule's prohibitions.[5] In studying the differences between the parties on the theory of poverty, one is reminded of St Francis de Sales's saying: how there are always some who wish to draw the

---

[1] E. Longpré, "Le Quolibet de Nicolas de Lyre, o.f.m.", *AFH* xxiii (1930), 54. In the course of this article Longpré edited the *quaestio* on the *usus pauper* to which we have referred. He wrongly attributed this to Nicholas of Lyra; in fact, it is a later redaction of the *quaestio* written by Pierre Auriol and is a strongly Conventual work. See F. Pelster, "Nikolaus von Lyra und seine Quaestio de usu paupere", *AFH* xlvi (1953), 212–14. Nicholas of Lyra himself defends the doctrine of Olivi, although without the extravagances of Ubertino and the Spirituals. Pelster believed that Nicholas was at Santa Croce c. 1300, where the influence of Olivi and others of similar views still lingered. Art. cit., p. 218.

[2] See above, p. 193, n. 1.

[3] For example, Richard of Conington's treatise, ed. Heysse, *AFH* xxiii (1930), 105.

[4] For example, "Ad primum igitur dicendum quod, quantum apparet ex verbis Regulae, restrictio in calceamentis et equitaturis non est necessitatis, sed condecentiae", ibid., p. 360. "Secundo videndum est, utrum frater Minor teneatur ad usum pauperem.—Dico quod non ex voto, sed ex decentia", Longpré, "Le Quolibet de Nicolas de Lyre", *AFH* xxiii (1930), 55.

[5] Holzapfel, *Handbuch*, p. 79.

net very tight, and others who want to make the meshes too wide.

But if the views of either side appeared exaggerated, the consequences of this mattered more for the Spirituals than for the Community. The burden of proof lay on the rigorists. It was up to them to impress the commission with their plans. They did not want a return to the *status quo*: twenty years of sufferings had already shown them the impossibility of observing their way of life under the old system. They had insisted on the *usus pauper*; in the event, the final commission of investigation, which sat at the Council of Vienne, found itself unable to agree on this point. Three differing opinions about it were reported to the Pope.[1]

It was not only these doctrinal issues which weakened the effect of the Spirituals' attack on the abuses of the Community. A tactical issue interposed between them and their objective. On 1 March 1311 the two new representatives of the Community, Raymond of Fronsiac and Bonagratia of Bergamo, who had replaced Gonsalvo and the ministers in the direction of the case, launched a formal *appellatio* against the Spirituals.[2] It was delivered before the Pope, in open consistory. The basis of the action was that the Spiritual representatives were fautors of heresy, and, as such, incapable of receiving the exemption from their superiors which the Pope had bestowed on them in 1310. Every one of them was a supporter of the doctrines of Olivi, whose works were proscribed in the order and had been condemned by the Franciscan masters and bachelors at Paris in 1283, and, more recently, by Murrovalle. In itself, the *appellatio* was purely a tactical device. As the Conventuals very well knew, the Olivi case was still *sub judice*. One of the questions of the investigation, which was still going on, ran: Are there errors in the works of Olivi? On the other hand, the Olivi question had of late been overshadowed by the question of the state of the observance, much to the advantage of the Spirituals. The *appellatio* brought Olivi, on whom the Community's case was stronger, back into the centre of discussion.

In the *appellatio* there was included yet another list of the errors

---

[1] G. Fussenegger, "Relatio commissionis in concilio Viennensi institutae ad decretalem 'Exivi de paradiso' praeparandam", *AFH* l (1957), 174-5.

[2] F. Ehrle, "Anklageschrift der Communität gegen die Spiritualen und im besondem gegen fr. Petrus Johannis Olivi (vom 1. März 1311)", *ALKG* II, 365-74.

of Olivi. Eight were given. They included some old points, such
as the *usus pauper*[1] and the question of the divine essence,[2] which
went back to the time of the commission of the seven masters.
They included one point from Murrovalle's persecutions in
Provence—the spear-wound.[3] They also included some new
material: Joachimism for the first time appeared in the lists
against Olivi.

> And he has spoken, written, and taught false and fantastic pro-
> phecies about the church in his books and writings, and especially
> in the postill which he has written on the Apocalypse, calling the
> church a great whore, and putting forward many other doctrines
> to the detriment of the church.[4]

More detail than before was given about Olivi's sect in Provence,
in an *excursus* to the eight errors.[5] But neither of these issues
carried much weight in Clement's investigation.

One distinguishing feature all the errors had: they were all
theological issues. It was clear that what the Community wanted
was a clear condemnation of Olivi in his theology; if possible, a
personal condemnation that would implicate his followers.

On all these points Ubertino was able to provide some sort of
answer. In the summer, he brought out an *apologia* for Olivi.[6]
First he turned the Conventuals' accusations back on their own
heads. Was the Community not a fautor of heresy, he asked,
equally with the Spirituals whom they were attacking? Had they
not made Olivi a *lector*, first at Florence, then at Montpellier?
These appointments had been made after, not before, the accusations of 1283.[7]

Then, he did what he could to defend Olivi's teaching. On most
issues he had something to say; on some he was effective. On the
spear-wound, by a curious chance, he had textual support for
Olivi's aberration. Olivi had suggested that John might be wrong
in putting the spear-wound after the death of Christ. In fact, there

---

[1] Ibid., pp. 369–70.
[2] Ibid., p. 369.
[3] Ibid., pp. 368–9.
[4] Ibid., p. 370, lines 16–19.
[5] Ibid., p. 371.
[6] F. Ehrle, "Ubertinos von Casale Vertheidigungsschriften des Petrus
Johannis Olivi und der Spiritualen", ibid., pp. 374–416.
[7] Ibid., pp. 381–2.

are excellent variants, recognized by Westcott and Hort, which insert in Matt. 27. 49 reference to the wound being inflicted before Christ's death.[1] Some supporters of Olivi had already noticed this: in 1300, four friars and a secular priest at Marseilles swore on affidavit that they had seen the variant in a book in the library of St Victor.[2] Ubertino took over their testimony.[3] On all the supposed errors he was notably moderate. He and the rest of the Spiritual representatives, he said, were not bound to Olivi.[4] It might be that individual points in his work needed correction. But if they did, was it necessary to prohibit all his works?[5] Yet Ubertino's defence, however skilful, could not conceal the fact that the Olivi case, which had troubled the order so long, needed still more investigation. Such an investigation might clear the Spirituals; it was more likely to draw attention away from the reform of the observance.

The Conventuals pressed their attack. In July, being refused another hearing in the consistory, they formally renewed their *appellatio* in private, in the presence of the chamberlain to Murrovalle, the cardinal protector.[6] A little later Bonagratia of Bergamo took an extreme course, and asked the auditors of the sacred palace whether it was legitimate for the Conventual representatives to have communication with the Spirituals, since they were excommunicated as supporters of the heresy of Olivi.[7] The Pope was angry, but by then it mattered less. The Community had got its way, and a new commission of three theologians had been set up to examine Olivi's teachings.

---

[1] See F. C. Burkitt, "Ubertino da Casale and a variant reading", *Journal of Theological Studies* xxiii (1922), 186–8.

[2] V. Doucet, "De operibus manuscriptis", *AFH* xxviii (1935), 441–2.

[3] Ibid., pp. 404–5. Burkitt believed the existence of this variant was a proof of Ubertino's veracity. Doucet, however, inclines to think that Ubertino merely took the evidence from the affidavit and passed it off as his own. "De operibus manuscriptis", *AFH* xxviii (1935), 431–3.

[4] ". . . idcirco semper premisimus, quod nos nichil defendebamus nec defendere intendebamus eroneum nec in dictis fratris Petri nec cuiuscunque alterius . . .", *ALKG* II, p. 413, lines 2–4.

[5] "Nam quod dicunt, errores eis sic immixtos, quod purum separari nequeat ab impuro, hoc est falsissimum, quia in paucis locis loquitur de illis opinionibus." Ibid., p. 388, lines 21–4.

[6] Ibid., p. 365.

[7] F. Ehrle, "Bonagrazias von Bergamo Gutachten über sein Verbannungsdecret", *ALKG* III, 37–8. "Raymund von Fronsac Actensammlung", ibid., p. 20, cap. xiii.

Soon the whole matter was held over. It was decided, very likely because of the doctrinal issues involved in the Olivi case,[1] to defer a settlement of the affairs of the Franciscans to the Council of Vienne, summoned for October 1311. This was a Conventual success. Time could not favour the Spirituals, who had already made their best points about the state of the observance and could expect to do little more.

The investigation of the poverty dispute now passed into the hand of another commission, appointed from among the members of the Council. They showed themselves favourable to the Spirituals in their attack on abuses, unfavourable to them in their doctrine of poverty. It was the *Rotulus*, more than any other treatise on either side, that held their attention. In their report, recently edited by Fussenegger in the *Archivum Franciscanum Historicum*,[2] they followed Ubertino's sequence of transgressions, repeatedly supporting his judgements.[3] On the other hand, the report said nothing of the literal observance of the intention of St Francis. Also much space was taken up with the words of precept in the Rule, a discussion of little interest to the rigorists, who seldom grasped the importance of grading accurately the obligations of the friars.

The settlement of the affair was made in May of 1312. Ostensibly, it was not a victory for either side. Two Bulls were issued. One, *Exivi de paradiso*, dealt with the doctrine and practice of poverty in the order;[4] the other, *Fidei catholicae fundamento*, settled the Olivi case.[5]

In the latter, two doctrinal positions, on the soul and on Christ's spear-wound, were condemned. Two views on the effects of baptism were described and one of them adjudged the more probable. The authorship of these points of doctrine remained anonymous. Some attempt has been made on these grounds to argue that the condemnations do not refer to the teachings of Olivi as they are found in his writings; but common sense and the opinions of the

---

[1] Müller's view: *Das Konzil*, p. 294. See *ALKG* III, p. 39, lines 2–5.
[2] G. Fussenegger, "Relatio commissionis in concilio Viennensi institutae ad decretalem 'Exivi de paradiso' praeparandam", *AFH* l (1957), 145–77.
[3] See Fussenegger's judgement, art. cit., p. 152.
[4] *BF* V, no. 195, pp. 80–6.
[5] Ibid., no. 196, p. 86.

neutrals at the Council of Vienne militate against this view.[1] We may take it that Olivi was envisaged.

The statements of the Bull were not entirely clear: the definition on the rational soul has been the subject of dispute ever since.[2] Ubertino's description of the views of the preparatory commission on Olivi suggests that theologians were confused and divided about Olivi's doctrine.[3] The definition can therefore be represented as a minimal decision, which skirted prolonged and difficult discussion of detail.

It can also be represented as an act of clemency towards the Spirituals. If Olivi was not mentioned by name, it would be made clear that no personal condemnation was envisaged, and the Spirituals could be freed from the accusation of fautorship of heresy. Three points were in any case a small result from the successive winnowings and threshings of Olivi's teachings, which had gone on since 1283.

As a whole, though, *Fidei catholicae fundamento* was a gain for the Community. *Exivi*, on the contrary, was divided: something was conceded to the Spirituals, something to the Community.

Like the report of the commission, the Bull reproduced the essentials of Ubertino's *Rotulus*. The transgressions were listed in the same order as in the *Rotulus*.[4] At the start a note was made that the Community had denied the existence of these offences, and

---

[1] L. Amorós, "Aegidii Romani Impugnatio doctrinae Petri Ioannis Olivi an. 1312, nunc primum in lucem edita (Disseritur de mente Concilii Viennensis in causa P. I. Olivi)", *AFH* xxvii (1934), 408–20.

[2] On this subject, see Müller's discussion of *Fidei catholicae fundamento: Das Konzil*, pp. 352–86. On Olivi's doctrine on matrimony, which was not mentioned in the Bull, see A. Maier, "Per la storia del Processo contro l'Olivi", *Rivista di Storia della Chiesa in Italia* vi (1952), 317–31.

[3] "Nam illa, que imponunt sibi, non inveniuntur ponderis notabilis per magistros visis suis dictis nisi in tribus articulis, scilicet de essentia divina, de anima rationali et de vulnere laterali; in quibus et in omnibus aliis positionibus et intentionem persone purgant ab omni heretica pravitate et in ipsismet tribus articulis varii et dubii conceptus ipsis magistris occurrunt." *Declaratio*, ed. Ehrle, *ALKG* III, p. 191, lines 12–18. Müller argues that Ubertino could not be lying here, because the work was submitted to a commission who had knowledge on this point.

[4] Among the points of similarity are the following. The *Rotulus*, *ALKG* III, 100, 101, complained of excess in clothing; the Community in their reply said that the injunctions of the Rule on this point were counsels only. But *Exivi*, *BF* V, 82b, said that they were precepts. The *Rotulus*, *ALKG* III, 115, said that annual rents were accepted in the order; *Exivi*, *BF* V, 83b, said the same. The *Rotulus* complained of excess in building (*ALKG* III, 115–116) and of the undue conservation of grain and wine (*ALKG* III, 115); *Exivi*, *BF* V, 83b-4a, did the same.

that they claimed that offenders were punished and statutes made
against them;[1] nevertheless, the listing of the offences, which
followed, and the language used in the descriptions of them,
clearly implied that they did take place. Ubertino's most anecdotal
points were included, down to the friars with the *bursarii* and the
keys to the purses.[2] The condemnations went surprisingly far.
No pleas of necessary development were allowed to stand against
the charge that buildings in the order were excessive; liturgical
necessity was not admitted as an excuse for excesses in church
ornaments.[3]

Once the intention of Francis was mentioned, when it was said
that he desired his order to be founded in poverty, both in spirit
and in deed.[4] This, however, was as far as the Bull went towards
meeting the desires of the Spirituals. Their *usus pauper* was not
accepted. Neither was the Conventual version. The Bull gave a
compromise solution. It laid down that the friars were specially
obliged to those poor uses expressed in the Rule, in the way in
which they were expressed. "Specialiter" still left some room for
manoeuvre. The imputation of heresy in connection with the
doctrine of the *usus pauper*, *pro* or *con*, was condemned; this went
against both sides.[5]

Exivi's decision on the obligation of the gospel for the friars was
on traditional lines. It was, in effect, an amplification of *Quo elongati*, and consequently against the Spirituals. Moreover, even the
discussion of the transgressions from the *Rotulus* did not support
the Spirituals all the way. When, for instance, Clement spoke
of the illegitimacy of the use of granaries and cellars for wine, or of
the clothing of the friars, he left an escape clause. The discretion of
the superior, under which the worst excesses had been palliated,
in the Spirituals' view, still remained.

There was a fundamental point. *Exivi* did nothing to undermine
the way of privileges. Ubertino had complained, for example, in
the *Rotulus* that the underlying cause of many offences against the
renunciation of dominion was the Papal privilege *Exultantes in
Domino*;[6] in *Exivi*, significantly enough, nothing was said of this.

---

[1] *BF* V, 84a.   [2] Ibid., p. 83a.   [3] Ibid., p. 85a.
[4] Ibid., p. 84b.   [5] Ibid., p. 85a.
[6] *ALKG* III, 113–14. *Exultantes* is not mentioned by name; but Ubertino
clearly must have it in mind.

Ubertino had stiffly criticized *Exiit qui seminat*. *Exivi* did nothing to criticize *Exiit*; the whole Bull was, indeed, a supplement to *Exiit*, following on the same lines of principle. Viewed in the light of the history of the order, *Exivi's* great function was its clarification of the points of obligation in the Rule. Its decision on this matter is to this day the foundation of the order's observance. In doing this the Bull was only giving practical expression to the principle laid down in the first clause of *Exiit*.[1] Finally, *Exivi* itself was another gloss on the Rule. What was the value of this to Ubertino and the rest of the Spirituals, who had pleaded for an end of Papal glosses?

The settlement, therefore, did not go as far as the Spirituals might have hoped. At one time, particularly in 1310, they had come very close to achieving their objective, only to have it snatched from their grasp by the skilful tactics of the Conventual representatives. But still one issue remained unsettled. The Bull said nothing about the permanent exemption of the Spirituals from their superiors. The rigorists continued to hope that it would be given to them, perhaps a little after the Council. It was, as Ubertino had said in his *Sanctitas vestra*, the one vital requirement for them.

[1] *Epitome*, ed. Eubel, pp. 291b–2b.

9

THE AFTERMATH

THE SPIRITUAL representatives, probably in 1312, withdrew from the Avignon convent, where they felt themselves threatened by the presence of the Conventuals, and made their home by a solitary church near Malaucène. The patron of the church gave them leave to stay; there were caves and water at hand; they had freedom to follow their own observance. In the winter of 1312–13 they moved to a settlement at St Lazare, in Avignon, and there, in their short, patched habits continued to observe the Rule to the letter.[1] Their hope was that this separate existence would shortly be permitted to all their confrères in the provinces.

Clement's first actions after the issue of *Exivi* revealed his displeasure with the Community. In July he cited to Avignon the provincial of Provence and fifteen others of the same province, who were known for their persecution of the Spirituals.[2] In an interview he threatened them and deprived them of office.[3] At the end of the month he gave orders for Bonagratia of Bergamo to be conveyed to the remote convent of Valcabrère and confined there at his will.[4]

This might have seemed a good augury for the Spirituals; but while the question of their exemption still hung in the balance, a group of Spirituals in Tuscany decided to take matters into their own hands.[5] The progress of the investigation had exacerbated the

---

[1] Angelo, *Historia*, ed. Ehrle, *ALKG* II, 140.

[2] *BF* V, no. 203, p. 89.

[3] We have this from a reputable witness, James Colonna. See L. Oliger, "Fr. Bertrandi de Turre processus contra Spirituales Aquitaniae (1315) et card. Jacobi de Columna litterae defensoriae Spiritualium Provinciae (1316)". *AFH* xvi (1923), 352.

[4] *BF* V, no. 204, p. 89.

[5] Angelo introduces his account of the Tuscan revolt in these terms: "Interea autem antequam questio a bone memorie papa Clemente terminaretur . . ." (*Historia*, ed. Ehrle, *ALKG* II, 139). By *questio* in this context he means, not the queries about the Rule, which were settled by *Exivi*, but the question of the

existing party feeling in the province. The Spirituals, pressed by persecution, applied for advice to a certain canon Martin, who, in his ignorance, assured them that it would be just to secede from the Community and form their own organization. They took his advice and rebelled. Some took refuge from their superiors in private houses.[1] Some apparently made off to Sicily, to seek refuge with Frederick.[2] A strong group left their various convents and took by force from the Community three convents, Carmignano, near Florence, and Arezzo and Ascania in the neighbourhood of Siena. They expelled Conventual sympathizers and defended the convents against them in the manner of war, "alberteschis cum propugnaculis et balistis . . ."[3] The news, when it reached Avignon, did much to discredit the Spiritual cause. Angelo says:

> And the pope and all the cardinals, even those who were on the Spiritual side, were disturbed and could easily believe of them all the evils which had been given in evidence against them by their enemies.[4]

The Pope in any case might not have granted them their exemption; but this episode, we may suspect, made a refusal certain.

Clement lectured both parties, then dismissed them from the curia. Each was to observe the Rule in unity, according to *Exivi de paradiso*. The superiors of the Community were to treat the Spirituals with kindness and promote them to office more frequently than others. The Spirituals were to obey their superiors, observe *Exivi*, and avoid all scandal and division. In other words, their exemption was refused. Ubertino made a last appeal; but

Spirituals' exemption. See his phrase on page 140: "Terminato namque consilio, negocium fratrum remansit indeterminatum. . . ." *Exivi* was issued in the third session of the Council of Vienne.

[1] Ehrle, "Die Spiritualen vor dem Inquisitionstribunal", *ALKG* I, p. 158, quoting N. Papini, *Notizie sicure della morte, sepoltura, canonizzazione e traslazione di S. Francesco d'Assisi e del ritrovamento del di lui corpo*, 2nd edn., Foligno, 1824, p. 246.

[2] On the Tuscan revolt, see F. Ehrle, "Die Spiritualen von Tuscien", *ALKG* IV (1888), 25–8; L. Oliger, "Beiträge zur Geschichte der Spiritualen, Fratizellen und Clarener in Mittelitalien", *ZKG* xlv (1926), 215–42. Oliger appears to suppose that there were two waves of Spirituals in flight to Sicily from Tuscany, one at the start of the revolt, and the other later, in the summer of 1313. This is uncertain: as he says himself, art. cit., p. 218, no historian has clarified all the details of this affair.

[3] Ehrle, *ALKG* I, p. 158, n. 1, quoting Papini, *Notizie*, p. 258.

[4] *Historia*, ed. Ehrle, *ALKG* II, 139.

in vain. The Pope said that he had confidence in the obedience of the brothers.[1]

In April 1313 Gonsalvo of Valboà died, and the generalate fell vacant. Clement wrote to the chapter-general, then assembling at Barcelona, and urged them, once more, to follow and not to exceed the limits of *Exivi*. As successor to Gonsalvo he asked them to appoint a superior who would, "velut pater benevolus", give favour to the Spirituals and nourish them in the unity of the order.[2] The chapter elected Alexander of Alexandria, provincial of Terra di Lavoro, and formerly one of the representatives of the Community at the curia, who set to work to fulfil Clement's policy. From the general chapter he went to the provincial chapter of Provence, held at Nîmes, and there saw that a new redaction was made of the provincial constitutions.[3] He assigned three convents, Narbonne, Béziers, and Carcassonne, to the Spirituals, and gave orders that they were to have sympathetic superiors set over them.[4]

In Tuscany the policy of integration naturally had no place; there was nothing for it but to force the Spirituals to return to their superiors. Proceedings were taken against them by the Bishop of Florence and an Inquisitor; the Spirituals protested.[5] In July Clement directed the Archbishop of Genoa and the Bishops of Lucca and Bologna to ensure that the Spirituals submitted and that the captured convents were returned to the Community.[6] But rather than surrender, the Spirituals fled by night and went to seek Frederick's protection in Sicily.[7] In the

---

[1] Ibid., pp. 140–1. Angelo says Clement made this refusal, "nolens fratribus displicere"; but the rest of his account suggests that the Tuscan revolt had weighed against the Spirituals. In the view of the Observants in the early fifteenth century, the refusal of the exemption was fatal for the hopes of reform. They said: ". . . Sic fuit in Concilio Viennensi factum, scilicet, quia non fuit bonis fratribus extra Ordinis communitatem provisum, eapropter ipsa reformatio modicam durationem habuit." L. Oliger, "De relatione inter Observantium querimonias Constantienses (1415) et Ubertini Casalensis quoddam scriptum", *AFH* ix (1916), 6.

[2] *BF* V, no. 212, pp. 93–5.   [3] Gratien, *Évolution*, p. 485.

[4] "Volo, inquit, quod vobis dentur prelati non displicibiles." See the account of these events given by the Spirituals in their appeal to the chapter-general of Naples, in 1316. *ALKG* II, 161.

[5] Ehrle, *ALKG* I, 157, citing Papini, *Notizie*, p. 264ff.

[6] *BF* V, no. 217, p. 96.

[7] For a supplication of the Spirituals, arrived in Sicily, to Frederick, see H. Finke, *Acta Aragonensia*, no. 418, pp. 661–6.

autumn Alexander wrote to James II of Aragon, asking him to use his influence and persuade his brother to expel the fugitives.[1] Frederick refused.[2]

Whether the new policy could have brought peace to Provence, it is impossible to say. No time was given for it to take effect. In April of the following year its prime author, Clement, died, and in October he was followed to the grave by Alexander of Alexandria. The deposed superiors had never accepted Clement's arrangements. Even at the time of the chapter at Barcelona, they were busy defaming the Spirituals.[3] Now they took their chance of revenge. Spirituals were punished, deprived of the sacraments, separated from contact with other brothers, pursued with mud and stones, and attacked publicly in sermons. The deposed superiors went as *discreti* to the provincial chapter at Carcassonne. There three of them were appointed diffinitors. Almost all were restored to their former offices, or like ones, and the sympathetic superiors formerly set over the Spirituals were absolved from office. Two most bitter Conventuals, William of Astre and Raymond Roverii, were made custodians of Narbonne and Montpellier, respectively.[4]

Against this attack the Spirituals had little defence, so long as both the Papacy and the generalate were vacant. They attempted appeals in legal form: we have the witness of James Colonna for this fact. They appealed to the future Pope; they appealed to the provincial, who was either unable or unwilling to help them.[5] Then, like their predecessors in Tuscany, they resorted to self-help. With the help of local citizens, they rose against the Conventuals and seized two of the convents, Narbonne and Béziers, that were formerly reserved for them. They expelled their opponents.[6] The sympathetic superiors returned, and Spirituals came to join the

---

[1] Ibid., no. 419, pp. 666–8.
[2] See James II's letter to Frederick of 25 Feb. 1314, which shows that Frederick had not expelled the fugitives: ibid., no. 422, pp. 670–1. Also, a letter of 1316, giving James II the news that the Spirituals had finally been sent to Tunis; but then only because of the objections of the townsmen of Messina. Ibid., no. 423, pp. 671–2.
[3] See the Spirituals' appeal of 1316: *ALKG* II, 163–4.
[4] Ibid., pp. 161–2.
[5] ". . . vel quia nolebat, vel quia non audebat . . .", ibid., p. 162.
[6] Ehrle, "Raymund von Fronsac Actensammlung", *ALKG* III, pp. 26–7, cap. i.

rebels from other convents of Provence, and even from Aquitaine, until, according to Angelo, there were one hundred and twenty in the two convents. They put on patched habits and resumed the literal observance.[1]

Counter-measures soon followed. The fugitives from Aquitaine were cited in their own convents, and at Narbonne, then excommunicated by their provincial, Bertrand de Turre.[2] William of Astre and Raymond Roverii obtained the aid of the Archbishop of Aix and the Bishop of Agen in taking action against the rebels of Provence. They in turn appointed as subdelegate the provost of Maguelonne. He repeated all the accusations of the Conventuals against the rigorists, and threatened them with excommunication and interdict, if they did not return to obedience. When they remained obdurate, William of Astre passed sentence.[3]

The Spirituals, meanwhile, issued appeals and counter-accusations. In the controversy they obtained the aid of James Colonna, who in February 1316 wrote letters on their behalf to the provost of Maguelonne, and to the rectors of the churches of the dioceses of Narbonne and Béziers.[4] In the letter to the provost he outlined the course of the Papal investigation, emphasizing Clement's good opinion of the Spirituals and their sufferings at the hands of the Community. He ordered the provost to desist from his action. The Archbishop of Aix revoked his commission, and the sentences against the Spirituals were quashed. The Community, however, was far from accepting the position.

It was now three years since the chapter at Barcelona, and preparations were being made for a chapter-general at Naples, which should elect a successor to Alexander of Alexandria. The Spirituals at Narbonne and Béziers through their leader accordingly drew up an appeal to the ministers and custodians assembled at Naples. Once more they recounted the events in Provence, and defended their seizure of the convents. They asked the chapter not to listen to the deposed superiors, or to admit any of them to attend their deliberations.[5] The appeal was taken to Naples by a messenger and delivered to the provincial of Terra di Lavoro who,

[1] Angelo, *Historia*, ed. Ehrle, *ALKG* II, 142.
[2] See the document ed. by Oliger, *AFH* xvi (1923), 339–49.
[3] See Ehrle's account, "Die Spiritualen der Provence", *ALKG* IV, 28–63.
[4] Ed. Oliger, *AFH* xvi (1923), 350–5.
[5] *ALKG* II, 159–64.

by right, presided over the chapter until it had elected a new minister-general. The messenger, according to the Spiritual account, was maltreated by the friars. The provincial read a part of the appeal, and refused to communicate it to the chapter.[1]

Settlement awaited the arrival of a new Pope and a new general.

[1] M. Bihl, "Aventures du messager envoyé par les Spirituels de Narbonne et de Béziers au Chapitre Général de Naples en Mai 1316", *AFH* v (1912), 777-9, and refs. given.

10

JOHN XXII AND THE CONDEMNATION OF THE DOCTRINE OF ABSOLUTE POVERTY

WE HAVE completed the task of providing a narrative account of the Spiritual–Conventual disputes from the time of *Exiit qui seminat* to the year of the accession of John XXII. We have seen how the situation became more complicated and more envenomed as successive friars and churchmen attempted to intervene to calm the disputes, to protect the Spirituals, or, alternatively, to aid the Community in destroying them. Now, in the light of our understanding of the long years of controversy within the order, we may turn to examine the policy of John XXII. Step by step, we shall see, he was led on from the settlement of the immediate troubles in the order to an examination of the theology of poverty which lay behind them.

First, he attacked the position of the Spirituals in the order; then, their lay supporters on the fringe; then, Olivi and the doctrine of his *Lectura super Apocalipsim*; then, finally, the accepted doctrine of the absolute poverty of Christ and the apostles. What we shall describe in this chapter is the greatest crisis in the history of the order: twelve catastrophic years in which John, with that magnificent contempt for human weakness which distinguished his pontificate, destroyed, turn by turn, the doctrine of poverty of the Spirituals, and the doctrine of poverty accepted by the whole order, Spiritual and Conventual alike.

But before describing John's actions, we should recall the possibilities open to him at his accession.

By 1316 the state of the order was parlous indeed. The settlement of *Exivi de paradiso* was in ruins. The system of separate convents for the Provençal Spirituals, which Clement had put into operation, was no longer in existence: what the Spirituals had, the two convents of Narbonne and Béziers, they were holding by force against the Community. Franciscans were litigating against each other, and obtaining the support of outside authorities to do so. The state of feeling between the Spirituals and the Community was certainly no better, and probably a good deal worse than it had been at the opening of Clement's investigation. Angelo was still waiting for a decision about his congregation. The Tuscan fugitives were at large. In Provence the suspicions remained about Olivi's lay following.

All waited on the views of the new Pope. Three ways of resolving the crisis were open to him. He could accept the Spiritual claims outright; he could accept their way of life as the most perfect observance of the Rule and declare that of the Community to be a secondary, mitigated form. This was Ubertino's solution; it was, moreover, the expedient adopted by Leo X in favour of the Observants in 1517,[1] in *Ite et vos*. In the fourteenth century, however, very few in authority were prepared to make the breach in the order which such a step would involve. Further, as we have seen, Clement's decision in *Exivi de paradiso* had, in essence, gone against the Spirituals; it would be a weighty matter to disregard such a precedent.

Or there was the way of compromise. The Pope, while refusing to admit the claims of the Spirituals *in toto*, could in practice give them a considerable measure of independence within the body of the order, with convents and superiors of their own. This had been Clement's solution; now it had foundered, partly through inherent difficulties, partly through the unlucky chance of a double vacancy in both the Papacy and the generalate. It would be possible to resurrect the scheme; but clearly it would be no easy task, after all that had happened, to force the Community, say in Provence, to recognize the Spirituals, and to ensure that they left them alone in future.

Finally, there remained a solution more drastic than anything yet attempted. The Pope could throw all his authority on the side of the Community, and, instead of restraining their persecuting superiors, as Clement had done, actually assist them to make an end of the Spirituals. It would be impossible to do this without

---

[1] This is not, of course, to suggest that the Observants of 1517 are to be equated with the Spirituals of 1316.

giving favour to the most doubtful elements on the Conventual side, men such as Bonagratia and the deposed Provençal superiors; on the other hand, it might well be argued that the Spirituals had discredited themselves since *Exivi* through their actions in Provence and Tuscany, and that now it would be less to the detriment of the order to suppress them than to give the victory to the Community.

The Pope still had freedom of choice between these alternatives, although, as Ehrle[1] and Oliger[2] have pointed out, the margin in favour of the Spirituals had much narrowed in the years since 1312. What finally tipped the scales, we may suspect, were the personal predilections of the new Pope. Almost all his effective experience had been in Provence, in an area, that is, where the Spirituals were most active and the division of opinion about them most clear-cut. As chancellor of the kingdom of Naples he had been close to Charles II, an avowed opponent of the rigorists. The evidence suggests that he arrived in office with his mind made up against the Spirituals. Clement had curbed persecution; John favoured the Inquisition. One of his first actions was to make a cardinal of Bertrand de Castenet, the Bishop of Albi, suspect to Clement V because of his work for the Inquisition. Temperamentally, as the events of his pontificate show, John favoured drastic action. There was therefore every reason for him to take up the third solution and to side with the Community.[3]

Once begun, events moved swiftly. John was elected in August and crowned in September 1316. At once he was confronted with petitions from both parties to the dispute. The rigorists of Narbonne and Béziers had made their appeal even before the election.[4] The Community delayed, in order to give the recalcitrants one more opportunity to return to obedience. Michael of Cesena, the new minister-general, sent a message to them from the chapter

---

[1] In his comparison between the actions of John XXII and Clement. "Even though the differences between them are not as great as might appear from the above, they cannot be completely explained away. Not a little, of this there can be no doubt, must be attributed to the conditions experienced by ecclesiastical authority during the years 1312 to 1316. . . ." "Die Spiritualen der Provence", *ALKG* IV, 43.

[2] "Spirituels", *DTC*, XIV, ii, 1941, coll. 2539–40.

[3] On John's background, esp., see N. Valois, "Jacques Duèse, pape sous le nom de Jean XXII", *Histoire littéraire de la France*, xxxiv (1915), 391–630.

[4] See their appeal, *ALKG* II, 162.

at Naples, offering pardon on condition that they submitted to their superiors.[1] Then, when they refused, he sent through the Conventual representatives at the curia a list of five supplications. In these he requested that unauthorized groups of Franciscans should be suppressed, that proceedings should be taken against the Tuscan fugitives, and that Ubertino da Casale should be punished. No more appeals should be allowed against superiors. Finally, a point of special significance for Provence, Beguins should not be confused with members of the third order. In sum, the Community asked for revenge and for a free hand to put down the rigorists.[2]

Investigation followed during the course of the winter of 1316–17. The proceedings were much shorter than those of Clement, and were weighted against the Spirituals. Their leaders—Ubertino, Angelo, Geoffrey of Cornone, who since the death of Gaufredi had been the principal of the Provençal group, and two other friars—were summoned to the curia. Angelo's account of the hearing, in the *Historia septem tribulationum*, makes it plain that the Pope's purpose was intimidation rather than inquiry. He himself was put in prison as a result.[3]

At about the same time the consistory was asked to give its views on the status of the Tuscan fugitives. The questions were weighted. Should favour be given to those who were in schism? Were the Tuscan fugitives, now in Sicily, to be considered schismatic?[4] The answers could not fail to fall against the Spirituals.

In March and April of 1317, a direct attack began against the two groups of Spirituals who were still wholly recalcitrant, in Provence, at the convents of Narbonne and Béziers, and Henry of Ceva's group from Tuscany, now sheltering under Frederick in Sicily. On 15 March the Pope wrote to Frederick, asking him to apprehend the group; on the same day certain cardinals wrote to the Sicilian bishops, requesting their aid.[5] On 5 April the letter to Frederick was repeated.[6] Two cardinals, Berengar Frédol and

---

[1] Gratien, *Évolution*, pp. 489–90.
[2] "Raymund von Fronsac Actensammlung", *ALKG* III, p. 27, cap. vii.
[3] *ALKG* II, 143–4.
[4] "Raymund von Fronsac Actensammlung", *ALKG* III, p. 28, cap. xi.
[5] *BF* V, no. 256, pp. 110–11; ibid., p. 111, n. 1.
[6] Ibid.

Arnald Novelli, were ordered to send a letter to the Spirituals of Narbonne and Béziers, demanding their submission. Both of them, being well-disposed to the Spirituals, excused themselves on the plea of business. On the 22nd three other Cardinals wrote in their place.[1] Five days later, on the 27th, orders were given for a list of friars from among the rebels of Narbonne and Béziers to be cited to Avignon. This summons, sent through the officials of the municipalities, could not be ignored; shortly afterwards, a group of some sixty-four began the journey to the curia.[2]

Douie, following Angelo,[3] has well described the interview with John XXII which followed. The Spirituals, with the lack of prudence which had distinguished all their activities, took as their spokesman Bernard Délicieux, a friar already well known in Provence for his agitation against the Inquisition.[4] Inevitably, he was discredited by his past record, prevented from completing his defence, and haled off to prison. Others, who tried to follow him, were silenced in the same way. Geoffrey of Cornone, a figure of repute, who tried to save his confrères, was drawn into a grim dialogue with the Pope, and incriminated. At length with the Spirituals crying "Pater sancte, iusticia, iusticia", John closed the hearing and ordered the rank and file to be detained, pending his decision, at the convent in Avignon. This settled the immediate problem of the convents at Narbonne and Béziers. It now remained for the Pope to work out a settlement, which would not only conclude these current disputes, but also act as a barrier against any recrudescence of them in the future.

The summer passed. The cardinals appear to have used the opportunity to rescue their protegés from the general shipwreck of the Spirituals. Angelo was released from prison, and went to the house of James Colonna. He appealed to Michael of Cesena to permit him the literal observance of the Rule within the body of

---

[1] "Raymund von Fronsac Actensammlung", *ALKG* III, p. 28, cap. ix, x, and, for the date, art. cit., p. 2.

[2] *BF* V, no. 266, pp. 118–20; no. 267, p. 120.

[3] *ALKG* II, 144–6. Douie, *Fraticelli*, pp. 18–19.

[4] M. de Dmitrewski, "Fr. Bernard Délicieux, o.f.m., sa lutte contre l'Inquisition de Carcassonne et d'Albi, son procès 1297–1319", *AFH* xvii (1924), 183–218, 313–37, 457–88, xviii (1925), 3–22. Originally, it seems, Délicieux had no special interest in the reform of the order; it was only from about 1310 onwards that he began to develop his Joachimism and Spiritual interests. art. cit., pp. 317–18, 463–4.

the order; failing there, he took the habit of the Celestinians.[1] Ubertino da Casale's future was settled by transferring him to the black monks; John, emphasizing that his action was not to be held to Ubertino's discredit, gave a cardinal the duty of clothing him with the Benedictine habit, and put him under the obedience of the Abbot of Gembloux, near Liége.[2] Ehrle believed, apparently, that such transfers were tantamount to an admission that the order had changed, through the successive modifications of poverty: when an order lost its individual character, its members were free, if they chose, to join other religious associations.[3] A more immediate point was that the order was rid of two intransigent rigorists.

By now the Spirituals had little to hope for from the Pope. The decision about Ubertino, promulgated on 1 October, was followed six days later by the Bull *Quorumdam exigit*.[4] It was the final settlement. In the preamble John explained how an excess of scruple among certain friars was threatening to destroy obedience. This, he said, has led him to add to the excellent interpretations of the Rule, *Exiit qui seminat* and *Exivi de paradiso*. He has long loved the Franciscan order: by removing such scruples, he hopes to bring peace to it.

In the text John referred back to two decisions made by Clement V in *Exivi de paradiso*, both on the words of precept in the Rule. In the first Clement had said that the order to the friars to wear vile clothing was a precept: the decision as to what constituted *vilitas* was laid on the consciences of superiors.[5] In the second Clement had decided that the Rule forbade the friars to have cellars or granaries for the storage of food and wine. Again, the prohibition had the force of precept: the duty of deciding when it might be dispensed was laid on the consciences of superiors.[6]

---

[1] Angelo da Clareno, *Apologia pro vita sua*, ed. V. Doucet, *AFH* xxxix (1948), 67–8.

[2] *BF* V, no. 287, p. 127.

[3] "Die Spaltung des Franciscanerordens in die Communität und die Spiritualen", *ALKG* III, p. 570, n. 1.

[4] *BF* V, no. 289, pp. 128–30.   [5] *BF* V, p. 82b.

[6] "Hoc autem ministrorum et custodum simul et separatim in suis administrationibus et custodiis (cum guardiani et duorum de conventu loci discretorum sacerdotum et antiquorum in ordine fratrum consilio et assensu) duximus iudicio reliquendum, eorum super hoc specialiter conscientias onerantes." Ibid., p. 84b.

John observed that disputes had arisen over the obligation to
wear vile clothing. Certain friars, obviously the Spirituals, had
insisted on wearing habits "curtos, strictos, inusitatos, et squali-
dos",[1] and, when asked to exchange them for the form of habit
general in the order, had appealed to Clement's words enjoining
vilitas at all times, and to a phrase addressed to the brothers in
Exiit qui seminat, "that holy poverty should always shine in the
brothers and their acts".[2] John now wishes to clarify the position.
He has had the question investigated at the curia, with represen-
tation given to both parties. He stresses that in the relevant clause
of *Exivi de paradiso* Clement had left full discretion over the form
of the habit to the Franciscan superiors. The friars must follow
the decisions of superiors on the *vilitas* of clothing. Obedience to
them will not involve transgression of the Rule: the exact nature
of the habit is not specified by it. John expatiates on the necessity
for superiors to be given discretion, and for their subjects to
render obedience.[3]

He followed the same theme on the question of the cellars and
granaries. *Exivi* has left the decision on their use in the hands of
superiors, and of the two *discreti* in each convent: the rest of the
friars must therefore give obedience to them.[4] Finally, in the dispositive section of the Bull, John exhorts all friars who do wear, or
have worn "strictos, curtos, et difformes habitus" in the curia to
return to obedience. No privileges of Clement V may be alleged
against this command. No appeals may be made against it. John
concludes with a eulogy of obedience, "Poverty is great, but
unity is greater; obedience is the greatest good if it is preserved
intact."[5] The Spirituals should not fear the return to obedience.

If any doubts as to the true meaning of this Bull remained in the
minds of the humbler zealots, they were dissipated by the actions
of the Community which followed. Five days after the issue of
Quorumdam exigit, Michael of Cesena set to work on the zealots of

[1] Ibid., p. 128b.
[2] *Epitome*, ed. Eubel, p. 294b.
[3] "Ne, si quisque regatur, ut appetit, confestim corruat, ut non quaerit,
neque taliter convenientibus non ordo sed horror inhabitet, adsit (quod absit)
discordia religans, religio relegetur; sententiae namque variantur ut capita, et
crescit in stolidis opinionibus phantasia." *BF* V, p. 129b.
[4] Ibid., p. 130a.
[5] Ibid., p. 130b.

Narbonne and Béziers. He summoned those who were in prison or in detention at the Avignon convent, showed them the Bull, and, in the presence of a notary and witnesses, asked them two questions. Would they obey the precepts contained in *Quorumdam exigit*? Did they believe that the Pope had the power to make such precepts as were contained in *Quorumdam exigit*?[1] The questions were well chosen. If they obeyed the Bull, they would abandon the short habits which had been their party badge, since at least the time of Crescenzio da Jesi.[2] They would return to their Conventual superiors. If they admitted the Pope's power to make such precepts, they would, in effect, be abandoning the Spiritual interpretation of the Rule as the *forma evangelicae vitae*, which, since it was laid down by Christ himself, was above the dispensing power either of the Franciscan superiors or, ultimately, of the Pope. To assent, therefore, was to abjure. But what was the alternative? By 6 November more than half the total had made their submission; these were sent back to their superiors. The twenty-five who were left were put into the hands of Michael le Moine, the Inquisitor of Provence.[3]

Under his care the number was drastically reduced. Twenty more submitted, made a public abjuration and were dispersed in the provinces. Five remained obdurate. A commission was appointed to decide whether their refusal of the Papal authority in this case could be considered as heresy.[4] They returned a favourable answer and the Inquisitor proceeded to extreme measures. One recanted; he was condemned to perpetual imprisonment. On 7 May the last four were burnt in the market-place at Marseilles.[5] Their fellow-sectaries, the Beguins of Provence, recorded their names as those of martyrs, and kept the anniversary of their burning as a feast of the Church.[6] This completed the overthrow of the Spirituals within the order.

But John had still to reckon with the Spirituals outside the

---

[1] "Raymund von Fronsac Actensammlung", *ALKG* III, p. 30, cap. xxiii.

[2] Crescenzio, as provincial of the March of Ancona, persecuted Spirituals there, who wore short habits—"portantes etiam mantellos curtos usque ad nates". *Chronica XXIV Generalium, AF* III, 263.

[3] *BF* V, no. 293, pp. 132–3.

[4] See Gratien, *Évolution*, p. 494, n. 34.

[5] For the Inquisitor's sentence, see E. Baluze, *Miscellanea*, ed. J. D. Mansi, II, Lucae, 1761, pp. 248–51.

[6] Bernard Gui, *Manuel de l'Inquisiteur*, ed. G. Mollat, I, Paris, 1926, pp. 132–5.

order, the Tuscan group under Henry of Ceva, the Celestinians, and their lay followers. At the turn of the year, he issued two more Bulls, which were intended to make an end of these last categories. The first, *Sancta Romana*, was published on 30 December 1317.[1] It employed a new phrase, *fraticelli*, for friars who formed associations of their own, outside the parent body. The Pope recalled how in various parts of Italy, in the island of Sicily, and in Provence, especially in Narbonne and Toulouse, certain men, commonly known as *fraticelli*, *fratres de paupere vita*, *bizzochi*, or *beghini* publicly begged from the faithful and acted as if they were one of the approved orders.[2] Many of them claimed to observe the Franciscan Rule to the letter, and either claimed an authorization from Celestine V or gave out that they were members of the third order. Some of them appeared to hold heretical views about the sacraments. The Pope excommunicated them and ordered them to be suppressed.

This Bull, it seems, was chiefly directed against the Celestinians; the object of the second, *Gloriosam ecclesiam*, issued on 23 January 1318, was to give formal condemnation to the Tuscan Spirituals.[3] The Pope first recapitulated the narrative of their revolt. He described the Spiritual agitation in Provence, the investigation at the curia, Clement's attempt at conversion by kindness,[4] the Tuscan Spirituals' use of the opportunity to break into revolt, and their flight to Sicily. Thence he passed to their theology. A first error was their belief that the Roman Church had become an *ecclesia carnalis*, and that they alone, with their accomplices, formed the *ecclesia spiritualis*. Another, the corollary of the first, was that all rights had passed from the *ecclesia carnalis* to the *ecclesia spiritualis*. Another again, which they shared with the Waldenses, was that oaths were unlawful; and that sinful priests could not administer the sacraments. A fifth error was the belief that in them alone was the gospel of Christ fulfilled. In addition, they held doubtful views on marriage, the Judgement, and the coming of Antichrist. The Pope concluded by invalidating all their acts and elections, and urging the bishops of Sicily to proceed against them.

[1] *BF* V, no. 297, pp. 134–5.
[2] Ibid., p. 135a.
[3] *BF* V, no. 302, pp. 137–42.
[4] ". . . huiusmodi homines benignitate magis quam severitate satagens emendare, illorum pestiferos conatus patientiae virtute tolerans." Ibid., p. 138b.

The Bull was significant, not so much for its effects on the Tuscan Spirituals, as for the insight it gives into the state of John's thought at this time. The exposition of the errors of the Tuscan group shows that he is no longer content with the purely administrative approach to the Spirituals, which he had adopted in *Quorumdam exigit*; he is beginning to consider the theology underlying their movement. Where will this take him? There cannot be much doubt about the answer: back to the writings of Olivi.

It is not difficult to demonstrate the affinity which exists between the errors attributed to the Tuscan Spirituals in *Gloriosam ecclesiam* and Olivi's Joachimite writings, above all the *Lectura* on the Apocalypse.[1]

Indeed, all roads led back to Olivi. In Provence the investigations of the Inquisition showed clearly how the errors of the Beguins, which were being uncovered at this time, stemmed from the writings of Olivi. Bernard Gui, the Dominican Inquisitor, wrote in the section of his Inquisitor's Manual, *de secta beguinorum*:

> It was found . . . that they acquired their errors and pestiferous opinions of this kind and collected them in part from the books or *opuscula* of brother Petrus Johannis Olivi . . . viz., from a postill of the same on the Apocalypse which they have both in Latin and also in vernacular translation; also from some treatises which the beguins say and believe that he composed, one on poverty, and another on begging, and one other on dispensations. . . . And they say and believe that brother Petrus Johannis had knowledge by revelation from God, especially in the postill or exposition of the same on the Apocalypse.[2]

The evidence of the Manual shows that the Beguins were, in fact, a part of the general Spiritual movement which John wished to destroy. It was apparent that if he was to deal, effectively, not only with the Spirituals in the first order, but also with their members outside and their lay followers, in Provence,

---

[1] J. Koch, "Vorschlag zu einer weiteren Ausgestaltung von Denzingers Enchiridion Symbolorum", *Theologische Quartalschrift* cxiii (1932), 145–7.

[2] *Manuel*, ed. G. Mollat, I, 110; quoted, Koch, *RTAM* v, p. 303, n. 7. The Manual was composed, probably, in the years 1323–4; but its evidence holds for the period from 1317, when judicial proceedings were first taken against the Beguins.

Sicily, and elsewhere, he would have to reopen the investigation of Olivi's writings.

The first step had already been taken. In 1317 John had given a Dominican cardinal, Nicholas de Albertis, the task of investigating the *Lectura super Apocalipsim*, and he in turn had appointed first a single theologian and then a commission of eight masters to report on its orthodoxy.[1] It was a more significant move than anyone can have realized at the time, for the inquiry into the *Lectura* led directly to a fresh controversy about the poverty of Christ, and so to a condemnation of the Franciscan doctrine and to yet another schism in the order. Historians and contemporaries alike have generally been puzzled to see how it was that a new controversy should have followed so hard on the heels of the old, with barely a three-year lull between the end of the Spirituals and the opening of the new dispute. Spirituals, like Angelo da Clareno, noticed the irony of the situation.[2] In our own time Douie, followed by Knowles, thought the cause lay in a fortuitous event which "seemed at first hardly more than an incident in the long rivalry between the two great mendicant Orders".[3] Ehrle related it in some way to the earlier, Spiritual–Conventual controversy, but only vaguely, as a result of the "perverse and unhealthy condition" of the observance brought about by the triumph of the worst elements in the Community.[4] Not until Koch in 1933 wrote an article on the investigations of the *Lectura* was any satisfactory reason brought forward to account for the close conjunction between the Spiritual dispute and the fresh controversy about the poverty of Christ.[5]

In Koch's hypothesis the starting-point of the new dispute should be sought in the report made on the *Lectura* by Nicholas de Albertis's commission of eight masters, somewhere between 1318 and 1320.[6] Their advice was, in effect, for a condemnation of the *Lectura*. They excerpted sixty passages of the original, and in almost

---

[1] J. Koch, "Der Prozess gegen die Postille Olivis zur Apokalypse", *RTAM* v (1933), 303–6.

[2] *Historia*, ed. Ehrle, *ALKG* II, 149.

[3] Douie, *Fraticelli*, pp. 153–4. ". . . an accidental spark set light to an old store of inflammable material", Knowles, *Religious Orders*, I, 246.

[4] "Die Spiritualen der Provence", *ALKG* IV, 45, 49–50.

[5] Koch, "Der Prozess", *RTAM* v (1933), 302–15.

[6] Ibid., p. 306. The text is given in E. Baluze, *Miscellanea*, ed. J. D. Mansi, II, Lucae, 1761, pp. 258–70. This is not a good edition.

every instance, among other errors and follies, found some item they adjudged heretical.[1]

As with Gerard of Borgo San Donnino, it was the Joachimite doctrine of ages which chiefly drew criticism. Despite the fact that Olivi's attitude to the doctrine differed very much from Gerard's,[2] and that certain ideas of Joachim, as, for instance, his Trinitarian conception of history, had been entirely eliminated,[3] the commission still believed that the doctrine was heretical as set down in the *Lectura*. In their comment on the first excerpt they condemned Olivi's application of the doctrine of ages to the history of the Church:

> Here it seems to us . . . that the division of the ages of the Church into seven . . . as for example that the sixth and seventh ages notably surpass the first five, and so reject them all, as the Church the Synagogue, should be adjudged heretical.[4]

In subsequent comments they demonstrated in detail how the doctrine of the sixth age subverted belief in the existing hierarchical Church. By a comparison of passages they showed that the *carnalis ecclesia*, or, in the language of the Apocalypse, Babylon, the great whore, to be destroyed in the sixth age, was in fact equated in Olivi's mind with the Papacy.[5] They showed how

---

[1] Whether these excerpts gave an accurate summary of Olivi's views, it is not our purpose to inquire. R. Manselli in his recent study (*La 'Lectura super Apocalipsim' di Pietro di Giovanni Olivi*, Roma, 1955), consulting the original, believes that they did not. He thinks that Olivi was more independent of Joachim than has been supposed, and also more orthodox. It should be noticed that he prefers *Lectura* for the title of the work: op. cit., pp. 144, n. 2, 177, n. 2.

[2] On Gerard, see above, p. 107. Manselli says of Olivi: "There is in him not even a shadow of the vital and impassioned tension of Gerardo da Borgo S. Donnino, or even of the ardent belief which Fra Salimbene tells us was possessed by Ugo di Digne. Even with regard to Joachim, Olivi retains his precise and detached agreement with which he accepts what others have said, but always with a guarded assent." Op. cit., p. 164.

[3] Manselli, op. cit., p. 187.

[4] Baluze-Mansi, *Miscellanea*, II, 258b.

[5] The decisive excerpt was no. xxxvii, ed. cit., p. 265b. See also the comments of the commission on no. iii, p. 259a; no. ix, p. 260a; no. xl, p. 266; no. xlvii, p. 268a. Manselli's interpretation is a different one. He says: "In fact, Olivi conceives the *carnalis ecclesia* and also the *ecclesia spiritualis* for that matter, not as an entity concretely recognisable in time and space but as outside history, living and unfolding itself within history, but not precisely identifiable with any of its manifestations. . . ." Op. cit., p. 221. For the sake of convenience, *status* in the texts of Olivi quoted by the commission, and in their comments, has been translated as "age"; it is recognized that this may be misleading, but our concern is rather with the commission's opinion than with the thought of Olivi.

Olivi supposed a transfer of primacy from Rome to the new form
of Church of the sixth age. He said, for example:

> . . . For as the glory which had been prepared for the synagogue
> and its rulers, if they had believed in Christ, was transferred to the
> primitive Church and its priests, so too the glory prepared for the
> final Church of the fifth age would be transferred, because of its
> adultery, to the elect of the sixth age. Wherefore also in this book
> it is called Babylon the whore, to be condemned about the beginning
> of the sixth age.[1]

They examined the nature of this new form of Church which
was to succeed the Papacy. As far as could be seen, it would consist primarily in the faithful remnant of the Spiritual Franciscans
and their lay followers. In Olivi's account the disputes among the
Franciscans, in which he had played so notable a part, were all
signs of the approaching end of the fifth age. In one passage, for
example, where he discussed the dating of the start of the new
age, he was inclined to place it with the opening of the Spiritual
disputes about the Rule. Some, he said, would date it from the
first issue of the Franciscan Rule, others from the revelations of
Joachim, others from the destruction of Babylon by the ten horns
of the beast, "others indeed from the raising up of the spirits of
certain men to the spirit of Christ and Francis, at a time when his
rule is to be wickedly and sophistically attacked by many, and
condemned by the Church of the carnal and proud, as Christ
was condemned by the reprobate Synagogue of the Jews."[2] The
last hypothesis seemed to him the most likely, for he thought it most
fitting that this condemnation should precede the destruction of
the carnal Church, in the same way that the condemnation of
Christ preceded the destruction of the synagogue.[3] Those who
would take part in the attack on the Rule would be not only carnal
doctors from the outside world but also pseudo-religious, that is,
Conventuals, from among the Franciscans.[4] The Spiritual disputes
had, of course, begun when Olivi was writing; it is clear that he
expected these to rise to a crescendo and to be accompanied by a
recrudescence of the attacks on the Rule by secular masters. He

---

[1] Ed. cit., p. 261a, no. xix.
[2] Ed. cit., pp. 261–2, no. xxiii.
[3] Ed. cit., p. 262a, no. xxiii.
[4] Ed. cit., p. 267b, no. xlv.

spoke of a new Herod of the carnal doctors, fairly plainly William of St Armour, condemning the state of evangelical poverty, in the infancy of the order, just as Herod tried to kill the child Jesus; there would have to be another attack of the same kind in the full age of the order so that the symbolism could be completed.[1]

After the persecutions, the appearance of the beasts and of the great and the mystical Antichrist, and the final destruction of the carnal Church, would come the victory of the elect of the sixth age. An evangelical order, which we shall have no difficulty in identifying with the Franciscans, purged of their Conventuals, would dominate the earth and rule all the other orders of the fifth age, as Adam ruled the fishes and birds in the Garden of Eden.[2] The Jews and the pagans would be gathered in, by means of the Franciscan order.[3] Francis would perhaps rise again: he had been the herald of the new age, the angel of the sixth seal foretold in the Apocalypse, and, as he had been made like Christ in the stigmata, so perhaps he would be like him in his resurrection.[4] The life of Christ would triumph: in the new age it would be observed, not only as far as the precepts, but also the counsels.[5] Finally, would come the seventh age, a "quaedam quieta et mira participatio futurae gloriae",[6] and then the end of all things.

What is most striking about this exposition is the importance of the part played by the doctrine of the poverty of Christ. In effect, it is the point on which Olivi's conception of the Church and his theological treatment of Church history rests.[7] In Olivi's account St Francis has become the herald of the new age because he brought back to the world the full knowledge of the poverty of Christ and the apostles. He is "the renovator of the evangelical life and rule to be propagated and magnified in the sixth and seventh age and the greatest observer of it after Christ and his mother".[8] His twelve early companions, like the twelve patriarchs or the twelve apostles of Christ, have become the apostles of the

---

[1] Ed. cit., p. 262b, no. xxvi.
[2] Ed. cit., p. 259b, no. viii.
[3] Ed. cit., p. 266b, no. xl.
[4] Ed. cit., p. 263b, no. xxviii. Put with caution: "quoddam huic scripturae consonum, quod nec assero, neque scio, nec censeo esse asserendum . . .".
[5] Ed. cit., p. 261a, no. xvi.
[6] Ed. cit., p. 258b, no. i.
[7] Koch, "Der Prozess", *RTAM* v (1933), 308; (free translation).
[8] Ed. cit., p. 263a, no. xxviii.

Church of the sixth age, because they have principally propagated this doctrine of poverty.[1] The disputes about the Rule, which threatened the purity of the observance of the poverty of Christ, then become the persecutions foretold in the Apocalypse, and the adultery of Babylon comes to consist in an attack on the doctrine of the poverty of Christ. Finally, the elect of the sixth age become those who hold fast to the true doctrine, that is, the Spiritual Franciscans. We thus arrive at the thesis: "Christ and the apostles had no property and the true Church is only to be found where this form of life is observed—among the Spirituals."[2]

What will be the basis for this revolutionary doctrine? Among the enactments of the Church, *Exiit qui seminat*. This Bull had formally accepted the doctrine that Christ and the apostles, as examples of perfection, had had no dominion. In Koch's view the report of the commission made it clear that *Exiit* presented an obstacle to the condemnation of the *Lectura*. In article twenty-two, in which Olivi had expounded the belief (which as we have seen is fundamental to his system) that the Franciscan Rule is a re-enactment of the life of Christ and the apostles, the commission had been obliged to hedge in their comments. Olivi had said:

> So by the authentic witness and confirmation of the Roman Church it is agreed that the rule of the Minors set down by St Francis is truly and properly that evangelical rule which Christ observed in himself, and imposed on the apostles, and had written down in the gospels. . . .[3]

In their comment the commission had to make a distinction. They said:

> About the rule of St Francis, that it is truly and properly the evangelical rule and so on, it seems that if he takes these words according to the understanding and declaration of the decretal *Exiit qui seminat*, he is right.[4]

Thus they had to approve this passage, taken in the sense of *Exiit*. On the other hand they condemned the extreme interpretation of

---

[1] Ed. cit., p. 264b, no. xxxi.
[2] ". . . dass Christus und die Apostel völlig besitzlos gewesen sind, und dass die wahre Kirche nur da zu finden ist, wo diese Lebensform geübt wird—nämlich bei den Spiritualen." Koch, "Der Prozess", *RTAM* v (1933), 308.
[3] Ed. cit., p. 261b, no. xxii.
[4] Ibid.

the passage, which they attributed to Olivi and his Spiritual followers:

> If by this he understands as he states elsewhere, and his followers say, that the rule of St Francis is truly and properly the same, identically, as the gospel of Christ, and vice versa, and that the Pope has no power over it, just as he has no power over the gospel, or that whatever is in the rule of St Francis, Christ observed it all to the letter and imposed it on the Apostles for them to observe, all this we think simply heretical and ridiculous and insane. . . .[1]

According to Koch this two-sided comment dissatisfied the Pope. He wanted a condemnation of the *Lectura* in order to make a thorough destruction of the Spiritual movement, and he saw that *Exiit* formed a barrier against it. He determined to see if a way could be found to get round this barrier. He abstracted the decisive question, "Whether to say that Christ and the apostles had nothing individually or in common is heretical?",[2] and put it forward for general discussion in the curia. Thus the fresh dispute about the poverty of Christ and the apostles was launched.

Between Koch's hypothesis and the traditional narrative of events there is no essential disagreement. According to this version, which is derived from the chronicle of the later Michaelist, Nicholas the Minorite,[3] the new dispute was occasioned by the activities of the Inquisition in Provence in 1321. The interrogation of a Beguin by John de Belna, a Dominican Inquisitor, had elucidated a series of heretical theses, among them the proposition that Christ and the apostles had nothing, either individually or in common. The Inquisitor, before passing sentence, summoned, as he was bound to do, a *consilium* of local notables, lawyers, and religious. To them he read out the list of condemned theses. When he reached the proposition about the poverty of Christ, he was challenged. Berengar Talon, *lector* at the Franciscan convent of Narbonne and a member of the *consilium*, objected that this was not a heresy, but a doctrine which had been accepted by the Pope in *Exiit qui seminat*. John de Belna counter-charged Talon with heresy; both appealed to the Pope; John, in order to settle the

---

[1] Ibid.
[2] "Utrum asserere quod Christus et apostoli non habuerunt aliquid sive in proprio sive in communi sit haereticum?"
[3] Baluze-Mansi, *Miscellanea*, III, Lucae, 1762, p. 207.

matter, circulated the suspect thesis and asked for the views of theologians. If we accept Koch's hypothesis, we may take this episode as the final occasion for action by John XXII. The ground had already been prepared by the report of the commission of eight masters: the appeals from Provence clinched the matter.

At the time of the opening of the dispute the Pope was about seventy-seven years old. He had been in frail health since his election—indeed the hope of a short reign had been a principal reason for the success of his candidature. But age and his apparent physical frailty had served to increase rather than to diminish his mental activity. He was an incomparable administrator. Already he had reorganized the Papal finances, and was substituting an unprecedented surplus for the debts of his predecessor. He had reformed two orders, those of Grandmont and the Hospitallers, in the latter case intervening personally to alter their statutes and to select and depose their superiors.[1]

Unquestionably, his was a personal rule. All spheres, finance, diplomacy, theology, felt the effects of his personality, powerful, shrewd, yet limited in certain directions. With all his powers of penetration, he had no suppleness. He could not bear contradiction. Although he made great use of commissions and consultations, he did not always wish to listen to their views. Berengar Frédol, one of his cardinals,[2] once gave some significant advice to an Aragonese ambassador on the way in which to approach the Pope. "Monseigneur Vidal," he said, "if you would defend the honour of the King of Aragon, do not make any proposals in the consistory, for you can be quite certain that the only matters the Pope will submit for discussion in the consistory are those in which he has determined to take no action."[3]

The Pope had never taken a degree in theology. His training had been exclusively in law, a fact which was to be of significance in the controversy which followed.

We have seen the sequence of events which led John to reopen

---

[1] G. Mollat, *Les Papes d'Avignon*, 9th edn., Paris, 1950, pp. 35–58; Y. Renouard, *La Papauté à Avignon*, Paris, 1954, pp. 18–19.

[2] Created by Clement V in 1305. See P. Viollet, "Berenger Frédol, canoniste", *Histoire littéraire de la France* xxxiv (1915), 62–178.

[3] Viollet, art. cit., p. 126, translating a letter of the Aragonese ambassador to James II, in Finke, *Acta Aragonensia* II, 586.

the question of the poverty of Christ. We may now turn from narrative to analysis: to examine the arguments which John put forward against the Franciscan position, and the exact nature of the condemnation of the Franciscan doctrine by which he ended the official controversy.

A fresh account of the controversy in the curia on the poverty of Christ between 1321 and 1323 is needed. The quantity of research devoted to it, over the years, has been comparatively slight. There is no lack of original material, both in published and in MS. form; the obstacle, one may suspect, has been the arid nature of the dispute itself. Nevertheless, the dispute does repay study. It led directly to the Michaelist revolt within the Franciscan order—a revolt which numbered among its members William of Ockham. On his own admission, Ockham was led into his radical criticisms of the medieval Church from his conviction that in the poverty of Christ controversy the Pope had imposed heresy on the Church. It would be hard to overestimate the effects of Ockham's criticism, directly and indirectly, on the history of the late medieval Church; and their starting-point lies in the Bulls of John XXII.

The greatest part of the modern work on this controversy has consisted in the editing of fresh MS. material. The central documents of the dispute are the Bulls of John XXII and the rival treatises of the Franciscans who came under his attack; these, in effect, continue in sequence long after the dogmatic decision of 1323, when the Michaelists braved the Papal ban in order to continue the argument on behalf of their order. The bulk of these were collected by a contemporary Michaelist, and will be found in the so-called Chronicle of Nicholas the Minorite. Baluze edited texts from the chronicle in his *Miscellanea*;[1] and Eubel has given a modern edition of documents selected from this collection in his *Bullarium Franciscanum*.

With these fundamental sources already in print, other scholars have turned their attention to the replies given by theologians, cardinals, and other churchmen to the formal question of John XXII, put forward in the curia. Published editions of these replies, in various forms, have been given by Tocco[2] and J. G.

---

[1] Baluze-Mansi, *Miscellanea*, III, 206–358.
[2] F. Tocco, *La quistione della povertà nel secolo XIV*, Napoli, 1910.

Sikes[1]; others remain in unpublished theses.[2] But although a start
has been made on the editing of these replies given in the curia,
and other, peripheral treatises composed by interested parties,
yet the central documents of the controversy, the Bulls of John
XXII and the works of the Franciscans who opposed him, still
require closer analysis. Existing accounts of them are defective,
partly because they have not given full weight to all the evidence.
If this is done, then a different picture will emerge from that
which is generally accepted.

Our first task will be to provide a list of the principal documents
exchanged between John and the Franciscan order, between the
opening of the dispute in 1321 and the dogmatic definition, *Cum
inter*, which ended it. This may be given in tabular form.

	JOHN XXII	FRANCISCAN ORDER
1322		
26 March	*Quia nonnunquam*	Chapter-General of Perugia issues:
4 June		Encyclical to the faithful (short version)
11 July		Encyclical to the faithful (long version)
8 December	*Ad conditorem* (first version)	
1323		
14 January		Protest made on behalf of order by Bonagratia of Bergamo
	Ad conditorem (second version, replaced, with same date as, first version)	
12 November	*Cum inter nonnullos*	

---

[1] Hervaeus Natalis, *Liber de paupertate Christi et Apostolorum*, ed. J. G. Sikes,
Archives d'Histoire Doctrinale et Littéraire du Moyen Âge xii–xiii (1937–1938),
209–97.

[2] M.-T. d'Alverny, "Les écrits théoriques concernant la pauvreté évangélique depuis Pierre Jean Olieu jusqu'à la bulle 'Cum inter nonnullos' 12 Nov.
1323", *Positions des thèses de l'École Nationale des Chartes*, Paris (vol. covering
1928), pp. 5–8; J. de Lagarde, "La participation de François de Meyronnes
à la querelle de la pauvreté (1322–1324)", op. cit. (vol. covering 1953), pp. 51–4.

Each of these documents is related. The controversy developed in a series of attacks and counter-attacks between John and the order. It is in this respect very unusual: the Pope, both now and in the later Michaelist controversy, descended into the arena to dispute with his opponents. His Bulls read as the work of one wholly committed to one side of the controversy, and may only be understood in the light of his opponents' attacks. The whole controversy was, of course, a much more complex affair than this. There are, as we have mentioned, the replies of the cardinals and other theologians to the question put forward in the curia by John XXII; amongst these, a series of attacks and replies by the Franciscan cardinals and the two principal Dominican theologians, Hervaeus Natalis and John of Naples; and, in addition, an unofficial controversy around the curia, between Franciscans and Dominicans.[1]

But the central thread remains in the exchanges between John and the order. In accord with the fundamental plan of this book, we may turn to examine these exchanges in their chronological sequence, giving attention only to John on the one hand and the official statements of the order on the other.

The opening of the battle can best be dated from the issue of John's Bull, *Quia nonnunquam*, in March 1322.[2] Its purpose was to abrogate the penalties prescribed by Nicholas III in *Exiit* for discussion of the contents of his Bull[3]—a move that was essential if theologians were to be free to state their views. But to the order it might well seem the first move in the destruction of their claims to the highest poverty. In the text John had insisted on his right to alter the edicts of his predecessors. He said in the opening words of the Bull: "Because sometimes, what conjecture believed would be of profit, subsequent experience has shown to be harmful, it ought not to be thought reprehensible, if the legislator takes steps to revoke canons issued by himself or his predecessors, if he sees them to be harmful rather than profitable. . . ."[4] *Exiit* was the

---

[1] On these points see M.-T. d'Alverny, "Les écrits théoriques", in *Positions des thèses*. It is the greatest tragedy that this work, which was the best of its year in the École des Chartes, should never have been published. I have not seen the work itself; but I am grateful to Mlle. d'Alverny for some valuable advice and references.

[2] *BF* V, no. 464, pp. 224b–225b.

[3] *Epitome*, ed. Eubel, pp. 299b–300a.   [4] *BF* V, 224b–225a.

rock on which the order's case rested. Their apologists said that this Bull had already settled the issue of the poverty of Christ in their favour; but their claim would be overthrown if John had the right to alter any edicts of his predecessors at will. John had abrogated one clause of *Exiit*—one which was clearly an administrative arrangement. But if his claim to revoke any edicts of his predecessors was upheld, then any other clauses of the Bull might be abrogated, even those carrying a dogmatic statement, and the whole Franciscan doctrine thereby overthrown.

The order determined to reply at once. At Pentecost the chapter-general, assembled at Perugia, issued three documents, the first a letter begging the Pope to restore Nicholas III's prohibition on discussion,[1] the others two versions of an encyclical to all the faithful, defending the position of *Exiit qui seminat*.

Of these, the letter has no further significance. The encyclical is vital. Only the short version has been given in a modern edition, by Eubel in the *Bullarium Franciscanum*.[2] The long version is only to be found in the old editions of Baluze-Mansi[3] and Wadding,[4] and has consequently been neglected. Yet it is of the greatest importance in elucidating John's arguments.

Undoubtedly, it was the encyclical which precipitated the crisis between John and the order. In both versions, it had all the appearance of an insolent reply to *Quia nonnunquam*. The concern of the chapter was to preserve inviolate the dogmatic clauses of *Exiit*, enshrining the doctrine of their order; the effect was to provoke the Pope to violent response. The encyclicals were addressed to all the faithful, and more than a hundred copies of them were broadcast in the Christian world before the end of the year.[5] They were delivered to the world, less in the manner of a reply to the question then being debated in the curia, than as a final judgement by some doctrinal authority.

The short version was nothing more than a declaration of the

---

[1] K. Müller, "Einige Actenstücke und Schriften zur Geschichte der Streitigkeiten unter den Minoriten in der ersten Hälfte des 14 Jahrhunderts", *ZKG* vi (1884), 106–8.

[2] Text given in a footnote: *BF* V, p. 233, n. 5, covering pp. 234b–5a.

[3] *Miscellanea*, III, 208b–11b.

[4] *Annales Minorum*, ad ann. 1322, no. lv, VI, Romae, 1733, pp. 397–401. This edn is superior to that of Baluze-Mansi.

[5] Douie, *Fraticelli*, p. 155, n. 7, and ref. given.

immutability of *Exiit*. The argument ran: the question of the poverty of Christ has already been settled in *Exiit*; *Exiit* has been received into canon law; John himself has commended it in *Quorumdam exigit*; therefore, it is clearly implied, he may not abrogate it now.[1]

The long version was a more academic treatise, intended for the consumption of the learned. It made the same point in essentials, but with the addition of more authorities and arguments. Two of these, in particular, deserve further attention if we are to elucidate John's reply. One is the traditional argument from the removal of *sollicitudo* from the heart. The chapter defined the highest and most perfect poverty as that which excludes the greater anxiety, or *sollicitudo*, about temporal goods. Even the holding of goods in common, they claimed, ensnared the spirits of those who possessed them, and rendered them anxious to conserve, defend, acquire, and amplify such goods.[2] Hence, a justification for the renunciation of common goods by Christ and the apostles. The terms differ, but the thought is in essence that of Bonaventura in the *Apologia pauperum*.[3]

The other argument represents the uttermost development of the Franciscan doctrine of the absolute poverty of Christ. Bonaventura, and *Exiit* following him, had said that Christ and the apostles, when showing the way of perfection, had made a total renunciation of dominion. *Exiit*, drawing out the implications of a passage in the *Apologia pauperum*, had said that the Franciscans had renounced all the rights of the civil law, and had only a *simplex usus facti* in their goods.[4] The encyclical now took the doctrine one stage further forward, and simply transferred the *simplex usus facti* to the life of Christ and the apostles. In this way it formed a comprehensive answer to all the "non-Franciscan" texts of Scripture. When Christ and the apostles held the bag, or when the apostles in the early Church had all things in common,

---

[1] *BF* V, 234b–5a (footnote).

[2] ". . . bona temporalia etiam in communi habita, mentes possidentium illaqueant . . . suos possessores reddunt sollicitos ad bona talia conservanda, defendenda, acquirenda, amplianda." *Annales Minorum*, VI, 399.

[3] Ed. cit., cap. vii, para. 1–3, pp. 272–3.

[4] *Apologia*, ed. cit., xi, 5, 312; *Exiit*, in *Epitome*, ed. Eubel, p. 293b. For further details on this point, and other issues relating to *Exiit* generally, see above, chap. 6.

they were acting only as administrators. They had renounced all rights in the civil law: they had, for themselves, only a *simplex usus facti*.[1]

Nothing could be better calculated to arouse John's anger than an attempt to restrict his freedom of action. He had not forgotten his anger some six years later, after the official controversy was over, when he taxed Michael of Cesena with presumption in issuing the encyclical.[2] His immediate reaction was to reassert his right to abrogate the edicts of his predecessors in the most forcible manner at his command. He issued the Bull *Ad conditorem*.[3]

No convincing explanation has hitherto been given for the issue of this remarkable document; but its meaning will become plain if we compare its opening words with those of *Quia nonnunquam*. John's first Bull claimed for the Pope the right to abrogate the edicts of his predecessors; the encyclical of Perugia denied it; now *Ad conditorem* claimed it again with greater emphasis: "To the legislator there is no doubt that it pertains when he sees edicts issued by himself or his predecessors doing harm rather than being of benefit, to take precautions that they have no power to do any more harm. . . ."[4]

Ad conditorem must be interpreted as a reply to the long version of the encyclical of Perugia. Its purpose was to abrogate another clause of *Exiit*, that in which Nicholas III formally received into the hands of the Roman Church the dominion over all the goods used by the Franciscans.[5] The encyclical had cast doubt on the

[1] *Annales Minorum*, VI, 400.

[2] ". . . & specialiter increpavit me de quadam littera Capituli generalis facta Perusii . . . increpans me, & ipsum Capitulum generale, quod pendente quaestione in Curia per ipsum proposita, praesumpseram una cum Capitulo generali eam determinare. . . ." Michael of Cesena's account of his interview with John XXII on 9 April 1328 in his *Appellatio*, Baluze-Mansi, *Miscellanea*, III, 238b.

[3] Text given in footnote, *BF* V, p. 233, n. 5; covering pp. 235b–7a.

[4] "Ad conditorem canonum non est dubium pertinere, cum statuta a se vel a suis praedecessoribus edita obesse percipit potius quam prodesse, ne ulterius obesse valeant, providere . . ." (*BF* V, 235b (footnote); 2nd version, 233b–4a). Compare the opening lines of *Quia nonnunquam*: "Quia nonnunquam, quod coniectura profuturum credidit, subsequens experientia nocivum ostendit, non debet reprehensibile iudicari, si canonum conditor canones a se vel suis praedecessoribus editos . . . revocare . . . studeat, si ea obesse potius viderit quam prodesse." *BF* V, 224b–5a.

[5] *Epitome*, ed. Eubel, p. 294a. John in his arguments dealt solely with the action of Nicholas III in *Exiit*—which, on this point, was in fact a re-enactment of *Ordinem vestrum*. See above pp. 97–9.

right of the Pope to alter *Exiit*; John answered this by abrogating another clause, thus at a stroke both asserting his freedom and knocking a hole in the Franciscan case.

In the first place, the Bull authorized a change in administration, which was a radical departure from precedent. The system of Papal ownership had been in operation for almost seventy years, since *Ordinem vestrum*. It was the basis of the defence of the Franciscan position. The encyclical, in its long version, claimed that the highest poverty consisted in the total renunciation of dominion. In practice, the order's right to observe the highest poverty was secured for them by the system of Papal ownership. Now it had been cancelled, and the order's position undermined. The Pope had refused to accept dominion over any goods which should come to the order in the future, and had declined to appoint any more procurators. If the order said that the highest poverty consisted in a total renunciation of dominion, then the order, after the issue of the Bull, was surely not observing such a poverty.

Secondly, the Bull made an attack on the argument of the encyclical drawn from the removal of *sollicitudo* from the heart. This was the basis of John's case against *Exiit* on this point. He argued that the arrangement made in *Exiit* ought to be revoked, because it was not a benefit but only a source of detriment to the order.

It was not a benefit in spiritual life,[1] since the reservation of dominion by the Papacy had not diminished but rather increased the *sollicitudo* of the order about their temporal goods.

> Since the perfection of Christian life consists principally and essentially in charity, which is called by the apostle the bond of perfection and which unites or connects man in some way to his end, and the way to it is prepared by the contempt of temporal goods and their renunciation, for this reason, in particular, that the *sollicitudo* which is caused by the acquiring, maintaining and administration of material goods and which militates against the act of charity, is thereby removed; it follows that if *sollicitudo* were to remain the same after such renunciation, as it is beforehand, such renunciation can have no contribution to make to perfection.[2]

[1] "Ipsis quidem prodesse ad statum perfectionis nequaquam potuit reservatio supradicta." *BF* V, 236a (footnote).

[2] "Cum enim perfectio vitae christianae principaliter et essentialiter in charitate consistat, quae ab apostolo 'vinculum perfectionis' dicitur et quae

In practice, John argued, this was the case with the Franciscans.

This all represents a reversal of the argument from the removal of *sollicitudo* from the heart in the long version of the encyclical of Perugia. The Franciscan argument had been up-ended by John. His case was pressed home, as we shall see, by *ad hominem* arguments designed to show that the *sollicitudo* of the Franciscans was not diminished in fact by the system of total renunciation of dominion. There is no sure ground for arguing from the evidence of this passage of *Ad conditorem, per se*, that Thomism played a part in the Bull.

The statement that perfection consists essentially in charity is not exclusively Thomist. Bonaventura has similar doctrine in his *Apologia pauperum*,[1] in a passage which anticipates the thought of the encyclical of Perugia. Although the claim has been made that Thomism played a part in John's Bulls, there would need to be more evidence than this before we could substantiate it.

Thirdly, the Bull reintroduced against the Franciscans the old argument of the consumables from Gerard of Abbeville.[2]

John said that *Exiit*'s arrangement was a detriment. It was an occasion for unjustified boasting by the Franciscans over all other mendicants. Because of the Papal ownership, they claimed that they had no dominion at all, only a *nudus usus*. In fact, it was rather the dominion of the Papacy that was naked than their use. By the terms of *Exiit*, the Franciscans under certain circumstances had

---

unit seu iungit aliqualiter hominem suo fini, ad quem per contemptum bonorum temporalium et ipsorum expropriationem via disponitur per hoc praecipue, quod sollicitudo, quam ipsa temporalia in acquirendo, conservando et administrando exigunt et quae plerumque ab actu charitatis retrahit, amputatur: restat, quod, si sollicitudo eadem post expropriationem huiusmodi, quae ante ipsam inerat, perseveret, ad perfectionem huiusmodi talis expropriatio nil conferret." *BF* V, 236a (footnote).

[1] "Christianae religionis fundamentum esse Christum Iesum, sapiens ille architectus Apostolus Paulus ad Corinthios asserit, docens, fundamentum aliud poni non posse praeter id quod positum est, quod est Christus Iesus. Hoc quidem in nostro intellectu collocatur per fidem, . . . in affectu per caritatem. . . . Ut igitur haec duo iungantur in unum, christianae religionis fundamentum et radix est fides, quae per caritatem operatur. . . . Huic autem fundamento sive radici directe adversatur cupiditas. . . . Et quoniam cupiditatis vitium et inordinatio radicatur in affectu mentis, occasio vero et fomentum sumitur a rebus extra possessis; ideo necesse est, quod perfecta radicis huius avulsio utrumque respiciat, ut avaritiae rubiginosa affectio et substantiae terrenae illecebrosa possessio tam spiritualiter quam corporaliter abdicentur." *Apologia*, ed. cit., cap. vii, para. 1–2, p. 272.

[2] See above, pp. 134–5.

the right to give, sell, and exchange those goods which lay under the dominion of the Papacy.[1] Did this not suggest that in fact they had, not *nudus usus*, but the rights of dominion?[2]

The Franciscans did not have *nudus usus* in things consumable by use. That there could be either a *usus iuris* or a *usus facti* without the rights of dominion in such goods was repugnant to law and reason. Nicholas III could not have intended to reserve to the Papacy the dominion over such goods: "For what sane man could believe that it was the intention of so great a father to preserve to the Roman church the dominion over one egg, one bean, or one crust of bread, which are often given to the brothers?"[3]

The Papacy held a dominion which was naked, verbal, and mathematical: the temporal benefit which accrued from it passed to the friars alone, and was intended to pass to them alone.[4]

The boast of the Franciscans, that through *Exiit* they had made a total renunciation of dominion, was therefore vain. The system harmed their internal life: it had caused schisms among them, which would last so long as it remained in force.[5] Their use of procurators acting in the name of the Roman Church was detrimental to the reputation of the Papacy.[6]

This theoretical disquisition was the more significant part of the Bull, because it questioned the validity of the whole concept of total renunciation of dominion. If these arguments were generally accepted, it would shake the doctrine of the absolute poverty of Christ. The Franciscans claimed that Christ and the apostles had observed a total renunciation of dominion; if it could be shown that such a renunciation was impossible or lacked spiritual value, then it would follow that they were wrong in believing this, and their claim to a unique imitation of Christ would fail. In this way the question of the poverty of Christ, which was at this time still under discussion, would be settled in advance, so to speak, by *Ad conditorem*.

Seeing their doctrine threatened, the order replied again with

---

[1] *Epitome*, ed. Eubel, p. 297.
[2] *BF* V, 236a (footnote).
[3] *BF* V, 236a.
[4] Ibid., p. 236b.   [5] Ibid.
[6] Ibid. We may note a striking similarity between John's complaints about the use of procurators and those of Ubertino. See the *Rotulus*, ed. Ehrle, *ALKG* III, p. 113, lines 11–20.

an *appellatio* from Bonagratia of Bergamo couched in terms as
personal as John's Bull.[1] He said the Pope had been misled and
the Bull contained lies. He quoted civil and canon law to show that
the principle of the consumables did not have a universal validity;[2]
also he claimed that it applied to usufruct, but not to the *simplex
usus facti* held by the Franciscans.[3] Alternatively, he appealed
away from positive to natural law, to the primeval state in which
there was no dominion and all things were common to all men,
when, clearly, use could be held without dominion in things
consumable by use.[4]

But the result of this intervention was only to strengthen the
Papal attack. After hearing Bonagratia, John took down his first
version of *Ad conditorem*. Then he replaced it with a new one, and
gave it the same date as the first.[5] In this, while softening some
personal criticisms and altering the dispositive clause in order to
retain dominion over churches and goods dedicated to divine use,
he yet maintained and extended the most damaging argument of
the consumables. In turn, he examined the civil law definitions of
usufruct, *ius utendi* and *simplex usus facti*, in order to demonstrate
how in each case it was incompatible with their nature that they
should be held in things consumable by use.[6] He said that for a
man to use an object, he must have a right of using. For example,
a man may not concede to another the act of riding on his horse,
he may only permit him to exercise that act on his horse, that is,
concede to him the right of using the horse. In fact, there must
always be a *ius utendi*, whether separate from or conjoined to
dominion, for there to be a legitimate use of an object. But *ius
utendi*, according to the civil law definition, could not be held
without dominion in things consumable by use. Therefore there
could be no use without dominion in things consumable by use,
and the Franciscan case failed.[7]

---

[1] Text given by Eubel in footnote, immediately after the first version of
Ad conditorem: *BF* V, p. 233, n. 5, covering pp. 237a–46b.

[2] Ibid., p. 242 (footnote). The standard examples: the slave, the *filiusfamilias*,
and the monk. Compare Bonaventura, *Apologia pauperum*, *Opera Omnia*, VIII,
cap. xi, para. 7, p. 312; para. 8, p. 313.

[3] *BF* V, 242–3 (footnote).

[4] Ibid., p. 241 (footnote).

[5] *BF* V, 246b (footnote). Text of the revised version ibid., no. 486, pp. 233–46.
See also Baluze-Mansi, *Miscellanea* III, 221b.

[6] Ibid., pp. 238b–40a.   [7] Ibid., pp. 240b–1a.

This new version of John's attack on the Franciscan theory contained two general arguments. One, which related to the successives, was later rejected by Ockham as an old error refuted by Aristotle in the fourth book of the Physics.

The other was of special significance, since it formed one of the arguments used in the dogmatic definition at the end of the controversy. It was the legal statement, that to have a simple use in an object without a right of using would make an act unjust.[1] This, the Michaelists later objected, was untrue, if John was speaking, as he appeared to be, of the *ius utendi* of the civil law: in that case he was overlooking the natural law, which allowed a man to have use without positive right under extreme necessity.[2]

The issue of the revised version of *Ad conditorem* virtually settled the fate of the doctrine of absolute poverty. Although replies on the question continued to come in, and although Franciscans made gallant attempts to adapt the arguments of Bonaventura to the new situation, the Bull had made it clear beyond doubt where the Pope's sympathies lay. The canonization of Aquinas, with his moderate views on poverty, was another blow to the Franciscans.

The definition, therefore, when it came, only confirmed the fears of the order. It was contained in a short Bull, *Cum inter nonnullos*[3] of November 1323, quite free of the polemic of *Ad conditorem* or the later Bulls directed against the Michaelists. Nevertheless, like *Ad conditorem*, it bears directly on the controversy with the Franciscans and cannot properly be understood without reference to it.

The text is short and may be translated in full.

Since it is the case that among various men of learning it is often doubted whether the persistent assertion—that our redeemer and lord Jesus Christ and his apostles did not have anything, either privately or in common—should be deemed heretical, as various people hold various and often contradictory opinions in the matter; we, wishing to put an end to this dispute, in accordance with the counsel of our brothers, declare by this everlasting edict that a persistent assertion of this kind shall henceforth be deemed erroneous and heretical, since it expressly contradicts holy scripture, which in a number of places asserts that they did have some things, and

[1] Ibid., pp. 242a–3b.
[2] See, for example, Michael of Cesena in Baluze-Mansi, *Miscellanea*, III, 256a–7a.   [3] *BF* V, no. 518, pp. 256–9.

openly supposes that holy scripture itself, from which undoubtedly the articles of the orthodox faith draw their authority, contains the seeds of falsehood with regard to the above-mentioned, and in consequence, by destroying its authority completely (as far as it can), makes the catholic faith doubtful and uncertain by removing its basis.

Again, to make a pertinacious assertion that our redeemer aforesaid and his apostles in no way had a right of using those things which holy scripture testifies that they had, or that they had no right of selling, giving, or exchanging them (yet holy scripture testifies that they did do this concerning the aforesaid things or it expressly supposes that they could have done so), since this assertion plainly defines the use and actions of Christ and the apostles in the case of the aforesaid things as unjust (which undoubtedly concerning the use, works, and actions of our redeemer the son of God is impiety, contrary to holy scripture, and inimical to the catholic faith): we declare, in accordance with the counsel of our brothers, that this same persistent assertion shall henceforth rightly be deemed erroneous and heretical.

Here two doctrines of absolute poverty are condemned. Each of them, we shall find, was put forward in the period 1321 to 1323.

The first doctrine to be condemned is the undifferentiated thesis of the Provençal Beguin: that Christ and the apostles had nothing, individually or in common. Taken literally, this was hardly sense. It was condemned because it implied a crude contradiction of Scripture, in much the same way that Olivi's doctrine of the spear-wound, condemned in *Fidei catholicae fundamento*, implied doubt of the evidence of St John's Gospel.[1] Strictly, the Franciscan position was not touched. In the controversy the apologists of the order had defended the thesis of the Beguin only provided that it was taken in some more precise sense.

In the second clause, John condemned as heretical a more concise thesis: that Christ and the apostles had no right of using, giving, selling, or exchanging the goods which they held. His ground, as we have seen, was that Scripture either witnesses that they did, or expressly supposes that they could perform these actions. To perform them without a right to do so would be unjust. Therefore, he concludes, to say that Christ had no right of using, selling, giving, and exchanging the goods he held is to suppose that his actions in this respect were unjust—which is heretical.

[1] See above, pp. 172–3.

No such term as *dominium* or *proprietas* was employed in the Bull; yet John specifically referred to those rights, of giving, selling, and exchanging, which were customarily comprehended in dominion or property. Did he thereby condemn in this clause the accepted Franciscan doctrine, that Christ and the apostles had made a total renunciation of dominion?

There is room for doubt about the answer. This was the thesis which John condemned in the second clause of *Cum inter*:

> . . . quod redemptori nostro praedicto eiusque apostolis [in] iis, quae ipsos habuisse scriptura sacra testatur, nequaquam ius ipsis utendi competierit nec illa vendendi seu donandi ius habuerint aut ex ipsis alia adquirendi. . . .[1]

Two witnesses may be selected, among others, who believed that this thesis was not to be equated with the traditional Franciscan doctrine.

Berengar Frédol, who was sympathetic to the Franciscan view, had a draft of *Cum inter* in front of him when he submitted his opinion on the poverty of Christ, and yet contrived to reconcile *Cum inter* with the traditional Franciscan belief in total renunciation of dominion.[2] In the seventeenth century, similarly, Wadding claimed that *Cum inter* did not condemn the traditional Franciscan doctrine contained in *Exiit*.[3] His argument ran on the following lines. *Exiit* and the Franciscans who followed it, he claimed, had not said that Christ did not hold dominion at all ("nequaquam"), only that he renounced dominion when showing the way of perfection. Nicholas's Bull, indeed, by admitting the doctrine of the condescension to the imperfect, had clearly implied that at certain times Christ had held a common dominion together with the college of apostles. Thus, as far as the words of *Cum inter* were concerned, it could be said that the Franciscan doctrine of total renunciation of dominion had not been condemned. Grammar was not wholly on Wadding's side: the emphatic negative (a characteristic usage of John), "nequaquam", cannot simply be equated with "numquam" ("not at any time"). Nevertheless, the expositions of Frédol and Wadding do suggest that the definition

---

[1] *BF* V, 257b–8a.
[2] See the "Dicta domini Berengarii Episcopi Tusculani" in Tocco, *La quistione della povertà*, pp. 143–52.
[3] *Annales Minorum* VII, 3–6.

of 1323 was not, so to speak, a water-tight condemnation of the traditional Franciscan doctrine.

There is some evidence that this was precisely John's intention. He was aware that *Cum inter* made no mention of *dominium* or *proprietas*: he reminded Michael of Cesena of this fact in a later Bull.[1] Moreover, according to one account, when *Cum inter* was read in consistory, a cardinal told him that he would be stating that it was heretical to say that Christ and the apostles did not have property and dominion, individually or in common. The Pope's reply was: "We shall not do this."[2] The element of ambiguity on the doctrine of *Exiit* may well have been intentional: it was still possible to reconcile the Bull with the thirteenth-century doctrine as set down in *Exiit*.[3]

But one doctrine, put foward in a contemporary source, was quite certainly condemned. In *Cum inter* John had not mentioned the rights of giving, selling, and exchanging alone. He had spoken also of the right of using. It would seem that by this he meant the *ius utendi* of the civil law, and not the right of natural law. If he had intended to speak of the latter, his statement would have been tautologous, since, by definition, the right of using held by natural law must be a just right. Time might be spent without giving, selling, or exchanging; a constant use of things, however, is necessary to existence. According to *Cum inter*, therefore, Christ must constantly have held the *ius utendi* of the civil law.

The doctrine of the *simplex usus facti* which was put forward in the long version of the encyclical of Perugia, implicitly denied this. The encyclical in the section containing this doctrine denied that Christ and the apostles held any civil law rights, even the *ius utendi*. There the chapter-general, after touching on the traditional "non-Franciscan" texts of Scripture, in which Christ and the apostles apparently exercised the rights of property-owners, said: "We say therefore to all the authorities which mention such acts, that the apostles did not do this as holders of

---

[1] *Quia vir reprobus. BF* V, 439b.

[2] "Responsiones ad oppositiones eorum, qui dicunt, quod Ioannes papa XXII sententialiter definivit in constitutione *Cum inter nonnullos*, haereticum fore censendum asserere illud, quod in decretali *Exiit qui seminat* § *Porro* continetur." Ibid., p. 258a (footnote).

[3] I hope to give a more thorough investigation of the meaning of the Bull at some later date, in the light of the whole Michaelist controversy.

dominion, but as mere and naked administrators of such goods: and having for themselves only a *simplex usus facti. . . ."* [1] *Cum inter*, in its second clause, condemned the doctrine of the *simplex usus facti* in all possible forms, for, since use is constant, the *ius utendi* of the civil law must constantly be held and cannot be renounced for a time, say, when showing the way of perfection.

To sum up, therefore, *Cum inter* condemned the thesis of the Provençal Beguin, and the doctrine of the *simplex usus facti* contained in the long version of the encyclical of Perugia. It was a condemnation of the doctrine of absolute poverty; but, strictly, it might perhaps be said that it condemned only its most advanced development. The Bull could still be reconciled with the thirteenth-century doctrine of absolute poverty as set down in *Exiit qui seminat*.

The course of the argument may now be briefly summarized. The dispute was opened by John's claim in *Quia nonnunquam* that he had the right to revoke the edicts of his predecessors at will. This claim was countered by the chapter-general in two versions of an encyclical to all the faithful; it was then restated by John in *Ad conditorem*, where he countered the academic arguments of the long encyclical, in particular the argument drawn from the removal of *sollicitudo* from the heart. In this Bull he reintroduced the argument of the consumables, used by Gerard of Abbeville. Bonagratia of Bergamo protested against *Ad conditorem*. John replied with a strengthened version of the Bull, in which he used the argument that use without right must be unjust. In the dogmatic definition, *Cum inter*, he condemned, firstly, the doctrine of the Provençal Beguin, secondly, the doctrine of the *simplex usus*

---

[1] The whole passage runs as follows: "Minor probatur, quantum ad singulas sui partes: primo quia oppositum illius non exprimitur evidenter in sacra scriptura secundum se accepta, quia si sic: hoc praecipue esset per hoc quod dicitur de loculis, Joan. 12. 12 & per hoc quod dicitur in actibus a.4 & 4 quod 'erant illis omnia communia'. Sed per nullum istorum aut per consilium habetur propositio praedicta evidenter ex sacra scriptura secundum se sumpta. Non primum, ubi agitur de emptione & venditione; quia emere & vendere non solum sunt actus habentium in se dominium, sed possunt esse actus dispensatorum, vel administratorum nullum habentium in re quae venditur, vel in pecunia de qua emitur, dominium. Dicimus ergo ad omnes auctoritates de talibus actibus mentionem facientes, quod Apostoli non faciebant hoc ut Domini, sed ut meri & nudi administratores talium: & pro seipsis solum simplicem facti usum habentes." Wadding, *Annales Minorum*, ad ann. 1322, no. lv, VI, p. 400.

facti in its application to the life of Christ which had been put forward in the long encyclical of Perugia. The argument against the first doctrine was, in effect, common sense; against the second, a legal principle, that use without right must be unjust.

What had happened to the doctrine of the absolute poverty of Christ? In its thirteenth-century form, as stated in Bonaventura and *Exiit qui seminat*, it was weak on the legal side. The Franciscans derived the legal side of their case, fundamentally, from Gregory IX in *Quo elongati*. In the fourteenth century, the chapter-general of Perugia put forward a more advanced doctrine of absolute poverty: the belief that Christ and the apostles had only a *simplex usus facti* in the goods they used. In a sense, by putting forward this argument in the encyclical, the order only made more obvious than before the shaky legal foundations of their doctrine. John with his legal training used this weakness to condemn them. His Bull *Cum inter*, in the strict sense, left intact the dogmatic statements about Christ's poverty contained in *Exiit qui seminat*, while destroying the version of Christ's poverty based on the *simplex usus facti*. But of his repudiation in practice of the order's cherished beliefs about poverty, there could be no doubt. The Franciscans who attended in the curia, or who heard versions of events from those who had, cannot have been left in any doubt of the feelings which John actually had about their doctrine of poverty, however cautious he may have been in avoiding a direct clash with the terms of *Exiit*. The definition, and the exchanges which preceded it, were in a real sense the death-blow of the traditional doctrine of the absolute poverty of Christ.

That these Bulls were the personal work of John seems highly probable. There is a common line of thought and style which runs through the whole sequence of major Bulls of his pontificate dealing with the affairs of the order, easier perhaps to detect than to describe concisely, but quite distinct from, for example, the Bulls produced in the pontificate of Clement V. There is evidence of personal interest in the existence of a copy of the Franciscan Rule annotated in the margin by the Pope's own hand.[1] One would place this work in the period of *Quorumdam exigit*, rather than later; but it nevertheless indicates that the later Bulls on poverty sprang

---

[1] A. Maier, "Annotazioni autografe di Giovanni XXII in Codici Vaticani", *Rivista di Storia della Chiesa in Italia*, vi (1952), 317–31.

in some measure from the personal knowledge of the Pope. This is confirmed by the great stress on law and on administration in these Bulls. It is characteristic of John that the settlement of the Spiritual disturbances should have been made in a Bull dealing with the essentially administrative questions of cellars, granaries, and the style of the Franciscan habit; and that his dogmatic definition of 1323 should have been preceded by a Bull, in some ways more important than *Cum inter*, which dealt with the administrative question of the Papal ownership of Franciscan goods.

This evidence of personal direction by John leads us on to a further conclusion, rather more tentative: that the Dominicans in the controversy played an essentially subordinate part, supplying arguments against the Franciscan position at the will of the Pope, but not fundamentally directing his course. If they had, then a more liberal admixture of Thomist theology might have been expected in John's Bulls; whereas, as we have seen, the arguments of these last are primarily legal and administrative, rather than theological.

There is, as yet, no clear evidence that John had been influenced by the Dominicans before the opening of the controversy. The Pope, it is true, did contribute funds to a work of Nicholas Trivet, the English Thomist and Dominican, in the period before 1321; but this work cannot be identified with Trivet's attack on the Franciscan doctrine of poverty.[1] John's accounts describe it as an "opus litterale",[2] and it has been identified with a commentary on Livy.[3]

What is known suggests that John, once the controversy was launched and his ire had been aroused by the encyclicals issued from Perugia, turned to the Dominican camp for effective arguments to overthrow the Franciscan case. His choice then fell on legal arguments—points such as the case of the consumables,

---

[1] F. Ehrle, "Nikolaus Trivet, sein Leben, sein Quolibet und Quaestiones ordinariae", *Festgabe zum 70 Geburtstage Clemens Baeumkers*, Münster-i.-W., 1923, p. 4, n. 2. Trivet's attack on the Franciscan position is not extant, but is known to us from the defences of two English Franciscans. See D. Douie, "Three Treatises on Evangelical Poverty by Fr. Richard Conyngton, Fr. Walter Chatton and an Anonymous", *AFH* xxiv (1931), 343, 345.

[2] "circa cuiusdam litteralis operis compositionem intendat." Ehrle, art. cit., p. 4, n. 2.

[3] W. A. Pantin, *The English Church in the Fourteenth Century*, Cambridge, 1955, p. 143.

which, though it must derive ultimately from Gerard of Abbeville in the thirteenth century, does appear in the reply on the question of poverty of Hervaeus Natalis, the Dominican master-general,[1] and the argument of *Cum inter*, that use without right must be unjust, which, similarly, will be found in Natalis's work.[2]

The logic of events and the Pope's concern with popular heresy in Provence led him to an attack on the doctrine of absolute poverty; the legal arguments he employed were a means to an end, the thorough extirpation, at the intellectual as well as the popular level, of a movement which he saw as a threat to sound doctrine and the state of the Church.

The effect of the dogmatic definition of 1323 lies, strictly, outside the scope of these pages; but it may be well to look forward beyond the limits of our period. The ultimate sequel to *Cum inter* was the revolt of the Michaelists in 1328. A group of friars, including Michael of Cesena, the minister-general, Bonagratia of Bergamo, and an English friar whose name was to be of fateful significance for the future, William of Ockham, broke into open revolt, and went to join the entourage of Lewis of Bavaria, the rebellious Emperor. Under his protection they launched attack after attack upon the Bulls of John XXII, whom they accused of having imposed heresy on the Church in *Ad conditorem* and *Cum inter nonnullos*. They were, inevitably, deposed from office, excluded from the order, and excommunicated. John, for his part, issued a lengthy refutation of their views in the *Quia vir reprobus*, only to be answered by Ockham in a work whose erudition and scope virtually precluded reply, the *Opus nonaginta dierum*. Although there is evidence that Ockham, after the death of his principal colleagues, sent back the seal of the order, the body of the Michaelists remained in schism till their death. Theirs was indeed the most spectacular defiance of any recorded in these pages.

But this was a movement without hope, and without future. The whole substance of the dispute was one which had already been fought over between John and the order in the period 1321-3. The subsequent work of John XXII and the manifestos of the Michaelists dealt, not with the fundamentals of poverty and the

[1] *Liber de paupertate*, ed. J. G. Sikes, p. 283.
[2] Ibid., pp. 295-6.

religious life, but with the *minutiae* of legal terms, dominion, usu-fruct, the *simplex usus facti*, and the like. The essential case on either side had already been stated; all that remained, after 1323, was to amplify existing arguments and to cast yet more widely a net of supporting authorities. If we are to understand the Michaelist movement, we should, rather, turn our eyes from the voluminous products of the post-1328 conflict, and look back on the course of Franciscan history before 1323. If we do that, we shall better comprehend both the causes of John's drastic action with regard to the Franciscan theory of poverty, and the obstinate refusal of the rebellious friars to accept his decisions.

As far as posterity is concerned, John has been his own worst enemy. The violence of his speech in the controversy, the evidence of hasty work in his Bulls, the unwillingness to brook any sort of opposition to his will, have tended to obscure the justice of his decisions on Franciscan poverty. Whatever the sympathy writers may feel for the Spiritual Franciscans who fell victim to his measures in 1317–18, or the Michaelist rebels who endured exile in order to protest against his decisions of 1322–3, can it be thought, seriously, that the interests of the Franciscan order or of the Church at large would have been better served if either group of friars had succeeded in gaining control of events? Can it be maintained that either the extreme Conventual or the Spiritual interpretations of poverty, as they had developed in the 1270s, represented a true understanding of the poverty which the friars were bound to observe?

Nothing now, it would seem, can re-create for us the motives which led John to undertake the work of surgery on the Francis-can body, of 1317–18, and 1322–3. But, without imposing an explanation of John's actions for which there is no evidence, it may be permissible to outline, as we have done, the course of the disputes in the order before John's accession, and to argue from these facts alone that John was faced with a situation which en-forced drastic action. If superiors in the order had been able to grapple more successfully with the Spiritual disturbances in the decades following *Exiit qui seminat*, if the disputes about poverty had not been confused with so many extraneous issues, such as nominalism, politics, and, ultimately, Joachimism, then the position might have been different; as it was, we may well feel that John's course was, in essentials, charted for him when he took the Papacy in 1316. What commands respect is the pertinacity with which John followed the thread which led from Olivi and the Spirituals, through the Beguin movement, to the absolute poverty of Christ. Surely here, we may say, logic was rather on the side of the Pope than on that of the Franciscans. It is unrealistic to say that poverty consists in the renunciation of property rights. Even the example of Francis, we have suggested, supported John rather than the friars; and the decisions of 1322–3 can be justified out of the purely religious needs of the order which he founded.

And yet, when all this is admitted, one may still feel sympathy with the Michaelist position. The friars who rebelled in 1328 were only repeating the opinions expressed by the whole body of the order before 1323. To say, as has more than once been done, that these men were Spirituals is to do violence to the facts. The leaders of the rebellion of 1328, so far from being the adherents of Spiritual doctrine, were their determined opponents. Michael of Cesena, the minister-general, had assisted John in the suppressions of 1317–18, and had forced the Spirituals to abjure after the issue of *Quorumdam exigit*. Bonagratia of Bergamo had been the venomous defender of the Community against the rigorists in the Council of Vienne. The third famous figure, William of Ockham, came from a province apparently untouched by the Spirituals; and there is no sign of particularly Spiritual doctrine in any of his writings. If other, Spiritual, friars joined the group, if, later on, the Michaelist rebels in Italy joined forces with former Spirituals, and the fraticelli *de opinione* became indistinguishable from the fraticelli *de paupere vita*, it nevertheless remains true that the heart of the rebellion lay in the academic Conventuals. It was they who continued the fight against John XXII. They represent the rump of the Community, and their arguments are little more than an expansion and a re-presentation of such statements as the long encyclical of Perugia and the protest of Bonagratia of 1323 against *Ad conditorem*. If we recognize this, then we can better understand the motives for the Michaelist revolt.

John, by his decisions of 1322–3, demanded from the order the most abrupt reversal of opinion. The belief that Christ and the apostles, when showing the way of perfection, had made a total renunciation of property rights, had been consecrated by long acceptance in the order and, to a certain extent, in the world outside. We have seen how Bonaventura's classic exposition of absolute poverty was accepted as orthodox doctrine by the Papacy in *Exiit qui seminat*; how the friars had defended the Bonaventuran doctrine with enthusiasm, and had been encouraged by the Papacy to do so. We have seen how, step by step, the brothers had been led to put their all into the doctrine of the absolute poverty of Christ. Even the Spiritual controversies had played their part. The latter, with all their fanaticism and extravagance, had yet insisted on the restriction of use being quite as essential a part of poverty as the renunciation of dominion. The Community had suppressed them. Those responsible were thus left with total renunciation of dominion as their title to poverty. If this went, it could be asked, what would remain for them? The attitude of the Michaelists becomes entirely credible if we recall the history of absolute poverty in the thirteenth century. Their tireless erudition in the examination of the *minutiae* of legal terminology, their unwavering belief that Christ's renunciation of common ownership was a vital doctrine of faith, becomes quite explicable in the light of the whole development of poverty in the Franciscan order in the century following the death of St Francis.

We have now, in effect, completed a survey of the history of Franciscan poverty from 1210 to 1323. This, the first century of the order's existence, was its formative period. The struggles over poverty are fundamental. The varied forms of Franciscan life, which reappear later, can be seen in this first century. Poverty had been discussed, and disputed over, from every angle. The renunciation of *dominium* had pride of place, as we have seen; but, alongside it, there had been prolonged investigation of the nature of the *usus* to which the friars were obliged. The exact relation had been discussed between the *usus pauper* and the vow of poverty; the legitimacy of mendicancy, the proper employment of intermediaries, the limits of dispensation from the Rule—all these, and other facets of the question of poverty, had been uncovered and brought into argument, both within and without the order.

If this constant debate is a sign of factiousness among the Franciscans, it is surely also a sign of vitality. One of the features of medieval religious life hardest for the modern historian to understand is the readiness of the religious to dispute and to litigate. In Franciscan history, this eagerness to hurry into controversy should not be misunderstood. The Franciscans fought over poverty because they cared about it. For a time the long series of conflicts assisted decline in the order. But the zeal still remained. The contemporary observance was not wholly collapsed in all parts. Nor had the Spiritual movement, despite its follies, been entirely in vain. The underlying care for poverty which remained in the order brought new reforms to birth, as it has done throughout Franciscan history. There is a peculiar appropriateness in the fact that it should have been the Spiritual Angelo da Clareno who assisted at the birth of the new movement for the reform of the order which succeeded where the Spirituals had failed. Under his influence a certain John of Valle, who entered the order in 1325, founded a hermitage for himself and four others in the Brugliano mountains in Umbria.[1] Here a primitive form of the observance was followed and the seed was planted which in later and happier times was to flower into the Order of Friars Minor of the Strict Observance.

[1] F. Ehrle, "Das Verhältniss der Spiritualen zu den Anhängern der Observanz", *ALKG* IV, 181–190. All that has been published since has confirmed Ehrle's view of the links between the Spirituals and the Observants. See the articles already cited of Blondeel d'Isegem in *Collectanea Franciscana* v and of Oliger in *AFH* ix, and, esp., Doucet's remark in his edition of Angelo da Clareno's *Apologia:* "However it may be, more and more as time goes on, it is being confirmed that the Observants and Reformed friars of the fifteenth century in some respects were nothing but continuators of the Spirituals of the thirteenth and fourteenth centuries, and were nourished on their writings which they sought diligently and read in secret." *AFH* xxxix (1948), 92.

BIBLIOGRAPHY

PRIMARY

Abbeville, Gerard of, *Contra adversarium perfectionis Christianae*, ed. S. Clasen, *AFH* xxxi (1938), 276–329, xxxii (1939), 89–202.

Acta Capituli Generalis Mediolani celebrati an. 1285, ed. A. Callebaut, *AFH* xxii (1929), 273–91.

Actus Beati Francisci et Sociorum eius, ed. P. Sabatier, Paris, 1902.

d'Alverny, M.-T., "Les écrits théoriques concernant la pauvreté évangélique depuis Pierre Jean Olieu jusqu'à la bulle 'Cum inter nonnullos' 12 Nov. 1323", *Positions des Thèses de l'École Nationale des Chartes*, Paris, (vol. covering 1928) pp. 5–8.

Amorós, L., "Series condemnationum et processuum contra doctrinam et sequaces Petri Ioannis Olivi (e Cod. Vat. Ottob. Lat. 1816)", *AFH* xxiv (1931), 495–512.

"Aegidii Romani Impugnatio doctrinae Petri Johannis Olivi an. 1312, nunc primum in lucem edita (Disseritur de mente Concilii Viennensis in causa P. J. Olivi)", *AFH* xxvii (1934), 399–451.

Baluze, E., *Miscellanea*, ed. J. D. Mansi, I–IV, Lucae, 1761–4.

Bellarmine, R., *Disputationes*, I, Ingolstadii, 1601.

Bergamo, Bonagratia of, *Tractatus de Christi et Apostolorum Paupertate*, ed. L. Oliger, *AFH* xxii (1929), 323–35, 487–511.

Bihl, M., "Statuta generalia Ordinis edita in Capitulis generalibus celebratis Narbonae an. 1260, Assisii an. 1279 atque Parisiis an. 1292", *AFH* xxxiv (1941), 13–94, 284–358.

Boehmer, H., *Analekten zur Geschichte des Franciscus von Assisi*, Tübingen, Leipzig, 1904.

Bologna, Peregrino of, "Chronicon abbreviatum de successione Ministrorum Generalium" in Thomas of Eccleston, *De Adventu Fratrum Minorum in Angliam*, ed. A. G. Little, Paris, 1909, Appendice II, pp. 141–5.

Bonaventura, *Opera Omnia*, V, Ad Claras Aquas, 1891; VIII, Ad Claras Aquas, 1898.

Bullarii Franciscani Epitome, ed. C. Eubel, Apud Claras Aquas, 1908.

Bullarium Franciscanum, ed. J. H. Sbaralea, I–III, Romae, 1759–65; ed. C. Eubel, V, Romae, 1898.

Casale, Ubertino da, *Arbor vitae crucifixae Jesus*, Venetiis, 1485. (The original has not been used.)

Super tribus sceleribus, ed. A. Heysse, *AFH* x (1917), 103–74.

"Catalogus ministrorum generalium", ed. O. Holder-Egger, *MGH Scriptores* XXXII, 653–74.

Chronica XXIV Generalium, *AF* III, Ad Claras Aquas, 1897.

Clareno, Angelo da, *Expositio Regulae Fratrum Minorum*, ed. L. Oliger, Ad Claras Aquas, 1912.

Apologia pro vita sua, ed. V. Doucet, *AFH* xxxix (1948), 63–200.

Corpus Iuris Civilis, ed. T. Mommsen, P. Krueger, I–III, Berolini, 1928–9.

Conington, Richard of, "Tractatus de paupertate fratrum minorum et abbreviatura inde a communitate extracta", ed. A. Heysse, *AFH* xxiii (1930), 57–105, 340–60.

Definitiones Capituli Generalis Argentinae celebrati anno 1282, ed. G. Fussenegger, *AFH* xxvi (1933), 127–40.

Definitiones Capitulorum Generalium Ordinis Fratrum Minorum 1260–1282, ed. A. G. Little, *AFH* vii (1914), 676–82.

Delorme, F. M., "Praevia nonnulla Decretali 'Exultantes in Domino' (18 Jan. 1283) de Procuratorum institutione", *AFH* vii (1914), 55–65.

Denifle, H., "Das Evangelium aeternum und die Commission zu Anagni", *ALKG* I (1885), 49–142.

"Die Denkschriften der Colonna gegen Bonifaz VIII und der Cardinale gegen die Colonna", *ALKG* V (1889), 493–529.

"'Diffinitiones' Capituli Generalis Narbonensis (1260)", ed. F. M. Delorme, *AFH* iii (1910), 491–504.

Digne, Hugues de, *De Finibus Paupertatis*, ed. C. Florovsky, *AFH* v (1912), 277–90.

Documenta Antiqua Franciscana, ed. L. Lemmens, Pars I *Scripta Fratris Leonis socii S.P. Francisci*, Pars II *Speculum Perfectionis* (Redactio I), Ad Claras Aquas, 1901.

Doucet, V., "De operibus manuscriptis Fr. Petri Ioannis Olivi in Bibliotheca Universitatis Patavinae asservatis", *AFH* xxviii (1935), 156–97, 408–42.

Douie, D., "Three Treatises on Evangelical Poverty by Fr. Richard Conyngton, Fr. Walter Chatton and an anonymous", *AFH* xxiv (1931), 341–69, xxv (1932), 36–58, 210–40.

Eccleston, Thomas of, *Tractatus de Adventu Fratrum Minorum in Angliam*, ed. A. G. Little, 1st edn., Paris, 1909, 2nd edn., Manchester, 1951.

Esser, K., Hardick, L., *Die Schriften des hl. Franziskus von Assisi*, Werl-i.-W., 1951.

Expositio Quatuor Magistrorum super Regulam Fratrum Minorum (1241–1242), ed. L. Oliger, Roma, 1950.

Finke, H., *Acta Aragonensia*, I–III, Berlin, Leipzig, 1908–23.

Fussenegger, G., "Relatio commissionis in concilio Viennensi institutae ad decretalem 'Exivi de paradiso' praeparandam", *AFH* l (1957), 145–77.

Giano, Jordan of, *Chronica*, ed. H. Boehmer, Paris, 1908.

Gratien, "Une lettre inédite de Pierre de Jean Olivi", *Études Franciscaines* xxix (1913), 414–22.

Gui, B., *Manuel de l'Inquisiteur*, ed. and tr. G. Mollat, I–II, Paris, 1926–7.

Heysse, A., "Descriptio codicis bibliothecae Laurentianae Florentinae S. Crucis Plut. 31 sin. Cod. 3", *AFH* xi (1918), 251–69.

"Anonymi Spiritualis responsio 'Beatus Vir' contra 'Abbreviaturam Communitatis'", *AFH* xlii (1950), 213–35.

Laberge, D., "Fr. Petri Ioannis Olivi O.F.M., tria scripta sui ipsius apologetica annorum 1283 et 1285", *AFH* xxviii (1935), 115–55, 374–407, xxix (1936), 98–141, 365–95.

Lagarde, J. de, "La participation de François de Meyronnes à la querelle de la pauvreté (1322–1324)", *Positions des Thèses de l'École Nationale des Chartes*, Paris (year covering 1953) pp. 51–4.

Legendae S. Francisci Assisiensis saeculis XIII et XIV conscriptae, *AF* X, Ad Claras Aquas, 1926–41.

Liber sententiarum Inquisitionis Tholosanae, ed. P. Limborch, Amstelodami, 1692.

Littera septem sigillorum, ed. G. Fussenegger, *AFH* xlvii (1954), 45–53.

Longpré, E., "Le Quolibet de Nicolas de Lyre, O.F.M." *AFH* xxiii (1930), 42–56.

Mansi, J. D., *Sacrorum Conciliorum . . . Collectio* XXII, Venetiis, 1778.

Marsh, Adam, *Epistolae*, ed. J. S. Brewer, *Monumenta Franciscana* II, London, 1858.

Natalis, Hervaeus, "Liber de paupertate Christi et Apostolorum", J. G. Sikes, *Archives d'Histoire Doctrinale et Littéraire du Moyen Âge*, xii–xiii, (1937–8), 209–97.

Novum Testamentum Latine, Evangelia, ed. J. Wordsworth, H. White, Oxonii, 1889–98.

Ockham, G. de, *Opera Politica*, ed. J. G. Sikes, I, Manchester, 1940.

Oliger, L. "Descriptio codicis capistranensis continens aliquot opuscula Fr. Petri Johannis Olivi (cod. conv. O.F.M. Capistr. xxvi)", *AFH* i (1908), 617–22.

"Die theologische Quaestion des Johannes Pecham über die vollkommene Armut", *FS* iv (1917), 127–76.

"Descriptio codicis S. Antonii de Urbe una cum appendice textuum de S. Francisco", *AFH* xii (1919), 321–401.

"Fr. Bertrandi de Turre processus contra Spirituales Aquitaniae (1315) et Card. Jacobi de Columna litterae defensoriae Spiritualium Provinciae (1316)", *AFH* xvi (1923), 323–55.

Olivi, P. J., *De renuntiatione Papae Coelestini V quaestio et epistola*, ed. L. Oliger, *AFH* xi (1918), 309–73.

Quodlibeta et impugnationes quorundam articulorum; item defensiones aliorum articulorum, Venetiis, 1509. (The original has not been used.)

Peckham, J., *Tractatus Tres de Paupertate*, ed. C. L. Kingsford, A. G. Little, F. Tocco, *BSFS* II, Aberdoniae, 1910.

Pelster, F., "Nikolaus von Lyra und seine Quaestio de usu paupere", *AFH* xlvi (1953), 211–50.

Salimbene, *Cronica*, ed. O. Holder-Egger, *MGH Scriptores* XXXII, Hannoverae et Lipsiae, 1905–13.

Sabatier, P., *Speculum Perfectionis seu S. Francisci Assisiensis Legenda Antiquissima auctore Fratre Leone*, Paris, 1898.

   Le Speculum Perfectionis ou Mémoires de Frère Léon sur la Seconde Partie de la Vie de Saint François d'Assise, I, *BSFS* XIII, Manchester, 1928, II, *BSFS* XVII, Manchester, 1931.

Supplementum ad Bullarium Franciscanum, ed. F. Annibali de Latera, Romae, 1780.

Tocco, F., *La quistione della povertà nel secolo XIV*, Napoli, 1910.

Tondelli, L., *Il Libro delle Figure dell'Abate Gioachino da Fiore*, I, 2nd edn., Torino, 1953.

Wadding, L., *Annales Minorum*, 2nd edn., Romae, 1731–45.

SECONDARY

d'Alençon, E., "Fr. Bonaventure d'Iseo Vicaire du Ministre Général des Mineurs au 1er Concile de Lyon, en 1245", *Études Franciscaines* xxxiii (1921), 519–28.

Attal, S., *Frate Elia compagno di S. Francesco*, Roma, 1936.

Auw, L. von, *Angelo Clareno et les Spirituels Franciscains*, Lausanne, 1952.

Balthasar, K., *Geschichte des Armutsstreites im Franziskanerorden bis zum Konzil von Vienne*, Münster-i.-W., 1911.

Bihel, S., "S. Franciscus fuitne angelus sexti sigilli? (Apoc. 7.2)", *Antonianum* ii (1927), 59–90.

Bihl, M., "Aventures du messager envoyé par les Spirituels de Narbonne et de Béziers au Chapitre Général de Naples en Mai 1316", *AFH* v (1912), 777–9.

   "Disquisitiones Celanenses", *AFH* xx (1927), 433–96, xxi (1928), 3–54, 161–205.

   "Contra duas novas hypotheses prolatas a Ioh. R. H. Moorman adversus 'Vitam S. Francisci' auctore Thoma Celanensi, cui substituere vellet sic dictam 'Legendam 3 Sociorum'", *AFH* xxxix (1946; pub. 1948), 3–37.

Blondeel d'Isegem, E., "L'Influence d'Ubertin de Casale sur les écrits de S. Bernardin de Sienne", *Collectanea Franciscana* v (1935), 5–44.

Borne, F. van den, "Zur Franziskus-Frage", *FS* vi (1919), 185–200.

Burkitt, F. C., "Ubertino da Casale and a variant reading", *Journal of Theological Studies* xxiii (1922), 186–8.

"Fonte Colombo and its traditions", *Franciscan Essays* II, BSFS Extra Ser. III, Manchester, 1932, pp. 41–55.

"St Francis of Assisi and some of his biographers", ibid., pp. 19–39.

Buscomari, Isidorus a, *S. Bonaventura, ordinis Fratrum Minorum minister generalis*, Roma, 1874.

Callaey, F., *L'idéalisme franciscain spirituel au XIVᵉ siècle. Étude sur Ubertin de Casale*, Louvain, Paris, Bruxelles, 1911.

Callebaut, A., "Saint François et les privilèges, surtout celui de la pauvreté concédé à Sainte Claire par Innocent III", *AFH* xx (1927), 182–93.

Cambell, J., "Les écrits de Saint François d'Assise devant la critique", *FS* xxxvi (1954), 82–109, 205–64.

Carvalho e Castro, L. de, *Saint Bonaventure, le docteur franciscain*, Paris, 1923.

Chérancé, L. de, *Saint Bonaventure (1221–1274)*, Paris, 1899; reviewed, F. van Ortroy, *Analecta Bollandiana* xviii (1899), 205–6.

Clasen, S., *Der hl. Bonaventura und das Mendikantentum*, Werl.-i.-W., 1940.

Clément, M.-M., "L'administration des biens chez les Frères mineurs des origines au milieu du XVIᵉ siècle", *Positions des Thèses de l'École Nationale des Chartes*, Paris, (year covering 1943), pp. 41–7.

Coulton, G. G., "The Story of St Francis of Assisi", F. J. Foakes Jackson and Kirsopp Lake, *The Beginnings of Christianity*, Part I, *The Acts of the Apostles*, vol. II, 1922, pp. 438–61.

Cuthbert, Father, *Life of St Francis of Assisi*, 2nd edn., London, 1914.

Dmitrewski, M. von, *Die christliche freiwillige Armut vom Ursprung der Kirche bis zum 12 Jahrhundert*, Berlin, Leipzig, 1913.

"Fr. Bernard Délicieux O.F.M., sa lutte contre l'Inquisition de Carcassonne et d'Albi, son procès 1297–1319", *AFH* xvii (1924), 183–218, 313–37, 457–88, xviii (1925), 3–32.

Douie, D., *The Nature and the Effect of the Heresy of the Fraticelli*, Manchester, 1932.

The Conflict between the Seculars and the Mendicants at the University of Paris in the Thirteenth Century (Aquinas Society of London, Aquinas Paper no. 23), London, 1954.

Ehrle, F., "Zur Quellenkunde der älteren Franziskanergeschichte", *ZKT* vii (1883), 323–52.

"Die Spiritualen, ihr Verhältniss zum Franciscanerorden und zu den Fraticellen", *ALKG* I (1885), 509–69; II (1886), 106–64, 249–336; III (1887), 553–623; IV (1888), 1–190.

"Zur Vorgeschichte des Concils von Vienne", *ALKG* II (1886), 353–416; III (1887), 1–195.

"Petrus Johannis Olivi, sein Leben und seine Schriften", *ALKG* III (1887), 409–552.

"Die ältesten Redactionen der Generalconstitutionen des Franziskanerordens", *ALKG* VI (1892), 1–138.

"Arnaldo de Villanova ed 'i Thomatiste', contributo alla storia
della Scuola Tomistica", *Gregorianum* i (1920), 475–501.

"Der heilige Bonaventura, seine Eigenart und seine drei Lebensaufgaben", *FS* viii (1921), 109–24.

"Nikolaus Trivet, sein Leben, seine Quolibet und Quaestiones
ordinariae", *Festgabe zum 70 Geburtstage Clemens Baeumkers*, Münster-
i.-W., 1923, pp. 1–63.

Esser, K., "Zu der 'Epistola de tribus quaestionibus' des hl. Bonaventura", *FS* xxvii (1940), 149–59.

   *Das Testament des Heiligen Franziskus von Assisi. Eine Untersuchung
über seine Echtheit und seine Bedeutung*, Münster-i.-W., 1949.

"Der Brief des hl. Franziskus an den hl. Antonius von Padua",
FS xxxi (1949), 135–51.

"Gestalt und Ideal des Minderbruderordens in seinen Anfangen",
FS xxxix (1957), 1–22.

Felder, H., *Geschichte der Wissenschaftlichen Studien im Franziskanerorden
bis um die Mitte des 13 Jahrhunderts*, Freiburg-i.-B., 1904.

Gilson, E., *La Philosophie de Saint Bonaventure*, Paris, 1924.

Goad, H. E., "Brother Elias as the leader of the Assisan party in the
order", *Franciscan Essays* II, *BSFS* Extra Ser. III, Manchester, 1932,
pp. 67–83.

Godefroy, "Ubertin de Casale", *DTC* XV, ii, 1950, coll. 2020–34.

Goetz, W., "Die Quellen zur Geschichte des hl. Franz von Assisi",
ZKG xxii (1901), 362–77, 525–65, xxiv (1903), 165–97, 475–519,
xxv (1904), 33–47.

   "Die ursprünglichen Ideale des hl. Franz von Assisi", *Historische
Vierteljahrschrift* vi (1903), 19–50.

Gratien, *Histoire de la Fondation et de l'Évolution de l'Ordre des Frères
Mineurs au XIIIᵉ siècle*, Paris, Gembloux, 1928.

Grundmann, H., *Studien über Joachim von Floris*, Leipzig, Berlin, 1927.

Heuckelum, M. van, *Spiritualistische Strömungen an den Höfen von Aragon
und Anjou wahrend der Höhe des Armutsstreites*, Berlin, Leipzig, 1912.

Holder-Egger, O., Schmeidler, B., "Zur Kritik minoritischer Geschichtsquellen", *Neues Archiv der Gesellschaft für ältere deutsche Geschichtskunde*,
xxxviii (1913), 483–502.

Holzapfel, H., *Handbuch der Geschichte des Franziskanerordens*, Freiburg-i.-
B., 1909.

Jeiler, I., "Armut", Wetzer and Welte's *Kirchenlexicon*, 2nd edn. by
J. Hergenrother and F. Kaulen, Freiburg-i.-B., I, 1880, coll. 1384–
1401.

Jordan, E., "Joachim de Flore", *DTC* VIII, ii, 1925, coll. 1425–
1458.

Jörgensen, J., *Den Hellige Frans af Assisi*, Koebenhavn og Kristiania, 1907, Eng. tr. T. O'Conor Sloane, 2nd edn., New York, 1913.

Jungmann, B., *Dissertationes selectae in Historiam Ecclesiasticam*, VI, Ratisbonae, Neo Eboraci, Cincinatii, 1886.

Knowles, D., *The Religious Orders in England*, I, Cambridge, 1948; II, Cambridge, 1955.

Koch, J., "Die Verurteilung Olivis auf dem Konzil von Vienne und ihre Vorgeschichte", *Scholastik* v (1930), 489–522.

"Philosophische und Theologische Irrtumslisten von 1270–1329. Ein Beitrag zur Entwicklung der Theologische Zensuren", *Mélanges Mandonnet* II, *Bibliothèque Thomiste* XIV, Paris, 1930, pp. 305–29.

"Der Sentenzenkommentar des Petrus Joannis Olivi", *RTAM* ii (1930), 290–310.

"Vorschlag zu einer weiteren Ausgestaltung von Denzingers Enchiridion Symbolorum", *Theologische Quartalschrift* cxlii (1932), 138–57.

"Der Prozess gegen die Postille Olivis zur Apokalypse", *RTAM* v (1933), 302–15.

Lampen, W., "De quibusdam sententiis et verbis in opusculis S.P.N. Francisci", *AFH* xxiv (1931), 552–57.

"De textibus S. Scripturae allegatis in opusculis S.P.N. Francisci", *AFH* xvii (1924), 443–5.

Lemmens, L., *Der heilige Bonaventura, Kardinal und Kirchenlehrer aus dem Franziskanerorden (1221–1274)*, Kempten, München, 1909; reviewed, L. Oliger, *AFH* iii (1910), 344–8.

Lempp, E., *Frère Élie de Cortone*, Paris, 1901.

Little, A. G., *The Grey Friars in Oxford*, Oxford, 1892.

Studies in English Franciscan History, Manchester, 1917.

"Some recently discovered Franciscan documents and their relations to the Second Life by Celano and the Speculum Perfectionis", *Proceedings of the British Academy* xii (1926), 147–78.

Franciscan Papers, Lists and Documents, Manchester, 1943.

Maggiani, V., "De relatione scriptorum quorumdam S. Bonaventurae ad Bullam 'Exiit' Nicolai III (1279)" *AFH* v (1912), 3–21.

Maier, A., "Per la storia del processo contro l'Olivi", *Rivista di Storia della Chiesa in Italia*, v (1951), 326–39.

"Annotazioni autografe di Giovanni XXII in Codici Vaticani", *Rivista di Storia della Chiesa in Italia*, vi (1952), 317–31.

"Zu einigen Problemen der Ockhamforschung", *AFH* xlvi (1953), 161–94.

Mandonnet, P., *Les origines de l'Ordo de Poenitentia*, Fribourg, 1898.

Manselli, R., *La "Lectura super Apocalipsim" di Pietro di Giovanni Olivi, ricerche sull' escatologismo medioevale*, Roma, 1955.

Mollat, G., *Les Papes d'Avignon*, 9th edn., Paris, 1950.

Moorman, J. R. H., *The Sources for the Life of S. Francis*, Manchester, 1940.

Müller, E., *Das Konzil von Vienne 1311–1312. Seine Quellen und seine Geschichte*, Münster-i.-W., 1934.

Müller, K., *Die Anfänge des Minoritenordens und der Bussbruderschaften*, Freiburg-i-B., 1885.

Nantes, René de, *Histoire des Spirituels dans l'Ordre de Saint François*, Couvin, Paris, 1909.

Oliger, L., "De origine regularum ordinis S. Clarae", *AFH* v (1912), 181–209, 413–47.

"De relatione inter Observantium querimonias Constantienses (1415) et Ubertini Caselensis quoddam Scriptum", *AFH* ix (1916), 3–41.

"Beiträge zur Geschichte der Spiritualen, Fratizellen und Clarener in Mittelitalien", *ZKG* xlv (1926), 215–42.

"Spirituels", *DTC* XIV, ii, 1941, coll. 2522–49.

De secta Spiritus libertatis in Umbria saec. XIV, disquisitio et documenta, Roma, 1943.

Onings, I., "De H. Bonaventura als 'Tweede Stichter' van de orde der Minderbroeders", *Collectanea Franciscana Neerlandica*, I, 's-Hertogenbosch, 1927, pp. 127–50.

Papini, N., *Notizie sicure della morte, sepoltura, canonizzazione e traslazione di S. Francesco d'Assisi e del ritrovamento del di lui corpo*, 2nd edn., Foligno, 1824. (The original has not been used.)

Pou y Marti, J. M., "Visionarios, beguinos y fraticelos catalanes (siglos XIII–XV)", *Archivo Ibero-Americano* xi (1919), 113–231; xii (1919), 8–53; xiv (1920), 5–51; xv (1921), 5–25; xviii (1922), 5–47; xix (1923), 25–40; xx (1923), 5–37, 289–320; xxi (1924), 348–68; xxii (1924), 281–326; xxiii (1925), 10–58, 349–69; xxiv (1925), 198–232; xxv (1926), 5–47.

Quaglia, A., *L'originalità della Regola francescana*, Sassoferrato, 1943.

Renouard, Y., *La papauté à Avignon*, Paris, 1954.

Sabatier, P., *Vie de S. François d'Assise*, Paris, 1894; Eng. tr. L. S. Houghton, London, 1904.

"Examen de quelques travaux récents sur les Opuscules de Saint François", *Opuscules de Critique Historique*, fasc. x, Paris, 1904.

"L'Originalité de Saint François d'Assise", *Franciscan Essays* I, *BSFS* Extra Ser. I, Aberdeen, 1912, pp. 1–17.

Vie de S. François d'Assise, Édition définitive, Paris, 1931.

Séjourné, Père, "Voeux de Religion", *DTC* XV, ii, 1950, coll. 3234–81.

Seton, W. W., *Blessed Giles of Assisi*, *BSFS* VIII, Manchester, 1918.

Thomas, A., "Le vrai nom du Frère Mineur Petrus Johannis Olivi", *Annales du Midi*, Toulouse, 1913, pp. 68f.

Valois, N., "Jacques Duèse, Pape sous le nom de Jean XXII", *Histoire Littéraire de la France* XXXIV (1915), 391–630.

Vidal, J. M., "Un ascète de sang royal, Philippe de Majorque",
   Revue des Questions Historiques lxxxviii (1910), 361–403.
Viollet, P., "Berenger Frédol, canoniste," *Histoire Littéraire de la France*
   XXXIV (1915), 62–178.
Völker, W., "Nachfolge Christi", *Die Religion in Geschichte und Gegen-
   wart*, 2nd edn., IV, Tübingen, 1930, coll. 396–401.

INDEX

Abruzzi, 168.

Ad conditorem, Bull of John XXII, 230–5, 239, 242, 244.

Agen, Bishop of, 206.

Agnellus of Pisa, 93.

Aix, Archbishop of, 206.

Albert of Pisa, 89, 92.

Albi, Bishop of, *see* Bertrand de Castenet.

Alexander IV, 95, 108.

Alexander of Alexandria, 204, 205, 206.

Alexander of Hales, 124.

Alphabetum catholicum, by Arnald of Villanova, 180.

Alverna, 46, 51, 174.

amicus spiritualis: origin in Rule of 1223, 41, 84; development in *Quo elongati*, 84–7; in *Ordinem vestrum*, 96f, in Franciscan observance, 84f, 94; relation to *nuntius*, 84f; to Papal procurator, 100f; development summarized, 102; *see fidelis persona*; *nuntius*; Papal procurator; *also* Papal privileges; poverty, among Franciscans.

Anagni, Papal commission at, 115.

Ancona: March of, 166f; province of, 52, 95, 160, 167, 170, 184; Spirituals in, *see* Celestinians.

Angela da Foligno, 159.

Angelo da Clareno: early history, *see* Celestinian Spirituals; approaches Celestine V for permission to secede, 168; for further wanderings, *see* Celestinian Spirituals; received by James Colonna, 182; imprisoned by John XXII, 211; released, and takes Celestinian habit, 212f; his independent congregation, 105, 209; link with Philip of Majorca, 181; and Observants, 246; views, 104, 176; as evidence for events, through *Historia septem tribulationum*, 18

95, 103, 104f, 109, 113, 115, 123, 168, 170, 173, 203, 206, 218; writings, *see Historia septem tribulationum*, Letters.

Anjou, royal house of: *see* Charles II; Louis of Toulouse, St; Raymond Berengar; Robert the Wise.

Annibali da Latere, 69.

Apologia pauperum, by St Bonaventura, 113, 127–31, 135–40, 143ff, 158, 193, 229, 232.

Aquinas, St Thomas, canonization of, 235; *see also* Thomism.

Aquitaine, province of, 163, 206.

Aragon: provincial of, 172; king of, and ambassador, 224; royal house of, *see* James II, Peter III.

Arbor vitae crucifixae Jesus, by Ubertino da Casale, 174ff, 185, 186.

Archiv für Litteratur und Kirchengeschichte, ed. Denifle and Ehrle, 156, 162, 185.

Archivum Franciscanum Historicum, 198.

Arezzo, 203.

Arlotto of Prato, 158.

Armenia, king of, 167.

Arnald of Rochafolio, 159.

Arnald of Villanova, 170, 179f, 182; writings, *see Alphabetum Catholicum; Rahonament*.

Ascania, 203.

Assisi, 48, 53, 57, 74; bishop of, 47; bishop's palace in, 13, 61; basilica at, 72, 74, 94, 99; building for the chapters in, 45; municipality of, 45, 47, 74; Portiuncula in, 25, 44–8, 53, 61; Sacro Convento in, 10; S. Rufino, canons of, 47; San Damiano in, 87; chapter-general of (1279), 141; (1289), 166; (1304), 176.

Attal, S., 74.

Augustine, St, Rule of, 35; as authority for St Bonaventura, 136.

UNIVERSITY
OF
GLASGOW
LIBRARY

Songs as old as time,
As old as my people.
Stirred by this rhythm,
The body moves in unison
To the call of my ancestors
From times of yore,
Through the years and eons of time,
Through the eternal music of the drum,
Through the spirit that pervades
Our lives and theirs, too.

The drum, the silent union,
Silent as a desert,
Silent yet and strong
As the elephant,
That binds today to yesterday,
Bridges the years that span
Their time and mine,
Uniting us as one;
Roll out your rhythms magical,
Old drum symbol of Africa,
That jumped the thick rich forests
Peopled by trees' gigantic growths,
That crossed great rivers
Not crossable,
Glided over rocks—
Swift-flowing currents did not hinder you—
Faithful to your call, breaking the distance
Barrier, transmitting sounds,
Meaningful sounds
In answer to your call.

And yet your task's not ended,
Nor ever will you sing
From boxes solid and firm,
Rhythms liquid
Bathing my people,
My ancestors and those of my own time,
In joy, rejoicing gaily
As supple bodies ebony
Schooled from earliest youth—
Nay, from before the womb—

Sensitive to your sounds
They move, mingling their bodies
With your sounds
In one harmonious effort grand.

Roll out your rhythms,
Drum solid and firm,
Rhythms melodiously liquid,
Drum symbol of Africa,
Bearing within your secret depths
The power magical
To stir this native soul,
This soul within here lodged,
The soul in you, in me,
In all our ancestors,
That live on from before all time
Toward the consummation of all time,
The grand finale of all things.

Roll out your rhythms;
Call out to Africa her sons,
Call out to Africa her daughters,

And those within whom still may dwell
The soul of Africa undoubtedly will heed.

Wole Soyinka

Born of Yoruba parentage in 1935 at Abeokuta in Western Nigeria, Wole Soyinka is an actor, musician, and producer, as well as one of the most talented of the African poets and playwrights. He was educated at Ibadan University and at Leeds University, where he took an English Honours degree. After leaving Leeds he was attached to the Royal Court Theatre, London, where his play, *The Invention*, was staged. In 1960 he returned to Nigeria, where his play, *A Dance of the Forests*, won the *Observer* competition. His courage and outspokenness are legendary and already a myth has developed around his name. In 1967 he was imprisoned in Nigeria for his activities during the Civil War, and two of his poems were smuggled out of prison to be published as a leaflet by Rex Collings under the title *Poems from Prison* in 1969. He is at present Director of the School of Drama at the University of Ibadan. He has contributed to a wide range of magazines and anthologies, and his poetry has been translated into many languages. His publications include: *Three Plays* (Mbari, 1962), *The Lion and the Jewel*, play (O.U.P., 1963), *The Dance of the Forests*, play (O.U.P., 1963), *Five Plays* (O.U.P., 1964), *The Road*, play (O.U.P., 1965), *The Interpreters*, novel (Deutsch, 1966), *Idanre*, poems (Methuen, 1967) and *Kongi's Harvest*, play (O.U.P., 1968). The last of these plays has now been made into a film.

Purgatory

(An extract from *Bearings*)

Wall of flagellation to the South
Strokes of justice slice a festive air—
It is the day of reckoning.

In puppet cast: first, by law compelled
The surgeon, bottle primed for the ordeal;

Next, a cardboard row of gaolers, eyelids
Of glue—the observation squad. And—
Hero of the piece—a towering shade across
The prostrate villain cuts a trial swathe
In air, nostalgic for the thumbscrew,
Rack, and nail extractors—Alas,
All good things shall pass away—he adapts
To the regulation cane. Stage props:
Bench for a naked body, crusted towel,
Pail of antiseptic yellow to impart
Wet timbres to dry measures of the Law.

    The circus comes to circus town
    A freak show comes to freaks
    An ancient pageant to divert
    Archetypes of Purgatorio

For here the mad commingle with the damned:
Epileptics, seers and visionaries,
Addicts of unknown addictions, soulmates
To the vegetable soul and grey
Companions to the ghosts of landmarks
Trudging the lifelong road to a dread
Judicial sentence.

And some have walked to the edge of the valley
Of the shadow, and, at a faint stir in memories
Long faded to the moment of the miracle of reprieve
To a knowledge of rebirth and a promise of tomorrows
And tomorrows, and an ever beginning of tomorrows
The mind retracts behind a calloused shelter
Of walls, self-censor on the freedom of remembrance
Tempering visions to opaque masonry, to rings
Of iron spikes, a peace of refuge, passionless
And the comfort of a gelded sanity.

Weaned from the moment of death, the miracle
Dulled, his mind dissolves in shadows, a look
Empty as all thoughts are featureless which
Plunge to that lone abyss—And
Had it there ended? Had it all there ended
Even in the valley of the shadow of Night?